新编英美文化教程

THE ESSENTIALS OF BRITISH AND AMERICAN CULTURE: A NEW COURSE BOOK

王恩铭 ◎ 主编

清华大学出版社
北京

内容简介

本书根据英、美两国的文化特性，以其民族构成和生活环境为开篇，描述和探讨了英、美两国民族特性形成的原因，然后在此基础上，针对英美两国的政治理念、宗教信仰、教育思想、价值观念、家庭生活、婚姻观念、休闲方式和社会福利等问题逐一讨论，在描述清楚现象的同时，挖掘这些现象的成因等更深层次的内容。

本书封面贴有清华大学出版社防伪标签，无标签者不得销售。
版权所有，侵权必究。举报：010-62782989，beiqinquan@tup.tsinghua.edu.cn。

图书在版编目（CIP）数据

新编英美文化教程 / 王恩铭主编. —北京：清华大学出版社，2016（2025.2重印）
ISBN 978-7-302-43730-7

Ⅰ.①新… Ⅱ.①王… Ⅲ.①英语—高等学校—教材 ②英国—概况 ③美国—概况
Ⅳ.①H31

中国版本图书馆 CIP 数据核字（2016）第 089175 号

责任编辑：娄志敏
封面设计：嘉泰利德
责任校对：王凤芝
责任印制：丛怀宇

出版发行：清华大学出版社
网　　址：https://www.tup.com.cn, https://www.wqxuetang.com
地　　址：北京清华大学学研大厦A座　　邮　编：100084
社 总 机：010-83470000　　邮　购：010-62786544
投稿与读者服务：010-62776969, c-service@tup.tsinghua.edu.cn
质 量 反 馈：010-62772015, zhiliang@tup.tsinghua.edu.cn

印 装 者：天津鑫丰华印务有限公司
经　　销：全国新华书店
开　　本：180mm×230mm　　印　张：17.5　　字　数：352千字
版　　次：2016年7月第1版　　印　次：2025年2月第12次印刷
定　　价：56.00元

产品编号：065624-01

前　言

伴随着全球化进程的加快和我国与世界各国交往程度的加深,"走出去"与"请进来"日益成为"地球村民"生活中的一部分。现代生活于是向我们这些"地球村民"们提出了新的挑战：在"走出去"与"请进来"的过程中,我们与"地球村"的其他居民能展开多大程度的思想和文化交流？对当代中国大学生来说,这一挑战更具直接和现实意义,因为他们肩负着"讲好中国故事",走向世界的重任。显然,要实现走向世界,我们必须首先了解世界,而要了解世界,最便捷同时也是最有效的路径莫过从理解他国文化开始。鉴于英语业已成为一种"世界普通话",且中国大学生又大多以英语为外语学习对象,所以,就大多数中国学生而言,了解和学习他国文化始于英语世界中的英美两国。这也是我们编写这本《新编英美文化教程》的动因和初衷。

长期以来,用于国内高等院校大学英语系列教材的英美概况教科书存在着诸多不足,如过多篇幅描述历史地理、人口分布、工农业经济、政府部门和教育机构等,很少甚至鲜有讲述文化观念、民族特性、宗教信仰、教育理念、家庭婚姻、休闲文化和社会福利等涉及一个国家普通百姓最直接、最相关、最关切的问题。作为一种新的尝试,本《教程》力图克服上述传统《英美概况》教程的编写思路和内容,重点突出英美两国的文化因子,在描述两国文化表现形式之同时,注意阐释和揭示这些文化表现形式背后的价值观念,让读者真正做到"知其然,又知其所以然"。换言之,本《教程》注重于贯彻和实现人类学对"文化"所做的最基本定义：1) 文化首先是一种生活方式 (a way of life)；2) 文化以一定的体制或制度形式表现出来 (expressed in the form of institution)；3) 文化的存在和表现反映出的是一个民族的价值观 (an expression of underpinning/undergirding values)。我们希望,呈现在读者面前的这本《教程》基本实现了这一宗旨。

基于这一考量,编写本《教程》时,我们在题材选取和内容编排上始终以反映英美两国文化精髓为准则、以突显英美两国思想理念为中心、以体现英美两国民族特色为重点,确保学生阅读使用了本《教程》之后,掌握英美两国文化的最基本特性,为与包括英美两国人民在内的英语世界人群开展跨文化交流做好足够的知识储备。沿此思路和理念,本《教程》在具体编写时,特别注意英美两国的民族特性及构成这些民族特性的历史成因、思维方式、政治理念、价值观念、社会环境、制度建设和生活方式等。我们认为，只有了解和弄懂这些真正体现英美两国民族文化特性的因素，我们才可以说基本掌握了"英美概况"。

为此，本《教程》在编写过程中，根据英美两国的文化特性，以其民族构成和生活环境开篇，描述和探讨英美两国民族特性形成的原因，然后在此基础上，针对英美两国的政治理念、宗教信仰、教育思想、价值观念、家庭生活、婚姻观念、休闲方式和社会福利等问题逐一分章讨论。在所有这些以具体主题思想为中心的每个章节里，我们兼顾描述和分析，不仅陈述清楚"What is it?"，而且试图说明"Why is it?"和"How is it?"。应该说，注重英美两国的文化特性及构成这些文化特性的因素，是本《教程》的两大最显著特点，也是它区别于国内其他同类教材的最鲜明标志。

为了使学生更有效和更便利地使用本《教程》，我们在编写此书时尽力做到 user-friendly，以帮助学生在最大程度上理解和掌握本《教程》提供的内容。为了实现这一目标，我们在每个章节前面先安排了 Focal Points 和 Discussion Questions，让本《教程》使用者在学习本章时从 Focal Points 处一目了然地知道本章的核心内容，并开始思考 Discussiou Questions 提出的相关问题。正文之后，我们安排了 Notes "栏目"，针对正文中出现的一些重要信息提供简明扼要的注解或解释。之后，作为教材，本《教程》为使用者设计了四种类型的练习题，它们分别为："多项选择"（Multiple Choices）、"判断题"（True and False）、"一般问题"（General Questions）和"思考题"（Essay Questions），旨在帮助学生准确理解和牢固掌握每篇课文的最基本内容。最后，为了使本《教程》使用者阅读方便，我们针对课文中出现的一些难词和词语，在页码边空白处提供了中文译文。总之，为了实现本《教程》的编写宗旨，我们集长期教学和研究之经验，在编写课本内容上历尽丰富厚实，在设计课后练习上历尽形式多样，希冀藉此让学生从中获益。

本《教程》编写者都从事英美文化教学和研究工作。从相当程度上讲，本《教程》的编写过程是我们研习、思考、总结的过程。基于我们各自的学术特长和教学经验，我们编写时做了分工，王恩铭负责美国文化部分，王卓负责英国文化部分，最后王恩铭负责统稿。这是我们第二次合作编写英美文化教科书，尽管已经历尽所能，但我们深知，书中错误也许难免，甚至还存在诸多遗憾。祈盼本《教程》使用者不吝指出纠正，以便我们今后修订完善。

王恩铭　上海外国语大学
王　卓　上海第二工业大学

个人简介

王恩铭

男，1957 年生。博士、教授、博士生导师，上海美国研究学会副会长、上海外国语大学美国研究中心主任、中华美国学会单位理事和中国美国研究联络会理事。

个人经历：

1982 年 7 月毕业于原上海外国语学院英语系英语语言文学专业，并留校任教至今。1982 至 1983 年在上外"美国学助教进修班"研修一年。1985 年获美国富布赖特青年学者奖学金赴美国威斯康星大学攻读美国学硕士学位，于 1987 年回国。1992 年作为富布赖特高级访问学者，再赴威斯康星大学，作为期一年的研究。1996 年，获美国"全国人文基金会"资助，赴美国堪萨斯大学，参加为期两个月的"美国黑人文化研讨班"。2000 年，获美国斯塔尔基金会资助，在香港大学美国研究中心做了十个月的访问学者。2004 年 1 月，受香港城市大学邀请，在该校做了一个月的"高级研究员"。2004 年 9 月，获美国斯塔尔基金会奖学金，赴香港大学美国研究中心，做为期六个月的高级访问学者。2014 年获中国国家留基委博士生导师奖学金赴德国拜罗伊特大学留学。

获奖情况：

1999 年 上海市高等教育优秀教材三等奖；2002 年 上海外国语大学首届"青年十佳教师"；2002 年 上海外国语大学教育奖励基金"申银万国科研"一等奖；2006 年 上海外国语大学科研学术专著三等奖；2006 年 上海外国语大学奖励基金"卡西欧专著奖"；2007 年 上海外国语大学奖励基金"卡西欧论文奖"；2008 年 上海外国语大学科研学术论文一等奖；2009 年 上海外国语大学教育奖励基金教学科研一等奖及"卡西欧专著奖"；2010 年 获上海外国语大学"卡西欧论文奖"；2011 年 获上海外国语大学"卡西欧论文奖"。2012 年 获上海外国语大学科研学术专著三等奖。

研究领域

主要从事美国文化、美国黑人政治思想与现代美国妇女的教学和研究工作。

主要学术成果

出版的论著包括：《美国文化史纲》（上海外语教育出版社）、《美国反正统文化运动—嬉皮士文化研究》（北京大学出版社）、《美国黑人领袖及其政治思想研究》（上海外语教育出版社)、《20世纪美国妇女研究》(上海外语教育出版社)、《当代美国社会与文化》(上海外语教育出版社)、《美国名校风采》(上海外语教育出版社)等。

  主编教材有《美国社会文化》(北京大学出版社)、《美国文化教程》(复旦大学出版社)、《美国文化与社会》(上海外语教育出版社)、《英语国家概况》及其《学生手册》(上海外语教育出版社)、《英美文化基础教程》(上海外语教育出版社)和《高级翻译教程》(上海外语教育出版社)。

  此外,在《世界经济与政治》、《美国研究》、《世界历史》、《世界民族》、《世界宗教文化》、《史学月刊》、《史学集刊》、《历史教学问题》、《妇女研究论丛》、《国际论坛》和《国际观察》等CSSCI检索源期刊及其他学术刊物上发表了60余篇美国文化、历史、政治和女性等方面的论文。其中主要包括《美国历史上的政教关系》、《从政治边缘走向政治中心》、《美国的新自由主义》、《美国嬉皮士文化运动》、《美国新左派运动》、《当代美国妇女运动》、《马尔科姆·爱克斯的黑人民族主义思想》、《论布克·T·华盛顿的妥协主义思想》、《也谈美国多元文化主义》、《当代美国新保守主义的兴起》、《试论美国新右翼》、《试论美国新宗教右翼》、《战后美国新保守主义的思想重构》、《论美国新型保守派》和《美国20世纪末的一场文化战争》等。另外还有译著《危机》《美国人的生活和社会制度》和《永不满足：特朗普传》等。

授课情况：

  本科生：美国经典作品选读、美国文化与社会、外报外刊选读；
  硕士研究生：美国文化、现代美国妇女、美国政治；
  博士研究生：美国思想文化史、美国研究导论、美国妇女研究及女性主义。

目 录

Part I The United States

Unit One The Land and the People ··· 1
   Focal Points ··· 1
   Discussion Questions ··· 1
   Text ··· 1
   A Land of Abundance ·· 2
   A Nation of Immigrants ·· 5
   In Search of the American Dream ······································· 7
   The National Character ·· 9
   Notes ·· 12
   Exercises ··· 12
   Reference Answers ·· 15

Unit Two American Politics ··· 17
   Focal Points ··· 17
   Discussion Questions ··· 17
   Text ··· 17
   Political Beliefs ·· 18
   Political System ·· 21
   Political Parties, Interest Groups and Citizenry ····················· 24
   Notes ·· 27
   Exercises ··· 28
   Reference Answers ·· 30

Unit Three American Values and Assumptions ··························· 32
   Focal Points ··· 32
   Discussion Questions ··· 32
   Text ··· 32
   Individualism ··· 33

    Equality ··· 35
    Achievement, Hard Work, and Materialism ······················· 37
    Optimism, Change, and Progress ······································ 39
    Notes ··· 41
    Exercises ··· 41
    Reference Answers ·· 44

Unit Four   Religion in American Life ······························ 46
    Focal Points ··· 46
    Discussion Questions ·· 46
    Text ··· 46
        "In God We Trust" ··· 47
    Religious Pluralism ·· 50
    Popular Religion ·· 53
    Notes ··· 55
    Exercises ·· 56
    Reference Answers ·· 59

Unit Five   Education in America ···································· 61
    Focal Points ··· 61
    Discussion Questions ·· 61
    Text ··· 61
    Guiding Principles ··· 62
    Goals of Education ·· 66
    Management of Education ·· 71
    Notes ··· 73
    Exercises ·· 73
    Reference Answers ·· 76

Unit Six   The American Family ······································ 79
    Focal Points ··· 79
    Discussion Questions ·· 79
    Text ··· 79
    The Changing Family ·· 80
    Marriage Relationship ··· 82
    Parenting ·· 86
    Notes ··· 88

  Exercises ··· 88
  Reference Answers ·· 91
Unit Seven Leisure Life in America ·· 93
  Focal Points ··· 93
  Discussion Questions ·· 93
  Text ··· 93
  Sports ·· 94
  Recreation ·· 97
  Weekends and Vacations ·· 100
  Notes ·· 105
  Exercises ··· 105
  Reference Answers ··· 108
Unit Eight Social Services ·· 110
  Focal Points ·· 110
  Discussion Questions ··· 110
  Text ·· 110
  Public Social Services ·· 111
  Voluntary Services ·· 115
  Health Care Services ··· 117
  Housing ··· 120
  Notes ·· 122
  Exercises ··· 123
  Reference Answers ··· 126

Part Ⅱ The Great Britain

Unit Nine The Land and the People ·· 129
  Focal Points ·· 129
  Discussion Questions ··· 129
  Text ·· 129
  The Land ··· 130
  The People ··· 134
  Notes ·· 140
  Exercises ··· 140

Reference Answers 143

Unit Ten   Government and Politics 145
   Focal Points 145
   Discussion Questions 145
   Text 145
   A Bird's-Eye View of British Political History 145
   Political System 149
   Political Parties and Citizenry 154
   Notes 157
   Exercises 158
   Reference Answers 160

Unit Eleven   British Values and Assumptions 163
   Focal Points 163
   Discussion Questions 163
   Text 163
   Senses of Irony and Humor 164
   Fair Play, Trust and Compromise 166
   The English Reserve and Politeness 167
   Class Consciousness 170
   Keeping Order, Work Ethic and Drink 174
   Notes 175
   Exercises 176
   Reference Answers 179

Unit Twelve   Religion in British Life 181
   Focal Points 181
   Discussion Questions 181
   Text 181
   A Bird's Eye View of Religious History 182
   Christianity and Other World Religions 184
   Religion and Society 189
   Notes 192
   Exercises 193
   Reference Answers 196

目 录

Unit Thirteen British Education 198
    Focal Points 198
    Discussion Questions 198
    Text 198
    Schools 199
    Colleges and Universities 202
    Changes and Trends in Education 206
    Notes 208
    Exercises 210
    Reference Answers 213

Unit Fourteen The British Family 215
    Focal Points 215
    Discussion Questions 215
    Text 215
    The Changing Family 216
    Marriage Relationship 219
    Parenting 222
    Notes 224
    Exercises 225
    General Questions 227
    Reference Answers 228

Unit Fifteen Leisure Life in Britain 230
    Focal Points 230
    Discussion Questions 230
    Text 230
    Leisure around the Home 231
    Public Entertainment 233
    New Patterns in Leisure 239
    Notes 241
    Exercises 242
    Reference Answers 245

Unit Sixteen Social Services 247
    Focal Points 247
    Discussion Questions 247

Text ··· 247
The Welfare State: An Overview ··· 247
The Welfare System ·· 251
Housing and Personal Social Services ····································· 254
Notes ·· 257
Exercises ··· 257
Reference Answers ··· 260
Bibliography ··· 262
Websites ··· 264

Part I The United States

Unit One The Land and the People

Focal Points

a vast and rich land
a nation of immigrants
the American Dream
salad bowl

a City upon a Hill
success story
the "melting-pot"
cultural diversity

the Great Plains
the Gold Rush
assimilation

Discussion Questions

1. What makes an American?
2. What is the American Dream?

Text

a varied land 多彩多姿的国家

the temperate zone 温带

Gulf of Mexico 墨西哥湾

The United States is **a varied land**—of forests, deserts, mountains, high flat lands and fertile plains. Almost every kind of climate can be found in the country, but, taken as a whole, the United States lies mostly in **the temperate zone**. The continental United States stretches 4,500 kilometers from the Atlantic Ocean on the east to the Pacific Ocean. It borders Canada on the north, and reaches south to Mexico and the **Gulf of Mexico**. With an area of 9,363,123 square kilometers, the United States is exceeded in size only by Russia, Canada, and China.

In this vast area there inhabit tens of millions of immigrants and their **descendents**, who, in search of the American Dream, have turned this vast stretch of wilderness into the most modern and most powerful country in the world within a short **span** of a few hundred years. Beginning as a **sparsely** settled land with about 10 million Native Americans living across the whole North America in **pre-Columbian** era, the present-day United States has now become a multi-ethnic, multi-racial, and multi-cultural country with an **estimated** population of 325,127,000 as of December 2015, making it the third-most populous country in the world.

descendent 后裔

span 一段时间
sparsely 稀疏地、稀少地
pre-Columbian 哥伦布"发现"美洲大陆之前
estimated 估计的

A Land of Abundance

The most **pronounced** feature of the United States is its vast size and great variety. Because of its vastness and diversity, American natural environment varies from the **Arctic** to the **tropical**, from **rainforest** to desert, and from vast **plains** to **rugged** mountains. Indeed, the present-day United States **comprehends** most of the physical conditions known to human beings: heat and cold, **swamp** and dry waste land, mountain ranges and endless plains, empty spaces and **megalopolis**, and above all, the world's largest river system. Given such great variations, it is not difficult to appreciate the fact that life in the hot southern sub-tropical forests can be in sharp contrast to that in the North, where winters may constitute an entirely different world to people living in the South.

Another advantage of American geography is its richness, in addition to its size and variety. When the early colonists came to the New World, they were all struck by the abundant supply of its natural resources. **The New England seas**, for example, were thick with fish, and a wealth of forest was found along the Atlantic coast and on the Appalachians. Even greater wealth lay in the Appalachian coal fields. Beyond that, the trans-Appalachians had a super-abundance of coal and oil, together with i-

pronounced 显著的、明显的

Arctic 北极
tropical 热带的
rainforest 雨林
plain 平原
rugged 崎岖的
comprehend 包含、包括
swamp 沼泽地
megalopolis 超大城市

the New England seas 新英格兰内海

Unit One   The Land and the People

ron, copper, lead and zinc, and above all, of **fertile and productive soils**. The Far West **abounded with** precious metals as well as forested **ranges** going down to its **irrigable basins**. So abundant were America's natural resources that they were thought to be boundless, capable of lasting for many, many years to come, if not forever.

Besides its enormous wealth of natural resources, the position of the United States has also been thought to be one of its chief **assets**. Over 2,000 miles from Europe (or 3,000 miles from Great Britain) and 7,000 miles from Asia, it was long isolated from the conflicts of these troubled continents, offering itself as a **haven** for those who wished to seek a new life. Not surprisingly, many of the first settlers were Pilgrims who ran away from their own country to build **a City upon the Hill** in this New World. However, as the settlers moved westward, striking inland first across **the Appalachians** and then across the Mississippi River, they isolated themselves further, enjoying a still greater opportunity to create a different and better life in the West than could have ever been imagined by their cousins left behind in the East or back home in Europe. In this sense, isolation helped America to **forge** many of its **traits**, not least of which was the **reckless** use of its abundant natural resources, creating what scholars later called "**throw-away culture**".

As the world grew less land-based and more ocean-centered, the position of the United States received fresh value. With improvements in transportation and communication, America ceased to be a **retreat** and instead became a **cross-roads**: a cross-roads between East and West, facing the two most **densely-populated** regions of the world—Western Europe and Eastern Asia. This shift has given the United States a vast scope of opportunity, for instead of being **gulfs** of separation, the Atlantic and the Pacific have become the **lifelines** of a new world in which Americans have made their country the focus of the world connections, reaping huge benefits from trades and commerce with Western Europe and Eastern Asia.

  Additionally, the geographical position has favored Americans in placing their country in the middle of **latitudes**. America, as a whole, is a warm-temperate land and only in northern Alaska is it under the **permanent** threat of frost. Moreover, with the Atlantic and the Pacific oceans on both sides, America is swept by **humid** and **maritime** airs and only in the extreme Southwest does it experience **chronic drought**. No other country has such a favorable climatic **disposition**—comfortable, **stimulating**, and productive. Take Russia and China for example. Two-thirds of Russia is in the **cool-temperate** and arctic zones, often frustrated by frost, and in the case of China, a large part of its land is so continental that they are virtually away from **rain-bearing** winds, frequently **plagued** by droughts. Evidently, both Russia and China **pale** in comparison with the United States in geographical position.

  While America's resources are plentiful, it does not mean that they would automatically yield beneficial results. Barriers of distance and **relief** and certain difficulties in the climate have all had to be overcome before the rich rewards could be won. So, there has been a strong element of challenge in each part of America in the **exploitation** of natural resources, evident from the beginning to the present. New England **fisheries** are set in a storm-swept sea where **storm-tracks** from the interior are carried out over the ocean. Virginia and the Carolinas have their "dismal swamps" to put up with: poor drainage and an all but tropical summer often meant fever of one kind or another in the past. And once the interior is reached, new hazards are there to be dealt with. A truly continental climate with strong heating in summer and intense chilling in winter brings July **thunderstorms** and **blizzards**. Before the arrival of science and technology, the killing of crops by severe winter frosts was quite common, and when spring came and snow melted, dangerous floods often rolled down the rivers and brought widespread ruin. Further

---

latitude 纬度

permanent 永久性的

humid 潮湿的
maritime 海洋性的
chronic drought 长久性干旱
disposition 布置、配置
stimulating 令人心情振奋的
cool-temperate 寒温带

rain-bearing 负载（裹挟）雨水的
plagued 苦恼、受灾
pale 显得逊色、相形见绌

relief（地形的）高低起伏

exploitation 开发、利用
fishery 渔业、养鱼业
storm-track 风暴路径

thunderstorm 雷暴雨
blizzard 冰风暴

Unit One The Land and the People

west in **the Great Plains** and the Pacific basins, rainfall is often unreliable and **drought** frequently hits the area. In short, based on the above descriptions of America's natural environment, it can be **safely** argued that every bit of America's natural resources has been brought into use through **strenuous** efforts. Without such diligent and persistent efforts, America's natural resources would not have been so fully exploited, nor would they have been put to such great use to the development of the United States.

A Nation of Immigrants

The United States has often been called "a nation of immigrants". There are basically two good reasons for this. Firstly, the country was settled, built, and developed by generations of immigrants and their children. Secondly, even today, the United States continues to **take in** more immigrants than any other country in the world. For this and many other reasons, America is among the most **heterogeneous** societies in the world. Many different cultural traditions, ethnic customs, national origins, racial groups and religious beliefs make up what we call "Americans". According to the data released by the U.S. Census Bureau in 2013, 77.7% of the U.S. citizens claim themselves to be Whites, 13.2% Blacks, 5.3% Asians, 1.2% Asian American Indians and Alaska Natives, 0.2% Native Hawaiians and other Pacific Islanders, and 2.4% two or more races. It should be noted that a separate listing for Hispanics is not included here because the US Census Bureau considers Hispanics to mean persons of Spanish/Hispanic/Latino origin, including those of Mexican, Cuban, **Puerto Rican**, **Dominican Republic**, Spanish, and Central or South American origin living in the U.S., who may be of any racial or ethnic group (white, black, Asian, etc.). It is estimated about 17.1% of the total US population is Hispanic. Excluding Hispanics or Latinos, White population will be reduced to 62.6%.

However, it would be very misleading to view America simply as a collection of different immigrant groups and ethnic or religious loyalties. Though tens of millions of Americans proudly acknowledge their ethnic roots, they are, in fact, more American than they are Irish, Jewish, German, or Cuban. Indeed, what they have in common is more significant than what makes them, as Americans, different from one another. However, it should be pointed out that although the variety of ethnic identities, immigration experiences, and cultural choices have all gone into the making of Americans, it is very difficult to describe what an average American is. For instance, the average American may be White, but not all Americans are White. Similarly, most Americans are Christians, but America cannot be called "a Christian country." **By the same token**, while the majority of Americans might claim European **ancestry**, such a description does not define Americans in general. More surprisingly, even though the United States is regarded as one of the major English-speaking countries in the world, and English is the common language by use in America, yet America has no "official" language, at least English is not the national language by law.

Immigrants came to the U.S. from different countries and at a different time, but over time **immigration patterns** have changed with regard to the **origin of emigration country**. These changing patterns do affect, and have affected, what America is today and how Americans view the rest of the world. It is generally believed that throughout American experience there have occurred altogether four waves of immigration, namely, the first wave: colonial immigration between 1680 and 1770; the second wave: the "old" immigrants between 1820 and 1890; the third wave: the "new" immigrants from 1890 to 1930; and finally, the fourth wave: from 1965 to the present. In each of these four waves of immigration, there were some discernable characteristics with regard to the origin of emigration countries.

---

by the same token 同样地

ancestry 祖先、祖宗

immigration pattern 移民模式

origin of emigration country 移民来源国

Unit One　The Land and the People

involuntary 非自愿的

For instance, during the first wave, the great majority of immigrants came from Great Britain, Germany, France and Ireland, plus **involuntary** blacks from Africa. This group of immigrants constituted the founders the United States.

Scandinavian 斯堪的纳维亚人

The so-called "old immigrants" in the second wave largely refereed to northwestern European immigrants, such as Germans, Irish, Britons and **Scandinavians**, plus French Canadians, Swiss, Chinese and Dutch. Since they basically came from the same countries as the first-wave immigrants, they were called "old immigrants". By contrast, immigrants during the third wave mostly **hailed from** southeastern rather than northwestern Europe, and hence they were **nicknamed** "new immigrants". This group of immigrants included primarily Italians, Jews, Poles, Hungarians, Russians, **Czechs**, and Greeks, marking a significant change in the origin of immigrants. However, with the passage of the Immigration Act of 1965, the largest share of immigrants since 1965 has come from Latin America and Asia, making the United States ever more heterogeneous in its racial, ethnic and religious composition. As a result of all these changes in the origin of emigration countries during the third and forth waves of immigration, the so-called **Anglo-Saxon** heritage of America has been undergoing a major change. With the nation growing increasingly multi-ethnic, multi-racial and multi-religious, America, more than ever before, has become truly "a nation of immigrants".

hail from 来自
nickname 起绰号

Czech 捷克人

Anglo-Saxon 安格鲁-撒克逊

In Search of the American Dream

Why did people from around the world emigrate to the U.S.? And, why do they still go there? A good way to approach these two questions is to look at the "push" and "pull" factors. By "push", it means the forces that "push" people to leave their own countries. They include, but not limited to, wars, revolutions, periods of starvation, persecutions, religious intolerance. In short, it could be any number of disasters which led people to believe there was no hope to stay where they were. By contrast, "pull" refers to the forces that "pull" people out of their own motherland and to the country they adopt as their new nation. Such forces include, among other things, political and religious freedom, economic opportunity, access to quality education, and a better life. **In a nutshell**, the "pull" factor can probably find its expression in the phrase—the American Dream. Only when the two factors combine to work together will immigration take place, because they are the two sides of the same coin.

Take the Chinese immigrants of the mid-19th century for example. At that time, in addition to local wars and natural disasters, land was scarce and opportunity was scanty in China. On the other hand, America seemed to offer abundant opportunity for personal improvement and economic betterment, let alone its attractive "Gold Rush". Thus, "pushed" by the miserable life back at home and "pulled" by the opportunity America offered, tens of thousands of Chinese went to the United States in search of a better life. Similarly, between 1846 and 1851, more than a million Irish emigrated to America in order to escape starvation and disease in Ireland in the 1870s, a wave of refugees left the political **turmoil** of Eastern and Southern Europe to seek freedom and a future in America. At other times when the "pull" force weakens, as during the Great Depression or during World War II, for example, smaller numbers of immigrants went to the United States. Since the 1960s, more and more people have fled the poverty and wars in Asia and Latin America in the hope of making a better living in the United States.

What then is the American Dream? While different people have different interpretations about it, the term "dream" can be defined as the hopes and ideals of a people, applied extensively to the American experience, and suggesting an ongoing, active creation, and a sense of new possibility and fresh hope. It could mean a decent job with good pay; it could also mean ownership

in a nutshell 概括地说

turmoil 动乱

of a car and a house. More importantly, it can mean freedom of speech, freedom of assembly, and freedom of religion. All of such dreams imply a sense of optimism, and a sense of aspiration. To be sure, other countries may have their own **success stories** and own dreams as well. What makes the American Dream unique is the coming together in one place of so many separate dreams: the search for liberty, the discovery of one's own potential, the betterment of one's life, and the exploration of new possibilities for happiness.

Of course, not all immigrants and their descendents realize their dream. Indeed, quite oftentimes, dreams turn into mere **illusions** or even **nightmares**. And, the nightmare of the corruption of ideals and failure of hopes reveals a different America, an America not so bright as portrayed in U. S. history books. For instance, dissenters and other groups perceived as un-American have faced repression of every kind throughout U. S. history, from the colonial **Quakers** to the Joseph McCarthy Communist **witch-hunt** of the 1950s. Indeed, immigrants often found barriers to opportunity: Irishmen seeking jobs saw signs reading "No Irish Need Apply," the West Coast had anti-Chinese **riots** in the 1870s, and the settler on the frontier, looking for the New **Eden** of his dreams, found, instead, only hardship and poverty. In short, at no time in U. S. history have the dream and ideal excluded illusion and nightmare, and **conversely**, at no time have the nightmare and illusion conquered the ideal and the dream. These two aspects of American life have always run hand in hand.

The National Character

Of all the many different racial and ethnic groups that have gone into the making of America, some have quickly **assimilated**. They have largely lost or intentionally given up many of those specific **markers** which would make them much different from their neighbors. This process of assimilation, or "Americanization", has characterized the immigrant experience in U.S. history. Many American-born Chinese (ABC), for example, are often **compared to** banana, meaning they look yellow outside but remain "white" inside. In other words, they have the appearance of Chinese, but in terms of values and lifestyle, they are very much like white Americans. In the United States, such a phenomenon is called the **"melting pot,"** meaning immigrants from foreign countries have been "melt" in the American "pot". As a **metaphor**, "melting-pot" suggests that America as a nation was created "out of many". Historians often use "one out of many" to refer to this process.

However, many other people, while becoming American in other ways, have managed to maintain a large degree of their ethnic identities. They either refuse to be "melted" into the "pot," or live far beyond the "melting pot." Take the Jewish people for example. While they are well positioned in American educational, financial, and scientific institutions, culturally speaking, they maintain their own religion, observe their own traditions, keep their own family values, and live their own way of life. In many ways, the Chinese, the Japanese, and other Asian Americans have done very much the same as Jews have in maintaining their ethnic identities. Such a phenomenon in the United States is often **likened to** a "**salad bowl**" as a way of **illustration**. According to this **interpretation**, American national character is better understood as "one and many" rather than "one out of many", meaning that America is "one" nation composed of "many" racial, ethnic, religious, and cultural groups.

Perhaps, a more interesting metaphor for American society than either the "melting pot" or the "salad bowl" is that of a "pizza," which has become, by the way, the single most popular food in America, among the young people in particular. Anyone who has tasted the pizza knows that the different ingredients in a pizza are often apparent and give the whole its particular favor, yet all are **fused** together into something larger. Like

---

compare to 比作

melting pot 大熔炉

metaphor 比喻

liken to 比作
salad bowl 色拉拼盘
illustration 解释、说明
interpretation 阐释、解读

fuse 融化、熔化

Unit One   The Land and the People

the metaphor of the "salad bowl," the metaphor of the "pizza" also implies that American society is composed of multi-ethnic groups with different cultural backgrounds. But unlike the metaphor of the "salad bowl", which merely indicates that all the ingredients in the "bowl" are mixed together with all the pieces separate from one another, the metaphor of the "pizza" suggests that all the ingredients in the "pizza" are **glued** to one another, forming an inseparable entity. In this sense, "pizza" is probably a better metaphor in characterizing the multicultural nature of present-day American society.

Still another factor to consider in describing "the American" is that the face of the nation is constantly, and often very rapidly, changing. As mentioned above, Hispanics, Blacks, Asians, Native Americans, and other ethnic minorities, when put together, represent about 38% of U.S. population. It is projected that by 2043, ethnic and racial minorities will outnumber the white population and become majority in the United States, while white Americans will become a minority group. Indeed, in a number of cities in the United States, Hispanics or Blacks now already represent the majority of citizens. In this context, the classical question—"What is the American, this new man?"—cannot be answered simply or conclusively. At best, one may say that an American is someone who meets the legal requirements of citizenship and who considers himself/herself to be an American. Of course, any person born on American soil automatically has the right to American citizenship. But is citizenship alone that defines an American, as citizenship in other countries defines a person's nationality? Till now, a great number of Americans tend to believe that it takes more than citizenship to become an American.

While what makes an American may be debatable, what can be drawn from the discussion above is relatively certain, that is, the older categories of nationality brought from the Old World—race, language, religion, and parents' ancestry—have

glue 黏合、粘牢

become increasingly less important to the meaning of being an American. To be sure, they can still be used to describe an American, but not to define one.

Notes

Pilgrims—They were also called Pilgrim Fathers, referring to, in American colonial history, settlers of Plymouth, Mass., the first permanent colony in New England (1620). Of the 102 colonists, 35 were members of the English Separatist Church (a radical faction of Puritanism) who had earlier fled to the Netherlands to escape persecution at home. Fearing that their children were assimilating into the Dutch culture, they decided to immigrate to America.

The Gold Rush—It refers to the Gold Rush of 1848-1955 in California, which captured the popular imagination in the United States and around the world. It led directly to the settlement of Californian by Americans and the rapid entry of that state into the Union in 1850. Additionally, it stimulated worldwide interest in prospecting for gold, and led to the new rushes in Australia, South Africa, Wales and Scotland.

Joseph McCarthy—(November 14, 1908—May 2, 1957) was an American politician who served as a Republican U.S. Senator from the state of Wisconsin from 1947 until his death in 1957. Beginning in 1950, McCarthy became the most visible public face of a period in which Cold War tensions fueled fears of widespread Communist subversion. He was noted for making claims that there were large numbers of Communists in the U.S. federal government and elsewhere. Ultimately, his tactics and inability to substantiate his claims led him to be censured by the U.S. Senate.

The Old World—It refers to Africa, Asia and Europe, used in the context of, and in contrast with, the "New World," i.e., the Americas.

The Immigration Act of 1965—The Act marked a radical break from the immigration policies of the past, ending the discriminatory system of national-origins established in 1914.

Exercises

Ⅰ. Multiple Choices

The following are questions or incomplete sentences. Below each question or sentence four possible answers marked A, B, C and D are provided. Choose the ONE that

Unit One The Land and the People

best completes the sentence or answers the question.

1. Black Americans represent about _____ of the U. S. population.

   A. 12%   B. 13%   C. 14%   D. 15%

2. Hispanics represent about _____ of the U. S. population.

   A. 13%   B. 14%   C. 15%   D. 16%

3. From the end of the Civil War to the 1920s, large numbers of new immigrants to the United States came from _____ and _____ Europe.

   A. Southern, Western   B. Eastern, Northern
   C. Northern, Western   D. Southern, Eastern

4. American society is becoming increasingly _____.

   A. unicultural   B. bicultural
   C. tricultural   D. multicultural

5. During the Great Depression, a smaller number of people immigrated to the United States because _____.

   A. America banned immigration.
   B. America did not welcome immigrants any more.
   C. America did not have much opportunity to offer to new immigrants.
   D. America hated immigrants.

6. Since the 1960s, more and more people have fled the _____ and _____ in Asia and Latin America in the hope of making a better living in the United States.

   A. famine, political persecution   B. natural disaster, dictatorship
   C. earthquake, flood   D. poverty, wars

7. In the sentence "The nightmare of the corruption of ideals and failure of hopes reveals a different America", "a different America" means _____.

   A. a differing America   B. a bright America
   C. an ugly America   D. a lovable America

8. Joseph McCarthy-led anti-Communist campaign happened in the _____.

   A. 1930s   B. 1940s   C. 1950s   D. 1960s

9. Many American-born Chinese (ABC), for example, are often compared to banana because _____.

   A. they look like banana
   B. they enjoy eating banana
   C. they prefer banana to other fruits
   D. they look yellow outside, but deep in their hearts they think like white Americans

10. "The face of the nation is constantly, and often very rapidly, changing." What does this sentence mean?

A. It means that the appearance of the United States is constantly, and often very rapidly, changing.

B. It means that the facade of the United States is constantly, and often very rapidly, changing.

C. It means that surface of the United States is constantly, and often very rapidly, changing.

D. It manes that the composition of U. S. population is constantly, and often very rapidly, changing.

Ⅱ. True and False

Read the following statements carefully and then decide whether they are True or False. Put a "T" if you think the statement is true and an "F" if it is not.

1. As "a nation of immigrants" the United States continues to take in more immigrants than any other country in the world.

2. As the metaphor of "melting pot" suggests, the United States is quite homogeneous.

3. Despite their deep ethnic roots, Americans have more things in common than what makes them different from one another.

4. Being intensely religious, the United States can be called a Christian country.

5. From the early settlement of North American colonies to the late 19th century, most of immigrants hailed from Eastern and Southern Europe.

6. The Chinese emigrants went to the United States in the mid-19th century in order to make their fortune there.

7. Between 1846 and 1851, more than a million Irish emigrated to America in order to escape political and religious persecution in Ireland.

8. What makes the American Dream unique is that it is within easy reach for all immigrants.

9. The process of assimilation is in fact the process of Americanization.

10. Ethnic minorities are expected to exceed the white people in number by the mid-21st century.

Ⅲ. General Questions

1. As a nation, what is the United States often called?

2. Who are Hispanics, according to the U. S. Census Bureau?

3. Is English the official language in the United States?

4. Why are changes in immigration pattern important to America?

5. What do we mean by "push" in explaining emigration?

6. Do all immigrants realize their American Dream?

7. What happens when immigrants are assimilated?

8. What is the key difference between these two metaphors?

9. What is the projected demographic change in US racial and ethnic composition for the year of 2043?

10. Is citizenship alone that defines an American, as citizenship in other countries defines a person's nationality?

Ⅳ. Essay Questions

1. Why is the United States regarded as "a nation of immigrants"?

2. To immigrants, what does the American Dream mean?

Reference Answers

Ⅰ. Multiple Choice

1. B   2. C   3. D   4. D   5. C   6. D   7. C   8. C   9. D   10. D

Ⅱ. True and False

1. T   2. F   3. T   4. F   5. F   6. T   7. F   8. F   9. F   10. T

Ⅲ. General Questions

1. The United States is often called "a nation of immigrants."

2. Hispanics mean persons of Spanish/Hispanic/Latino origin, including those of Mexican, Cuban, Puerto Rican, Dominican Republic, Spanish, and Central or South American origin living in the US who may be of any racial or ethnic group (white, black, Asian, etc.).

3. No, it is not, though English is the common language by use in the United States.

4. Because these changing patterns do affect, and have affected, what America is today and how Americans view the rest of the world.

5. By "push", we mean the forces that "push" people to leave their own countries. They include, but not limited to, wars, revolutions, periods of starvation, persecutions, and religious intolerance.

6. No, not all immigrants or their descendents realize their American Dream. In fact, quite oftentimes, their dreams turn into mere illusions or even nightmares.

7. When immigrants are assimilated, it means that they have largely lost or intentionally given up many of those specific markers (such as their traditions, customs, beliefs and even language) which would make them much different from their neighbors.

8. Yes, as a metaphor, the "melting pot" implies homogeneity, while the metaphor of "salad bowl" suggests heterogeneity. Or, the former means "one out of many", and the latter "one and many."

9. It is projected that by 2043, ethnic and racial minorities will outnumber the white population and become majority in the United States, while white Americans will become a minority group.

10. Legally, yes, but a great number of Americans tend to believe that it takes more than citizenship to become an American.

Ⅳ. Essay Questions

1. There are basically two good reasons for this. Firstly, the country was settled, built, and developed by generations of immigrants and their children. Secondly, even today, the United States continues to take in more immigrants than any other country in the world.

2. The term "dream" can be defined as the hopes and ideals of a people, applied extensively to the American experience, and suggesting an ongoing, active creation, and a sense of new possibility and fresh hope. It could mean a decent job with good pay; it could also mean ownership of a car and a house. Additionally, it can mean freedom of speech, freedom of assembly, and freedom of religion. All of such dreams imply a sense of optimism, and a sense of aspiration.

Unit Two　American Politics

Focal Points

the Bill of Rights
the ideal of compromise
the Supreme Court
the rule of law
judicial review
citizenry
popular sovereignty
interest group

Discussion Questions

What is the key to the understanding of American politics?

Text

In general, Americans are quite proud of their political system. They seem to revere their Founding Fathers like George Washington and Thomas Jefferson, their Constitution, and their **Bill of Rights**. Whether they are well informed about politics, or whether they participate actively in political matters, most Americans believe their political system has advantages that many other political systems lack. Even though most Americans have a rather negative view of politics and politicians, they are convinced that the system itself is well designed and has functioned relatively well, capable of protecting their individual freedom, and responsive to their wishes in ways other political systems may not be. More importantly, Americans feel quite free to criticize their political leaders **in ways they see fit**.

Bill of Rights. 人权法案

in ways they see fit 他们认为合适的方式

Political Beliefs

Like any other nation's political system, the U.S. political system is also based on a set of political beliefs, among which are the rule of law, popular sovereignty, the ideal of compromise, and the protection of individual rights.

The Rule of Law

The idea behind the rule of law is that **impartial** laws, not human beings with their irrational and **arbitrary** tastes and judgments, should govern the formal aspects of social interaction. American youngsters are taught in their school that they live under the rule of law, not **the rule of people**. As they grow up, they gradually have such a belief internalized in their hearts, believing that no person is or should be above the law, and that laws apply equally to all people regardless of their wealth, personal connection, or **social station**. Their faith in the rule of law is so strong that not even the person holding the highest office in the nation, or the person possessing the largest amount of wealth, they think, should **be immune from** it. In the 1970s, for example, President Richard Nixon was removed from office as a result of his behavior in connection with what was called the "**Watergate Scandal**". Similarly, Standard Oil Co. Inc., then the largest oil refiner in the world, was ordered to break up into 34 companies in 1911, when the United States Supreme Court ruled that it was an illegal monopoly. While there have been quite a few cases in U.S. history where the rich and the powerful managed to escape legal punishment for the wrong deeds they had committed, the rule of law, on the whole, has **prevailed** in its **enforcement** both **in letter and in spirit**, giving Americans unshakable confidence in it.

Popular Sovereignty

Sovereignty, be definition, means the greatest authority to command all others. Every **nation-state** in the modern world has sovereignty. It may **reside in** a king, in a parliament, or in the state. In the case of the United States, sovereignty resides

---

the rule of law 法治
impartial 公平的、公正的
arbitrary 武断的、专制的

the rule of people 人治

social station 社会地位

be immune from 免于

Watergate Scandal 水门事件

prevail 占上风、胜过
enforcement 执行、落实
in letter and in spirit 在字面意思和精神实质上
popular sovereignty 主权在民
nation-state 民族国家
reside in 存在于

in the people, hence, popular sovereignty. By residing sovereignty in the people, it suggests, in theory at least, that a government can always be changed, preferably by majority rule, and if necessary, by revolution, when the government loses the consent of the governed. Still, however, the concept of popular sovereignty is ambiguous, because it does not say clearly who are these "people" in whom sovereignty resides. Obviously, when American Founding Fathers were drafting the Constitution, they did not include women, blacks, Indians or youth under 18 in the "people", for these groups of people were not given the voting right for a long time after the founding of the new nation. Without the voting right, these "people" could not **participate in** politics, and when denied **access to** politics, they could not exercise sovereignty **accorded** them by the Constitution. Even nowadays, when all the people at or above 18 can vote in the U. S., popular sovereignty is still far from being fully realized, for oftentimes it is money that dictates the outcome of political election. At best, it can only be hoped that participatory democracy will keep improving until Americans eventually turn their government into what Abraham Lincoln said of it: "**government of the people, by the people, and for the people**". Only then can Americans truly feel that they are sovereignty **in every sense of the word**.

The Ideal of Compromise

In the U. S., politics is believed to be the art of compromise, by which Americans mean that for the sake of reaching agreement, compromise is not only necessary, but also desirable. By definition, a compromise is a settlement of differences in which both parties make some **concessions** to the other side. When neither side is willing to compromise, the parties involved will **end up** in a **deadlock**, as is the case with the Democratic and Republican parties in U. S. Congress in recent years. On the whole, compromise is viewed quite positively in America, where people are taught early on in their life that to be able to make compromises is a good thing. A person capable of making right compromises is often deemed as an efficient person, for he gets things done, and thereby achieves success. Mature people, in the eyes of most Americans, resolve their differences through discussion and compromise, enjoying a "win-win" outcome. Of course, there are different views on what constitutes an acceptable level of compromise. If it is a matter of principle, many people would find it difficult, if not impossible, to make a compromise. However, when no fundamental **creeds** are involved, compromise is welcome. Therefore, a political agreement that results from a compromise is generally viewed by Americans as something good, indeed even **cherishable**. That partially explains why the U. S. Congress has been held in such low public respect in recent years. One chief reason, **among other things**, is that neither of the two major parties is willing to reach compromises and take action on such major issues as global climate change, immigration, health care, and budget. Of course, not all Americans share the assumption that compromise is good. To them, compromise may be seen as abandoning ones' principle. But to the majority of Americans, compromise is considered positive for a simple reason—it works. Being practical and pragmatic, Americans are more interested in getting things done than wasting time keeping arguing with each other.

Protection of Individual Rights

Of all the people in the world, Americans are probably most jealous of their individual freedom. To secure this individual freedom, American people, when ratifying the newly drafted Constitution, demanded that it be made part of the Constitution in the form of the Bill of Rights. Based on the concept of dignity of the individual, this principle reverses the common notion that the individual is **subordinate to** the state, and declares the most important characteristic of a just society should be the recognition of individual worth, hence individual freedom. The Bill of Rights contains the most **sweeping** and **substantive** pro-

creed 信条

cherishable 值得珍惜的

among other things 除了其他原因之外

subordinate to 从属于

sweeping 广泛的、彻底的
substantive 实质的、坚固的

tection for the individual rights in the United States. Included, among other things, are rights to freedom of speech, freedom of press, freedom of religion, freedom of assembly, as well as the **right to a recognizable procedure in criminal law**. Each of the rights contained in the Bill of Rights is worthy of lengthy discussion, but just by noting one, the right to the freedom of religion, one can see how advanced the **framers** of the U. S. Constitution were. Until 1787, no major state in the West had ever had the courage or inclination to separate the institution of government from the practice of religion. By forbidding all religious tests for office holding, and by **separating church and state**, the United States Constitution represented a significant milestone in the history of individual liberty.

Political System

The political system largely refers to the governmental system, which, in the United States, is characterized by federalism. By federalism, it refers to a dual form of government in which there is a functional and territorial division of power or authority. In other words, in a federal country, there are local and state units of government, as well as a national government. Given the limited space here, attention will be given only to the national government, which, in accordance with the principle of checks and balances, is divided into the Executive (the President), the Legislative (Congress) and the Judiciary (the Supreme Court).

The President

The President of the United States is elected every four years to a four-year term of office, with no more than two full terms allowed. As is true with Senators and Representatives, the President is elected directly by the voters (through state electors). In other words, the political party with the most Senators and Representatives does not choose the President. This means that the President can be from one party, and the majority of those in the House of Representatives or Senator from another party. And, this is not uncommon in American experience.

As the head of the state of the most powerful country in the world, President of the United States enjoys enormous power. He, first of all, is the chief executive of the United States, responsible for taking care that the laws are faithfully executed. Secondly, as the chief diplomat, he is responsible for U. S. foreign policy, oftentimes working in collaboration with Congress. Thirdly, he is the commander in chief of the U. S. armed forces. In peace and war, he is the unchallenged, and indeed, unchallengeable director of the **military might** of the country. Fourthly, he holds the position of chief legislator, responsible for presenting to the annual budget to Congress, introducing and seeking passage of legislative programs. Beyond all this, there are other roles the President has assumed. For example, he is the head of his political party, and he is also responsible for the economic health of the country.

military might 军事力量

Congress

As a law-making body, Congress is made up of the Senate and the House of Representatives. There are 100 Senators, two from each state, representing all the people in a state and their interests. One third of the Senators are elected every two years for six-year terms of office. The House, on the other hand, has 435 members, elected every two years for two-year terms. They represent the population of "congressional districts" into which each state is divided. The number of Representatives from each state is based on its population. For instance, Californian, the state with the largest population, has 45 Representatives, while Delaware has one 1 Representative. There is no limit to the number of terms a Senator or a Representative may serve.

Congress makes all laws for the United States, hence the name: law-making body. According to the U. S. Constitution, each house of Congress has the power to introduce legislation, and each can also vote against legislation passed by the other. Because legislation only becomes law if both houses agree, compromise between them is necessary. Additionally, since no bill passed by both houses becomes law until the President signs it, compromise between Congress and the President is also sometimes required. **Not for nothing**, as stated previously, is politics deemed the art of compromise in America. In general, Congress decides upon taxes and how money is spent. In addition, it regulates commerce among the states and with foreign countries. Finally, it also sets rules for the **naturalization** of immigrants.

The Judiciary

Following the Executive, and the Legislative, the Judiciary is the third branch of federal government of the United States. Its main instrument is the Supreme Court, which watches over the other two branches, determining whether or not their laws and acts are in accord with the Constitution. Congress has the power to fix the number of judges sitting on the Court, but it cannot change the powers given to the Supreme Court by the Constitution itself.

The Supreme Court consists of a chief justice and eight associate justices. They are nominated by the President, but must be approved by the Senate. Once approved, they hold office as Supreme Court Justices for life. A decision of the Supreme Court cannot be appealed to any other court. Neither the President nor Congress can change their decisions. In addition to the Supreme Court, Congress has established 13 federal courts of appeal and, below them, 94 federal district courts. Together, they constitute the federal judiciary system.

The Supreme Court has direct **jurisdiction** in only two kinds of cases: those involving foreign diplomats and those in which a state is a party. All other cases which reach the Court are appeals from lower courts. The Supreme Court chooses which of these it will hear. Most of the cases involve the interpretation of the Constitution. Perhaps, the most distinctive feature about the Supreme Court is its power of **judicial review**, i. e., it has the right to declare laws and actions of the federal, state, and local governments unconstitutional. In no other country in the world does the Supreme Court play such a large role in making public policy as it does in the United States.

Political Parties, Interest Groups and Citizenry

If we take politics as a play, we may say that political beliefs provide the idea, the Constitution the **script**, political system the stage, and political parties, interest groups and citizens the players. In order for the play to perform well, all these three groups need to take part in and act out their own roles.

Political Parties

Political parties are the basis of the American political system. Curiously, the U. S. Constitution says nothing about political parties, but over time the U. S. has developed a two-party system. The two major parties are the Democrats and the Republicans. There are other parties besides these two, but they are usually too small to be significant in American politics. Such minor parties have occasionally won offices at lower levels of government, but seldom are able to make their presence felt at the national level. As a matter of fact, in the United States, one does not need to be a member of a political party to run in any election at any level of government. Also, people can simply declare themselves to be members of the two major parties, or to be independent, when they **register** to vote in a district. Party members in America do not carry membership cards, nor do they pay membership fees, as is the case in many other countries in the world.

Generally speaking, the Democrats are believed to be associated with labor, ethnic minorities, and women, and the Republicans with business, industry, and investors. Additionally, Republicans tend to favor limited government and balanced

judicial review 司法审核

script 剧本

register 登记

budget, opposing in particular the greater involvement of the federal government in some areas of public life which they consider to be the responsibilities of the state and local governments. By contrast, Democrats tend to favor a more active role of the national government in both economic life and social matters, especially in social welfare programs. In political terms, those favoring a smaller role for the government are labeled "conservative", while those favoring a larger and more active government are labeled "liberal".

These are all generalizations, for in real life, to distinguish between the two parties is often difficult. In the case of ordinary people, for example, they can switch their party **affiliation** whenever they find it necessary. Similarly, for those elected politicians, they, too, are not **bound to** a party program, nor are they subject to any party discipline when they disagree with their party. On the whole, though the Republican Party is usually considered the more conservative of America's two major political parties, while the Democratic Party is believed to be more liberal.

Interest Groups

Americans, always concerned that politicians work to serve or advance their own interests rather than the interests of the people who elect them, often form **interest groups**. Interest groups are of many types. Some are formal associations; others have no formal organization at all. Several interest groups may exist within a single formal organization. Whatever the size or form interest groups may be, their purpose and function are the same, i.e., seeking to shape the political agenda and influence the outcome of policy-making by putting pressure on politicians. Such political action is called **lobbying**. That is why interest groups are also called "**pressure groups**" or **lobbing organizations.**

Interest groups lobby virtually on every imaginable subject. One group may campaign for a nationwide, federal gun-control law, while another group may just as vigorously get itself organized to oppose it. Some conservative religious groups call for pupils being allowed to pray, if they wish, at school. But another group, more liberal and **secular** minded, may demand that school pray be banned, because such a practice, they argue, violates the principle of separation of church and state. In short, driven by their own interests, Americans, according to the law, can organize themselves as a political group to seek and protect their own interests.

Such political activities by interest groups have, in many ways, helped weaken the political parties. Imagine a politician who does not pay close attention to the special concerns of his voters? He will be thrown out of office in the next election. Yet, imagine an interest group exercising tremendous political influence? Its interests are likely to be served at the expense of the public interest. Clearly, interest group as a political player is double-edged. It can hold politicians more accountable to their voters on the one hand, and provide powerful people with a legitimate tool to server their own interest on the other hand.

Citizenry

As citizens of the United States of America, Americans enjoy all the **privileges** and freedoms accorded them by the Constitution. However, such privileges and freedoms are balanced by the duties and responsibilities of citizenship. Foremost among the responsibilities of citizenship is the wise use of the power of the **ballot**. A well-informed **electorate** is the surest guarantee of the survival of American democracy. Whether the issue is paving a street in the town in which they live or approving a major change in U.S. immigration policy, American voters have the duty to cast their votes on the basis of all the information available. Only when the majority of Americans participate in election and cast their votes in an informed fashion, can the general interest of the public be served.

A second major responsibility of citizenship is public service.

The term public service, as we know, comes in many forms. It can mean military service, civil service, voluntary service, and social service. If politics is understood narrowly, public service may refer to government jobs. A relatively small number of Americans choose politics as a lifetime career, but there are literally millions of citizens who have entered government service at all levels. They are the ones who keep American government functioning on daily basis. However, if politics is defined broadly, public service may include many **non-government-sponsored** activities. From parent-teacher associations at the local level to consumer protection organizations at the national level, American citizens are all expected to contribute freely of their time, energy, and talents in support of causes in which they believe. Additionally, the American judicial system relies on the service of citizens as members of juries in federal, state and local courts. **It goes without saying** that without the vigorous support of citizenry in the form of public service, American government could not function the way as it was designed by the Founding Fathers, nor could American democracy continue as it was intended by them.

non-government-sponsored 非政府赞助的

it goes without saying 毋庸说

Notes

The Bill of Rights—it is the collective name for the first ten amendments to the U.S. Constitution. These amendments guarantee a number of personal freedom, limit the government's power in judicial and other procedures, and reserve some powers to the states and the public.

The Founding Fathers—They were political leaders and statesmen who participated in the American Revolution by signing the Declaration of Independence, taking part in the Revolutionary War, and establishing the U.S. Constitution.

Richard Nixon—Nixon (1913-1994) was the 37th President of the United States of America, serving from 1969 to 1974, when he became the only president to resign the office.

The Watergate Scandal—It was a major political scandal that occurred in the United States in the 1970s as a result of the June 17, 1972 break-in at the Democratic National

Committee headquarters at the Watergate office complex in Washington D. C. , and the Nixon administration's attempted cover-up of its involvement.

Exercises

Ⅰ. Multiple Choices

The following are questions or incomplete sentences. Below each sentence or question four possible answers marked A, B, C and D are provided. Choose the ONE that best completes the sentence or answers the question.

1. Most Americans believe their political system has _____ that many other political systems lack.

 A. shortcomings   B. disadvantages

 C. merits   D. demerits

2. Americans feel quite _____ to criticize their political leaders in ways they see fit.

 A. comfortable   B. necessary   C. ready   D. unrestricted

3. The essence of the rule of law is _____.

 A. laws should be applied to all people without biases, regardless of wealth or social status.

 B. laws should be biased when applied to different people based on wealth or social status.

 C. laws should be partial when applied to different people according to wealth or social status.

 D. laws should be applied impartially only when the parties involved are equal in both wealth and social status.

4. Sovereignty, by definition, means the greatest authority to command _____.

 A. the military force   B. the government

 C. the country   D. all the above

5. In American politics, compromise is believed to be not only _____, but also _____.

 A. unnecessary, undesirable   B. necessary, desirable

 C. unimportant, unavoidable   D. insignificant, useless

6. The most desired result of a compromise is a _____ outcome.

 A. no-lose   B. one-lose   C. no-win   D. win-win

7. Of all the people in the world, Americans are probably most jealous of their individual freedom. Here, the word "jealous" means all the following, except _____.
   A. envious   B. desirous   C. protective   D. cautious

8. Until _____, no major state in the West had ever had the courage or inclination to separate the institution of government from the practice of religion.
   A. 1778   B. 1878   C. 1787   D. 1788

9. American government is characterized by _____.
   A. federal system   B. confederate system
   C. unitary system   D. centralized system

10. In a federal country, power is divided between _____.
    A. local and state governments
    B. local, state and national governments
    C. state governments
    D. local governments

Ⅱ. True and False

Read the following statements carefully and then decide whether they are true or false. Put a "T" if you think the statement is true and an "F" if it is not.

1. American youngsters are taught in their school that they live under the rule of men, not the rule of law.

2. Americans believe that the person holding the highest office in the nation, or the person possessing the largest amount of wealth, can be treated differently when they are caught committing crime.

3. Most Americans tend to view compromise positively if no fundamental principles are betrayed.

4. The Bill of Rights was part of the U. S. Constitution when it was drafted, rather than amended after it was drafted.

5. The President of the United States can serve two terms at most.

6. Like the President, a Senator or a Representative can serve no more than two terms at most.

7. The decisions made by the Supreme Court cannot be overturned by anyone.

8. There are only two political parties in the United States.

9. In general, the Democratic Party is in favor of a more active role for the federal government to play, while the Republican Party is in favor of a more limited role.

10. Interest groups can play both a positive and negative role in American politics.

Ⅲ. General Questions

1. How do most Americans view politics and politicians?

2. Where does sovereignty reside in the United States?

3. What is the chief reason for the U.S. Congress to be held in such low public respect in recent years?

4. What are some of the fundamental rights stipulated in the Bill of Rights?

5. How many Senators are there in the U.S. Senate? And, how are they allocated among the 50 states of the United States of America?

6. What kinds of cases does the U.S. Supreme Court have direct jurisdiction in?

7. Why do Americans form interest groups?

8. What do Americans enjoy as citizens of the United States of America?

9. What is the surest guarantee of the survival of American democracy?

10. What does public service include?

Ⅳ. Essay Questions

1. The President of the United States is said to be the most powerful person in the world. Do you agree? Why and/or why not?

2. What are the major differences between the Democratic Party and the Republican Party?

Reference Answers

Ⅰ. Multiple Choices

1. C 2. D 3. A 4. D 5. B 6. D 7. C 8. C 9. A 10. B

Ⅱ. True and False

1. F 2. F 3. T 4. F 5. T 6. F 7. T 8. F 9. T 10. T

Ⅲ. General Questions

1. Most Americans have a rather negative view of politics and politicians.

2. In the United States, sovereignty resides in the people, in theory at least.

3. The main reason is that neither of the two major parties is willing to reach compromises and take action on such important issues as global climate change, immigra-

tion, health care and budget.

4. They include, but not limited to, rights to freedom of speech, freedom of press, freedom of religion, and freedom of assembly.

5. There are 100 Senators in the U.S. Senate, each of the 50 states having two seats in the Senate.

6. The Supreme Court has direct jurisdiction in only two kinds of cases: those involving foreign diplomats and those in which a state is a party.

7. Americans form interest groups largely to protect their own, or in some cases, public interests, when they are concerned that politicians are only interested in advancing interests of their own.

8. As citizens of the United States of America, Americans enjoy all the privileges and freedoms accorded them by the Constitution.

9. A well-informed electorate the surest guarantee of the survival of American democracy.

10. Public service includes military service, civil service, voluntary service, and social service. Such services are sometimes government-sponsored, but more often than not non-government-sponsored.

Ⅳ. Essay Questions

1. Yes, I do. At present, the United States is the most powerful country in the world, and President of the United States holds the highest office in the country, and thus he enjoys the greatest power in the world, so far at least. Specifically, the President is the chief executive of the United States, the chief foreign policy maker, the commander in chief of the U.S. armed forces, and the chief legislator, capable of rallying political, economic, military and financial resources behind him to achieve the goals he sets his sights on.

2. Differences between the Democratic Party and the Republican Party are manifold. In terms of political support groups, for example, the Democrat Party relies upon labor, women and ethnic minorities, while the Republican Party relies upon business, industry and investors. Regarding the role of the federal government, the Democrats favor a more active government, while the Republicans are in support of a more limited government. Finally, on many of social and cultural issues in America today, such as welfare, abortion and gay marriage, the Democrats are more liberal, and the Republicans are more conservative.

Unit Three   American Values and Assumptions

Focal Points

individualism	equality	achievement
materialism	hard word	progress
change	optimism	

Discussion Questions

In American value system, which value Americans hold dearest?

Text

As people grow up, they learn certain values and assumptions from people and the media around them, such as their parents, teachers, friends, television, films, books, newspapers and the Internet. Values and assumptions are closely related, though there are some differences between them. By "values", we mean ideas about what is right and wrong, desirable and undesirable, normal and abnormal, proper and improper. By "**assumptions**", we mean the unquestioned **givens** about life, the way things are, and the way things are done, i. e., we "assume" that this is the way it should be. In the following space, some of the most important American values and assumptions are provided to help readers understand how Americans **perceive** and relate to the world around them.

assumption 假定、假设
given 已知的事实

perceive 认识、察觉

Unit Three American Values and Assumptions

Individualism

The most important thing to understand about Americans is probably their devotion to individualism. They are trained from very early in their lives to think of themselves as separate individuals who are responsible for their own situations in life and their own destinies. They are advised not to see themselves as members of a **close-knit**, interdependent family, religious group, tribe, nation or any other collective group. To help **instill** this value in the minds of children, parents and teachers will **see to it that** the young children are provided every possible opportunity to make their own choices and express their own opinions. For example, a parent will ask a one-year-old child what color balloon she wants. Similarly, a school teacher will ask a seven-year-old boy whom he wants to sit next to. Usually, the child's preference will be respected. **Trivial** as all this may seem to be, it demonstrates that **self-autonomy** is encouraged early on in childhood in America.

Philosophically speaking, the American concept of an individual self is rooted in the liberal tradition of John Locke, who asserted that the biological individual is the basic unit of nature and social systems derive from the interaction of individuals who exist **prior to** the social order and who are acting in their self-interest. Historically speaking, the American attachment to individualism as a value comes from early settlers' colonial experience. After the "discovery" of the New World, Europeans, English in particular, came to the North American continent to establish colonies free from the controls of kings and governments, priests and churches, noblemen and aristocrats in European societies. **In the wake** of the victory of the War for Independence, American founding fathers not only **expressly** forbade titles of nobility, but also managed to establish a central government with limited power. Such historic decisions had a profound effect on the shaping of the American character. By limiting the power of the national government, and by **eliminating** a formal aristocracy in the new nation, they created a climate of freedom where emphasis was put on the individual. Gradually, the United States came to **be associated with** the concept of individual freedom. This is probably the most basic of all the American values.

Scholars often call this value individualism, but most Americans prefer the word freedom. By freedom, Americans mean the desire and the ability of all individuals to control their own destiny without outside interference from the government, the church, the ruling class, the political party or any other organized authority. The desire to be free of controls was a basic value of the new nation in 1776, and has continued to be the most **cherished** one till today in America. **On the positive side**, individualism means independence, self-reliance, self-autonomy, self-quest, self-respect, self-help and self-realization. For this and many other reasons, Americans consider the ideal person to be an individualistic, self-reliant and self-autonomous one. That is why Americans regard as heroes those individuals who "stand out from the crowd" by doing something first or best, or those individuals who managed to rise from **"rags to riches"** in their lives under **adverse** circumstances. In Great Britain, there is a proverbial saying—"it takes three generations to make a gentleman", meaning that one has to rely upon his family to succeed. In America, however, a more preferred phrase is what is said to be Benjamin Franklin's advice to his fellow Americans—"God helps those who help themselves", indicating that **self-made man** is held in great respect and admiration by most Americans.

On the negative side, individualism may mean selfishness, because individualism, by definition, tends to **give top priority to** the individual. Therefore, when **driven to extremes**, an individual can be so self-centered and so self-serving that he/she is likely to put his/her interests above those of his/her family

---

eliminate 去除、消除、废除

be associated with 与……联系在一起

cherish 珍视、珍惜

on the positive side 积极的方面

rags to riches 从穷光蛋到大富豪

adverse 不利的

self-made man 自我奋斗成功的、白手起家的

give top priority to 给予最高优先

driven to extremes 走向极端

members, classmates, and fellow countrymen. Americans have learned from their historical experiences that if an individual does not **exercise restraint** in his/her hot pursuit of happiness, he/she tends to develop two kinds of **indifference**: indifference to the preservation of natural reserve, and indifference to the people in need of help. While the first kind of indifference results in the destruction of natural environment, the second one leads to the damaging of human relationship in society. Fully aware of such negative consequences, Americans, while still worshipping individualism as a fundamental value in their belief system, have made a great deal of effort over the past century to educate and encourage the younger generation to be more community-conscious and less self-centered so as to **strike a good balance** between individualism and collectivism. In short, individual freedom remains a most highly cherished value for most Americans, but people have become increasingly persuaded that it should be exercised with restraint.

Equality

Second to individual freedom, equality is another value that Americans **hold dear**. Indeed, it can be argued that if individualism means individual freedom, collectivism implies equality. For immigrants and their descendents alike, America is a symbol of not only freedom, but also equality, as **eloquently** stated in the Declaration of Independence that "all men are created equal". Despite frequent violation of this sacred principle in American experience, particularly in matters of racial, **ethnic**, gender, and religious relationships, Americans, by and large, have a deep faith that in some fundamental way all people (at least all American people) are of equal value, that no one is born superior to anyone else, that no one is entitled to any **privileges**, and that no one is above anyone else merely because of birth. In politics, Americans say: "one person, one vote", meaning that any person's opinion is as **valid** and worthy of attention as any other person's opinion. In doing business, Americans emphasize the rule of free competition and the principle of fair play, suggesting that everyone is equal in the playing field. In social life, Americans **address** each other in their first names, seeing no need to use **titles** to distinguish one from another in social status. Many of American expressions, such as "he is a regular guy", "he is a great commoner", and "he is an average person", exactly **convey** the sense of equality that people feel about each other. Those who "**put on airs**" or "show off" often end up being laughed at.

address 称呼
title 头衔

convey 传达、传递
put on airs 摆架子

Convinced of the equal value of human beings, Americans tend to feel uncomfortable when someone treats them with obvious **deference**. They dislike being the subjects of open displays of respect, for instance, being bowed to or being treated as though they could do no wrong or making no unreasonable requests. So strong is their belief in the ideal of equality that they may sometimes even feel **offended** at the suggestion that there are social classes in America. Due to such a prevailing conception or misconception of American society, some American scholars and politicians even go so far as to claim that America is basically a class-free or classless society. While there is no historical or realistic basis to argue that America is truly class-free, what all of this suggests is that Americans hold the principle of "all men are created equal" so highly that they cannot accept or tolerate any legally **sanctioned** social classes. In this sense, American President Andrew Jackson's political slogan—"equal opportunity for all, special privileges for none" truly captures the essence of Americans' strong faith in the ideal of equality, even though in real life Americans have time and again **violated** the ideal in practice, as has been shown in racial, gender and class inequality throughout U.S. history.

deference 敬重、敬意

offend 冒犯

sanction 认可、批准、赞同

violate 违背、违反

What needs to be emphasized is that Americans do make **distinctions** among themselves as a result of such factors as wealth, level of education, gender and occupation. However,

distinction 区别、甄别

such distinctions are acknowledged in relatively **subtle** rather than open ways. Tone of voice, order of speaking, choice of words, seating arrangements, these are the means by which Americans acknowledge **status** differences. For instance, people of higher status are more likely to speak first, louder, and longer. Also, they sit at the head of the table or in the most comfortable chair, feeling free to interrupt other speakers more than others feel free to interrupt them. If there is touching between the people involved, the high-status person will touch first. In short, what is **distinctive** about the American outlook on the matter of equality are the two key **underlying** assumptions: 1) no matter what a person's initial **station** in life, he/she should have the equal opportunity to achieve high standing;

2) everyone, no matter how unfortunate, deserves some basic level of respect. Viewed **in conjunction with** the ideal of individualism, the ideal of equality in America should be understood as equality of opportunity, not equality of result.

Achievement, Hard Work, and Materialism

The ideals of individualism and equality discussed above are closely related to the ideal of "the pursuit of happiness" expressed in the Declaration of Independence. In other words, when Americans talk about individual freedom and equality, they often mean to say that everyone is free to pursue his/her happiness on equal basis. And, by "the pursuit of happiness", Americans largely mean achievements. It can be achievement in one's political career; it can also be achievement in one's academic research. But, for most ordinary Americans, achievement simply means success in one's education, occupation, marriage and family life. These are all part of their "pursuit of happiness". Since America provides more freedom and greater equality for its people to pursue their happiness than most other countries do in the world, Americans are known to be **highly-**

motivated and **achievement-oriented**.

"He's a hard worker", one American might say in praise of another. Or, "She gets the job done". These expressions convey the typical American admiration for a person who **approaches** a task conscientiously and persistently, **seeing it through** to a successful conclusion. Additionally, these expressions convey an admiration for achievers, whose lives center on accomplishing some physical and measurable task. Living in a relatively free and equal society, Americans have an urgent need and a strong desire to prove to the people around them that they are as good as anybody else. In order to realize it, they need to attain an identity through success and achievement. Since America rejects the notions of **inherited** privileges, titles, and **nobility**, one's success and achievement often come **in the form of** visible and measurable attainments, such as a big house one owns, a fancy car one drives, a **high-salaried job** one holds or a **prestigious** position one occupies. Individuals with high achievement motivations are **portrayed** as people who enjoy **taking the initiative** in making decisions. They prefer to participate in activities that challenge their skills and abilities. They are usually confident of their success, but they tend to be too optimistic when the conditions for a successful performance are unknown. Because of their willingness to **take risks** and their confidence in achieving targeted goals, people with high achievement motivation are oftentimes described as **risk-takers**.

What needs to be pointed out is that in American culture, achievement is given a material meaning. For society as a whole, it leads to an emphasis on technology and publicity, i.e., making achievements measurable and visible. **Acting on** these assumptions, Americans rend to define progress as technological change. Eventually, social progress comes to mean the number of schools set up rather than the quality of teaching itself or quality of teaching staff. For individuals, it leads to a stress on **accumulation** of material goods. Around the world,

Americans are criticized for being too materialistic, i.e., too much concerned with material possessions, viewing material wealth as an end rather than as a means. For Americans, however, this materialistic **bent** is natural and proper. They have been taught that it is good to achieve, to work hard and to acquire more material **badges** of their success and in the process ensure a better future for themselves and their families. Such a keen concern with visible achievement may lead Americans to **lose sight of** main issues. Consequently, many Americans **settle for** a sensation, a personal **triumph over** a **counterpart**, or a specific accomplishment that can be reported as an achievement.

Optimism, Change, and Progress

Americans' notions of achievement, hard work and materialism, in many ways, reflect their optimism, believing that change is possible and progress can be made. Unlike people in other nations with a long history, Americans are generally less concerned about history or traditions. "History does not matter", many of them will say, or "It is the future that counts". Always hopeful for a better future, they look ahead, believing that what happens in the future is within their control or at least **subject to** their influence. The mature and sensible person, they think, set goals for the future, writes them down and works hard toward them. When asked about their goals, as they are commonly asked in job interviews, say, "Where do you want to be in ten years?" most Americans have a ready answer. If they don't, they are likely to apologize for their apparent inadequacy, replying "I am sorry, but I haven't figured that out **as yet**".

As a young nation with abundant natural resources, America offers plenty of opportunity for its citizens to **bring their potential to the fullest degree possible**. Accordingly, Americans believe that people, as individuals or as a group, can change most aspects of their physical and social environment, if they decide to do so, make appropriate plans, and then work hard at them. Historically speaking, such optimism was planted in the minds of Americans when the early settlers came to the Now World with the conviction that the virgin land was **a promised land** for them. Later, it kept growing as the nation expanded westward across the **vast stretches of** the continent. Finally, the remarkable industrial growth and the amazing technological revolution seem to bring to Americans one new hope after another. To the average American, new possibilities are always there, and obstacles exist merely to be overcome. As along as one keeps trying and working hard, he/she will eventually **turn things round**. Such expressions as "the difficult takes a while" and "the impossible takes a little longer", in many ways, **embody** the Americans' confidence in **bringing about** desirable changes for themselves in the future.

　　Closely associated with their assumption that they can turn things round is the Americans' assumption that changes are always possible and that they can always make changes for the better, both of which will lead to progress. To most Americans, their physical and social environments are subject to human **alteration** or control. Early Americans cleared forest, **drained swamps**, and changed the **course** of rivers in order to "build" their country. Contemporary Americans have gone to **the outer space** and landed on the moon in part just to prove that they could do so. "If you want to be an American", American parents often say to their children, "you have to believe you can fix it", meaning to be an American, one has to have the confidence that he/she can and should make things happen. This statement reflects the fundamental American belief in progress and a better future. For this reason, Americans are generally rather impatient with people they see as passively accepting conditions that are less than desirable. "Why don't you do something about it?" Americans will ask. Anyone who tends to settle for anything less than desirable is not likely to be held in respect by Americans, if not laughed at or condemned. To most

a promised land 希望之地、应许之乡

vast stretches of 茫茫无际的一大片……

turn things round 改变形势、改变局面、使情况转变

embody 体现

bring about 带来

alteration 改变

drain 排（水）

swamp 沼泽地

course（河）道

the outer space 太空

Unit Three   American Values and Assumptions

equate with 把……等同于……

Americans, one can and should be able to shape his/her own future. This is usually accomplished by changing the conditions in which one found oneself. For this reason, Americans tend to **equate** change **with** progress and equate progress with a better future. The key point is to always remain optimistic.

Notes

John Locke—(1632—1704) was an English philosopher and physician regarded as one of the most influential of Enlightenment thinkers and known as the "Father of Classical Liberalism".

Benjamin Franklin—(1706—1790) was one of the Founding Fathers of the United States of America. A world-renowned polymath, Franklin was a leading author, printer, statesman, scientist, inventor, philosopher and diplomat in early America.

Andrew Jackson—(1767—1845) was the 7th President of the United States of America. He was elected to both the U.S. House of Representatives and the Senate, but did not get known in the country until the War of 1812, when he led the U.S. military forces to win victories at two crucial battles against Great Britain.

Exercises

Ⅰ. Multiple Choices

The following are questions or incomplete sentences. Below each sentence or question four possible answers marked A, B, C and D are provided. Choose the ONE that best completes the sentence or answers the question.

1. In early childhood, Americans are advised to see themselves as

   A. a member of a group

   B. a dependent person

   C. a self-reliant and responsible individual

   D. a follower

2. In the sentence "parents and teachers will <u>see to it that</u> the young children are provided every possible opportunity to make their own choices and express their own opinions", what does "see to it that" mean?

   A. see it as it is   B. make sure that

C. see it through   D. see and get it

3. In building their new nation, American founding fathers explicitly _____ titles of nobility or aristocracy.

A. rejected   B. kept   C. accepted   D. inherited

4. Americans regard as heroes those individuals who "stand out from the crowd". What does the phrase "stand out from the crowd" mean?

A. step out of the crowd

B. leave the crowd

C. outstanding among a group of people

D. run out of the crowd

5. In American value system, if individualism means _____, collectivism implies _____.

A. equality, freedom   B. freedom, equality

C. rights, protection   D. protection, rights

6. In social life, Americans address each other in their first names, because _____.

A. they want to be friendly and informal to one another.

B. they find it too bothersome to use both first and last names.

C. they don't like other people to know their last name.

D. they think first name is usually better than last name.

7. Americans believe that everyone, no matter how unfortunate, deserves some basic levels of _____.

A. attention   B. consideration

C. admiration   D. respect

8. By "the pursuit of happiness", Americans largely mean _____.

A. the pursuit of material comforts   B. the pursuit of wealth

C. the pursuit of honor and glory   D. A and B

9. When many Americans say, "history does not matter", what do they mean?

A. They mean Americans have no respect for history.

B. They mean since the United States has a short history, it is of little importance.

C. They mean history only tells what happened in the past; what is really important is the future.

D. They mean Americans do not trust their history.

10. Americans are generally rather _____ with people they see as passively ac-

cepting conditions that are less than desirable.

A. impatient   B. patient   C. satisfied   D. dissatisfied

II. **True and False**

Read the following statements carefully and then decide whether they are true or false. Put a "T" if you think the statement is true and an "F" if it is not.

1. American young children are provided few opportunities to make their own choices and express their own opinions.

2. In the United States, children's preference is always respected, no matter what.

3. The American concept of an individual self is rooted in the liberal tradition of an Englishman by the name of John Locke.

4. By freedom, Americans mean the desire and the ability of all individuals to control their own destiny without outside interference from any organized authority, such as political, religious, business, financial or educational authority.

5. "All men are created equal" is stated in the U.S. Constitution as a principle.

6. In America, Those who "put on airs" or "show off" often end up being ridiculed.

7. Americans make no distinctions among themselves despite their differences in wealth, level of education, race, gender or occupation.

8. Americans are known to be highly-driven in their pursuit of achievements.

9. Americans are ready to take risks and therefore they are often described as risk-takers.

10. Generally speaking, Americans, whites and non-whites alike, tend to view their country as a promised land, even though that promise oftentimes gets broken.

III. **General Questions**

1. What is the difference between "value" and "assumption"?

2. What is probably the most important thing to understand about Americans?

3. What are Americans trained to think of in their early childhood?

4. What immigrants and their descendents alike, what does the United States symbolize?

5. In American politics, when people say "one person, one vote", what do they mean?

6. What kind of ideal expressed in the Declaration of Independence are the ideals of individualism and equality closely related to?

7. In American culture, what kind of meaning is achievement given?

8. How do Americans measure one's success or achievement in general?

9. What do Americans' notions of achievement, hard work and materialism reflect?

10. What do most Americans think of their physical and social environments?

Ⅳ. Essay Questions

1. What is the historical origin of American commitment to individualism?

2. Why are Americans so full of optimism?

Reference Answers

Ⅰ. Multiple Choices

1. C   2. B   3. A   4. C   5. B   6. A   7. D   8. D   9. C   10. A

Ⅱ. True and False

1. F   2. F   3. T   4. T   5. F   6. T   7. F   8. T   9. T   10. T

Ⅲ. General Questions

1. Value and assumption are both related to and different from each other. Value refers to ideas about what is right and wrong, desirable and undesirable, normal and abnormal, proper and improper. Assumption refers to the unquestioned givens about life, for instance the way things are, and the way things are done, i.e., we "assume" that this is the way it should be.

2. The most important thing to understand about Americans is their devotion to individualism.

3. They are trained from very early in their lives to think of themselves as separate individuals who are responsible for their own situations in life and their own destinies.

4. For immigrants and their descendents alike, America is a symbol of freedom and equality.

5. In American politics, "one person, one vote" means that any person's opinion is as valid and worthy of attention as any other person's opinion.

6. The ideals of individualism and equality are closely related to the ideal of "the pursuit of happiness" expressed in the Declaration of Independence.

7. In American culture, achievement is given a material meaning.

8. Americans measure one's success and achievement by looking at visible and measurable attainments he has made, such as his house, car, job or position.

9. Americans' notions of achievement, hard work and materialism reflect their optimism, believing that change is possible and progress can be made.

10. To most Americans, their physical and social environments are subject to human alteration or control.

Ⅳ. Essay Questions

1. Historically speaking, the American commitment to individualism as a value comes from early settlers' colonial experience. After the "discovery" of the New World, Europeans, English in particular, came to the North American continent to establish colonies free from the controls of kings and governments, priests and churches, noblemen and aristocrats in European societies. In the wake of the victory of the War for Independence, American founding fathers not only expressly forbade titles of nobility, but also managed to establish a central government with limited power. Such historic decisions had a profound effect on the shaping of the American character. By limiting the power of the national government, and by eliminating a formal aristocracy in the new nation, they created a climate of freedom where emphasis was put on the individual. Gradually, the United States came to be associated with the concept of individual freedom. This is probably the most basic of all the American values.

2. Unlike people in other nations with a long history, Americans are generally less concerned about history or traditions. Instead, they tend to look forward to the future, believing that what happens in the future is within their control, or at least subject to their influence. Such a conviction has a lot to do with the fact that as a young nation with abundant natural resources, America offers plenty of opportunity for its citizens to bring their potential to the fullest degree possible. To the average American, since America provides such a high degree of social mobility, new possibilities are always there for people to explore, and obstacles exist merely to be overcome. In short, as along as one keeps trying and working hard, he/she will eventually turn things round.

Unit Four   Religion in American Life

Focal Points

Puritan	Protestantism	Catholicism
separation of church and state	state church	religious pluralism
denomination	Judeo-Christian tradition	popular religion

Discussion Questions

How important is religion in American life?

Text

In a land first settled by the Puritans in New England and Anglican Protestants in the South, religion has always been a centerpiece in American life, influencing the way Americans perceive and react to the environment in which they live. While almost all Western countries have experienced sharp decline in religious **observance** as a result of industrialization, consumerism, materialism, and **secularization**, America seems to move in the opposite direction. Instead of becoming irreligious, America has witnessed several religious revivals sweeping across the country over the past forty-plus years. In 1992, for example, 90 percent of Americans said that they were religious. In recent years, however, there has been a slight decline in the number of believers. In 2010, for instance, 80 percent of adult Americans regarded themselves as religious in one form or another, and by the December of 2013, that figure dropped to 74

observance 奉行、遵循、礼仪
secularization 世俗化

percent, according to a Harris Poll of that year. However, despite such a decline, America still remains the most religious country in the industrialized world.

"In God We Trust"

The American view on religion is **paradoxical**. They honor the separation of church and state, meaning that one is free to believe or not to believe in God, and that one is also free to worship at the church of one's own choice, but in public life few Americans would ever openly admit having no religious belief at all. There are many reasons for being timid in making such a public claim. For one thing, since vast majority of Americans are religious, claiming no belief in God publicly is like making oneself an **outcast**, or a **deviant**, at best. For another, the presence of God can be felt almost everywhere in the United States. When one uses money, for example, he/she finds the phrase "In God We Trust" cast on coins and paper currencies. When one drives one's car around, he/she is likely to see on the **rear** of a car running before him/her such **bumper-sticker** statements as "America, Bless God", "**Honk** if you love God", "Smile, God loves you", "Jesus is the answer" and "Beware of God". And, when one turns on TV on Sunday, he/she often finds a TV preacher on the screen. For still another, there is a widespread feeling among Americans that **decent** people generally believe in God, and that **ethical** standards **spring from** religion. More significantly, on many solemn occasions, the word "God" is always uttered. For instance, the President of the United States may begin his **State of the Union Address** with a **supplication** to God, and virtually all American politicians end their **campaign speeches** with the phrase "God Bless America". Also, the recitation of **the Pledge of Allegiance to the Flag**, in Congress at the beginning of its each session, or in school at the beginning of every school day, is a constant reminder to every American that the United States is "One Nation, Under God".

The reasons for American strong attachment to religion are **manifold**. To begin with, the history of American religion is as long as that of the United States, or longer if one counts the year of 1776 as the beginning of the founding of the United States, when the Declaration of Independence was published. Such a long history has laid a solid foundation for the flourishing of religious beliefs in America. Secondly, the principle of separation of church and state removes any possibility of government intervention in American religious life, making it possible, or rather necessary, for religious organizations to compete with one another for new members in the religious market, from whom they **derive** funding. Such competition between religious organizations, as competition between business organizations, tends to **boost** the growth of religious organizations. Thirdly, in the course of American experience over the past 300-plus years, there have been several religious revivals nationwide, each one of them producing a **surge** in membership **in its wake**. Such repeated religious revivals help **infuse** new vigor and fresh vitality into the religious **scene** in the United States. Fourthly, as a nation of immigrants, and more importantly as a nation that stands for freedom of belief, America has attracted numerous people around the world who escaped from religious persecution in their own countries. These groups of religiously motivated immigrants have contributed tremendously not only to the growing population of religious believers in the United States, but also to the increased diversity of religious beliefs in the country. In short, the above-mentioned four reasons, among other things, combine to help America maintain a high degree of religious intensity among its population, not found in other industrialized nations in the Western world.

Since Americans generally believe "In God, We Trust" and since the United States regards itself as "One Nation, Under God", it can be well imagined that Americans take religion quite seriously. However, seriously taken as it is, religion is sup-

---

manifold 多方面的

derive 获取

boost 促进

surge 上升、上冲
in its wake 在它之后
infuse 向……注入
scene 活动领域

posed to be primarily a private matter, between the individual, his conscience and his church. Government, according to the Constitution, is not allowed to give special favors to any religion or to hinder the free practice of any religion. As a result, there are no church taxes in the United States, nor is there an official state church or a state-supported church. Likewise, there are no legal or official religious holidays. Christmas, for example, is an important religious holiday for Christians. However, Congress cannot proclaim it, or any other religious observance. To do so would violate the principle of separation of church and state. In short, in "One Nation, Under God", religion is seen basically as providing spiritual guidance, helping people lead a life according to the **tenets** of their faith. For Christians, for example, this means following the principle of brotherly love, forgiveness, charity, righteousness, and humility.

However, there are some important exceptions to the general view of religion being deemed as largely a private matter. First, there are certain religious groups in America, notably **fundamentalist** or **evangelical** Christians, whose members consider it their duty to **convert** others to their faith. Members of these groups will readily try to bring up the subject of religion and will try to **induce** people who do not belong to their group to become members. Second, there are some communities in the United States, for instance, **Mormons** in Utah, and **Lutherans** in Minnesota, where virtually everyone belongs to the same religious **denomination**. In such communities, people's religious views are likely to be known by many people, and religion is talked about rather openly and freely. Third, political candidates for and holders of electoral offices at the national and state level often make their religious views and activities quite public. For instance, they may announce what religious traditions they belong to, and they often have themselves photographed attending religious services, usually **in the company of** their families. Sometimes, they even express their views on political, social and cultural issues **couched in** religious terms. All this is usually regarded as part of an effort to **portray** themselves as **wholesome**, right-minded people who deserve the public's trust.

Religious Pluralism

Unlike other nations in the world where religion tends to be **monolithic**, America is characterized by pluralism in its religious belief, or "**poly-piety**" as one colonial called. There are many reasons making American religion pluralistic, chief among which are: 1) absence of an **established church**; 2) freedom of religion; 3) immigration. Without an established church, Americans are never forced to join any particular church; instead, they are left free to form any religious organization as they wish. Similarly, guaranteed the freedom of conscience, Americans can choose or even create any religious denomination at their will. Finally, being a nation of immigrants, America has immigrants coming ashore from every corner of the world, bringing with them religious belief of every type. The 2012 Yearbook of American and Canadian Churches, for example, provided a directory of 235 U.S. local and regional **ecumenical** bodies with program and contract information, meaning that as of 2012 there were as many as 235 Christian organizations in the United States, not including non-Christian religious organizations and those Christian groups not officially listed.

According to a 2007 survey conducted by **the Pew Research Center**, the majority of Americans (78.4%) identify themselves as Christians, and the rest either belong to other religions (4.7%) or are non-affiliated (16.1), or simply "Don't Know" (0.8%). Of the Christians, according to the survey, about 51.3% claim themselves to be Protestant, 23.9% Catholic, 1.7% **Mormon**, and 0.7% **Jehovah' Witness**, 0.6% Orthodox, and remaining 0.3& other Christians. Among 4.7% other religions, Jews represent 1.7%, with the Buddhism and Muslim accounting for 0.7% and 0.6% respectively. What is interest-

---

couch in 以……措辞表达

portray 描写、描绘

wholesome 健全的、无污点的

monolithic 单一的

poly-piety 多重虔诚性

established church 国教

ecumenical 全基督教的

the Pew Research Center 皮尤研究中心

Mormon 摩门教

Jehovah' Witness 耶和华见证人

ing to note is that in 1963, 90% of Americans claimed to be Christians, and only 2% professed no religious affiliation. However, half a century later, the percentage of Christians was just a bit over 70%, while 13% claimed no religious identity at all. All these figures tell us that 1) as late as 1963, America was still largely a Christian country; when 90% Americans identified themselves as Christians; 2) even though America was largely a Christian country prior to 1963, American Christianity was characterized by diversity, with **denominations** of every kind in Protestantism; 3) Immigrants from Asia and Latin America since the 1960s have significantly transformed the religious landscape of the United States, not only promoting such new religious beliefs as **Buddhism**, **Muslims** and **Hinduism** in the U.S., but also expanding such old religious beliefs as Catholicism and Judaism.

Despite all these changes, the large majority of religious Americans today are still within the **Judeo-Christian** tradition, and U.S. religion largely consists of three main faiths in terms of their history, numbers and influence: Protestantism, Catholicism and Judaism. Protestantism is the largest and most diverse of the U.S. faiths. Although a majority of adult Americans identify themselves as Protestants, they can be divided into many denominations and **sects**, with conservative, mainstream and liberal outlooks. There is no one single denomination for all Protestants; instead, each denomination follows its own beliefs and practices. For example, within the Protestants, such well-known denominations as the **Presbyterian**, **Lutheran**, the **Baptist** churches, **Methodists**, the Southern Baptist Convention, and the National Baptist Convention, are all independent churches. By contrast, the Roman Catholic Church in the U.S. is not denominational at all. Therefore, even though Catholicism is the second largest religion after Protestantism in the U.S., its Roman Catholic Church is the biggest church in terms of a single religious denomination. Still, even though it is one single religious denomination, institutionally speaking, the Roman Catholic Church, like Protestantism, is divided between liberals and conservatives on a wide range of issues, like abortion, gay marriage, and birth control. As for Judaism, it, in some ways, presents a paradox, for "Jew" refers to both a religion and a people. Because of this inter-connection between religion and nationality, Jews, more than any other people within the Judeo-Christian tradition in America, feel most strongly about this interplay, leading eventually to divisions among Jews. Some Jews insist that they should be made inseparable, others they be compromised, and still others they be reformed. As a result, Judaism in America finds itself divided into Reform, Conservative, and Orthodox Judaism.

In addition to the three main faiths mentioned above, there are other significant religious groups in the United States, with their number close to 9 million. They include, but not limited to, **Islam**, **Buddhism**, **Hinduism** or **Sikhism**. It is said that Islam is now the fourth largest faith in the United States, with a good potential to grow bigger **down the road**. Also, there have grown in America a quite significant number of **cults**, or non-conventional religions, as some people call them. Researchers do not agree on the exact number of such cults. The Cult Awareness Network claims that there are as many as 2500 cults and that number is growing. The Institute for the Study of American Religion cites **approximately** 700. Whatever the figure they may be, cults have been very much in American media in recent years, suggesting that they do have an appeal to many Americans. Finally, according to a Statistical Abstract of the United States, 2012, about 1.6 million American adults described themselves as **atheist**, more than 2 million as **agnostic**, over 30.4 million as having no religious, and 11.9-plus million giving no religious identification. All this indicates that the challenge to Christianity in America does not come simply from non-Christian religious groups, but more significantly from a rejec-

Islam 伊斯兰教
Sikhism 锡克教
down the road 今后、将来
cult 邪教

approximately 大约、接近

atheist 异教徒
agnostic 不可知论者

tion of all forms of organized religions by a growing number of non-believers in the country.

Popular Religion

What has been discussed above may be said to be institutional religions, for they are all structured social institutions or organizations. However, apart from these formal religions, there is another aspect of religion in the United States that is at least equally significant. This is called popular religion, i. e., religion that occurs outside the formal boundaries of established religious institutions. It is widespread, **pervasive** and influential. The existence of a wide variety of popular religion alongside the institutional ones indicates that what counts religion is not the sole **prerogative** of a few academics.

To be sure, most Americans belong to some sort of religious community. They can be Protestants, Catholics, Jews, Buddhists or Muslims, for example. However, many American believers **supplement** their formal membership and church attendance with a variety of other religious activities. Such activities, generally speaking, do not come directly from their community of faith, such as revivals, watching religious television programs, listening to religious talks, and various devotional activities like private prayer, reading, **chanting** and **meditation**. These examples of "popular religion" are all present in the common culture in which most Americans grew up, and they have become familiar with all of this by **hearsay** if not by direct experience. They are popular in two senses, at least. First, they have mass appeal, meaning they "sell" well to a great number of people. Second, they are not taught by **theologians** in **seminaries**, but rather offered to a wide variety of people of no special knowledge but common sense.

Widespread as it is, popular religion is very difficult to describe, for there is no agreed-upon definition. Still, however, there are enough common features of it to make it distinctive.

For instance, popular religion is more practiced by ordinary people than by theologians or religious leaders. Also, it exists alongside formal institutional religions as a complement to it, rather than a replacement. Furthermore, it offers people more direct access to the **sacred** than formal religious groups. More significantly, formal religious organizations impose order and structure on religion, while, popular religion, by contrast, provides a lively sense of the supernatural without the imposition of formal structure. Finally, it **draws on** the core religious institutions of the culture, Christianity for example, but **blends** this with other sources of tradition to make it a reflection of both mainstream and alternative values.

In the commercialized culture of the U.S., the strength of popular culture **manifests** itself in the amount of money it **generates**. It is estimated that Christian retail is a yearly three-billion-dollar-plus industry. For instance, Americans buy cross symbols and put them on their cars, or purchase statues of Jesus, Mary, or the Buddha and place them in their yards. They all cost money. Also, many Americans buy and wear **religious-theme** shirts, and they, too, promote business. More significantly, religious music in America has a big market, where such **musicals** as "Jesus Christ, Superstar" and "Godspell" continue to enjoy great popularity among a great number of Americans, **pious** or not pious. Beyond all this, gift items such as religious-theme **figurines**, decorative items, and greeting cards sell well in both religious book and supply stores and secular stores. Most amazing of all, there are computer games and educational software based on **biblical** stories and teachings to help children learn about the Bible!

Although the most popular religion in the United States is Christian, it is not exclusively Christian. A number of catalogs offer a variety of items for people to devise their own spirituality. One such catalog has an umbrella that features the eight major symbols of Buddhism, as well as items reflecting Native A-

sacred 神圣的

draw on 汲取
blend 与……融于一体

manifest 显示
generate 产生

religious-theme 宗教主题的

musical 音乐剧

pious 虔诚的
figurine 用陶土、刻石等制作的小人像

biblical 圣经的

merican religions. In another catalog, those of Jewish faith can choose from a vast assortment of Jewish religious items such as **prayer shawls**, **menorahs** and **Passover** plates. Several sources exist for Buddhists to obtain statues, meditation cushions and benches, and audiotapes or videotapes. *Hinduism Today*, a magazine for North American Hindus, routinely advertises Hindu religious articles such as deity statues, beads and incense. Indeed, just as American religion becomes increasingly diversified, so will American popular religion become more and more pervasive and influential. Perhaps, the most notable development in popular religion at the beginning of the 21st century is the rapidly expanding presence of religion on the Internet, where ordinary people conduct "**cyber-rituals**" and discuss religious matters at chat rooms, making religion more informal, more accessible, and hence more popular.

prayer shawl 祷告披巾
menorah 九千支大烛台
Passover 逾越节

cyber-ritual 网络礼仪

Notes

The State of the Union Address—The State of the Union Address is presented by the President of the United States to a joint session of the United States Congress, typically delivered annually. The address not only reports on the condition of the nation, but also allows presidents to outline their legislative agenda and their national priorities.

The Pledge of Allegiance to the Flag—The Pledge of Allegiance of the United States is an expression of fealty to the Flag of the United States and the Republic of the United States of America. Its official version reads as follows: "I pledge allegiance to the flag of the United States of American and to the Republic for which it stands, one nation under God, indivisible, with liberty and justice for all".

Fundamentalism—Fundamentalism is the demand for a strict adherence to the orthodox theological doctrines, usually understood as a reaction to modernist theology. The term was originally coined by its supporters to describe five specific classic theological beliefs of Christianity, and that developed into a Christian fundamentalist movement with the Protestant community of the United States in the early part of the 20th century.

Evangelicalism—Evangelicalism is a world-wide Protestant movement, maintaining that the essence of gospel consists in the doctrine of salvation by faith in God's atonement.

Mormons—Mormons are a religious and cultural group related to Mormonism, principal branch of the Latter Day Saint Movement of Restorationist Christianity, which began with the vision of Joseph Smith in upstate New York during the 1820s. Today, most Mormons are understood to be members of The Church of Jesus Christ of Latter Day Saints.

Exercises

Ⅰ. Multiple Choices

The following are questions or incomplete sentences. Below each sentence or question four possible answers marked A, B, C and D are provided. Choose the ONE that best completes the sentence or answers the question.

1. Almost all Western countries have experienced _____ decline in religious observance as a result of industrialization, consumerism, materialism and secularization.

　　A. steady　　　　B. slow　　　　C. steep　　　　D. gradual

2. In 2010, for instance, _____ percent of adult Americans regarded themselves as religious in one form or another, and by 2013, that figure dropped to _____ percent.

　　A. 74, 80　　　　B. 80, 74　　　　C. 84, 70　　　　D. 70, 84

3. When Americans uses money, they find the phrase _____ cast on coins and paper currencies.

　　A. "In Jesus, We Trust"　　　　B. "My God, We Trust"
　　C. "In God, We Trust"　　　　D. "One Nation, Under God"

4. There is a widespread feeling among Americans that _____ people generally believe in God.

　　A. hard-working　　B. ambitious　　C. smart　　　　D. honest

5. The principle of separation of church and state <u>removes any possibility of government intervention in American religious life.</u> The underlined phrase means:

　　A. there is some possibility for government intervention in American religious life.

　　B. there is no possibility for government intervention in American religious life.

　　C. the possibility of government intervention in American religious life is relocated.

　　D. the possibility of government intervention in American religious life is recognized.

6. Christmas is an important religious holiday for _____.

A. all religious believers   B. all Americans

C. Christians and non-Christians alike   D. Christians

7. U. S. religion largely consists of three main faiths in terms of their history, numbers and influence, namely:

A. Protestantism, Catholicism and Judaism

B. Catholicism, Protestantism and Buddhism

C. Protestantism, Muslim and Judaism

D. Hinduism, Catholicism and Judaism

8. "Jew" refers to both a religion and a _____.

A. country   B. language   C. culture   D. people

9. By "popular religion", it largely means _____.

A. it is a kind of religion that is very popular among religious believers.

B. it is a kind of religion that has been popularized in the country.

C. it is a kind of religion that occurs outside the formal boundaries of established religious institutions.

D. it is a kind of religion that has gained popular approval.

10. The strength of popular religion can be measured by _____.

A. the degree of its popularity among the believers

B. the amount of money it generates in the consumer market

C. the intensity of its belief as a doctrine

D. the scope of its influence in society

Ⅱ. True and False

Read the following statements carefully and then decide whether they are true or false. Put a "T" if you think the statement is true and an "F" if it is not.

1. In the early 1990s, 90 percent of Americans said that they were religious.

2. In public life, most Americans would openly admit having no religious belief at all.

3. School children in America cite the Pledge of Allegiance to the Flag at the beginning of every school day.

4. Religion in America is like a market, where different religious denominations compete with each other for new followers.

5. Religion in America is supposed to be primarily a public matter between the

church and the state.

6. Without an established church, Americans are free to join or not to join any particular church.

7. Over the past half a century, there has been a steady decline in the number of Christians in the United States.

8. Islam is now the fifth largest faith in the United States after Protestantism, Catholicism, Judaism, and Buddhism.

9. The number of cults in America is alarmingly large and difficult to determine.

10. Popular religion is basically a kind of supplementary religious activity, informal and unorganized.

Ⅲ. General Questions

1. Why do we say that the American view on religion is paradoxical?

2. How does one feel the presence of God in everyday life in America?

3. Since no church in the United States is funded by the government, where do churches get their financial support?

4. Why are there no church taxes, no religious holidays, or a state church in the United States?

5. What are the two most active religious groups in contemporary America that tend to consider it their duty to convert others to their faith?

6. Where are Mormons most heavily concentrated in the United States?

7. What are the chief reasons for religious pluralism in America?

8. How come Catholicism is the single largest religious denomination in the United States, when there are more Protestants than Catholics living in the country?

9. What are some of non-major religious groups in the United States?

10. What may be the most amazing thing about popular religion?

Ⅳ. Essay Questions

1. Why are Americans so intensely religious?

2. What are some of the common features of popular religion?

Unit Four Religion in American Life

Reference Answers

I. Multiple Choices

1. C 2. B 3. C 4. D 5. B 6. D 7. A 8. D 9. C 10. B

II. True and False

1. T 2. F 3. T 4. T 5. F 6. T 7. T 8. F 9. T 10. T

III. General Questions

1. Because on the one hand they are free to believe or not to believe in God, and yet on the other hand few Americans would ever openly admit having no religious belief in public life.

2. One feels the presence of God in everyday life in America when he uses U.S. money, drives a car around or watches TV programs on Sunday.

3. Churches in the United States get financial support mostly from their memberships.

4. Because they are forbidden by the U.S. Constitution, according to which the state and the church should be separated from each other, meaning the government cannot pass any law establishing a state church, or designating a particular religion's holiday as a national religious holiday, or deciding taxes for any particular church.

5. They are fundamentalists and evangelicals.

6. Mormons are most heavily concentrated in the state of Utah, USA.

7. They are absence of an established church, freedom of religion, immigration.

8. Because Protestants in the United States are divided into numerous denominations, such as Baptists, Presbyterians, and Methodists, while the Roman Catholic Church in the United States is a solidly unified church.

9. They are Islam, Buddhism, Hinduism, and Sikhism.

10. Perhaps, the most amazing thing about popular religion is that there are computer games and educational software based on biblical stories and teachings designed to help children learn about the Bible!

IV. Essay Questions

1. There are many reasons for Americans being so religiously intense. To begin with, the United States has a long history of religion, which helps to lay a solid founda-

tion for the flourishing of religious beliefs in America. Secondly, the principle of separation of church and state makes it possible for religious organizations to compete with one another for new members in the religious market, which tends to boost the growth of religious organizations. Thirdly, there have been several religious revivals in U. S. history, each of which produces a surge in membership in its wake. Fourthly, as a nation of immigrants, America has attracted numerous people around the world to come to the U. S. These immigrants brought with them their religious beliefs and practices. In sum, the above-mentioned four reasons combine to help America maintain a high degree of religious intensity among its population.

2. Some of the common features of popular religion include: 1) it is more practiced by ordinary people than by theologians or religious leaders; 2) it exists alongside formal institutional religions as a complement to it, rather than a replacement; 3) it offers people more direct access to the sacred than formal religious groups; 4) in comparison with formal religious organizations which impose order and structure on religion, popular religion, by contrast, provides a lively sense of the supernatural without the imposition of formal structure; finally, 5) while it draws on the core religious institutions of the culture, Christianity for example, it blends this with other sources of tradition to make it a reflection of both mainstream and alternative values.

Unit Five Education in America

Focal Points

access to education
well-rounded people
educational ladder

equal opportunity in education
social/individual goals in education
No Child Left Behind

Discussion Questions

What are the most important guiding principles in the American educational system?

Text

Americans have shown a great concern for education since early colonial times, and at the same time have also expected a great deal from their educational institutions. To them, education does not merely function as a **vehicle** to **pass on** knowledge to children; it also serves the purpose of instilling values in the **plastic** minds of the young. **Viewed in this light**, American schools can best be understood as a kind of social institutions that reflect the basic values and fundamental principles of the United States, rather than simply as a kind of skill-training places where students are taught to prepare themselves for jobs upon graduation.

vehicle 工具
pass on 传递、传输
plastic 可塑性强调、易受影响的
viewed in this light 以此观之

Guiding Principles

Like any other institution, education in the United States also has its own guiding principles under which its system operates. To understand these principles is, in fact, to understand the beliefs and values of the American people as a nation. In this section, some of the key guiding principles of American education are **singled out** to illustrate the ideals that Americans **cherish** and **embrace** in their educational system.

single out 挑出、选出
cherish 珍视
embrace 信奉

Access to Education

The American educational system is based on the idea that as many people as possible should have access to as much education as possible. Such an idea, as can be imaged, is an outcome of Americans' assumptions about equality among people. While these assumptions about equalitarianism do not mean that everyone has an equal opportunity to enter Harvard, Yale, Standard, or other **highly prestigious** universities, they do suggest that everyone in the United States has access to **institutions of higher learning** as long as he/she is academically qualified. Admission to Harvard or Yale is highly competitive and selective, generally restricted only to those with the most impressive academic records and the most outstanding personal accomplishments. However, numerous post-secondary institutions like state universities and community colleges across the country are accessible to virtually every American student, if he/she is willing to push himself or herself a bit hard for higher education.

highly prestigious 威望崇高的

institutions of higher learning 高等教育机构

In order to make sure that all American children can actually "enjoy" access to education, including higher education, all fifty U.S. states have "compulsory attendance" laws, requiring young people to attend school or to be home-schooled. According to the National Conference of State Legislatures, twenty-six states require students to continue attending school at least until the age of 16. Other states set the age at 17 or 18, or else they require completion of a specified grade. Most states, under the influence of a 2000 federal law known as **No Child Left Behind**, have developed examinations intended to prevent students from graduating from secondary school without attaining **prescribed** test scores. However, it should be pointed out that the U.S. educational system has no standardized examinations whose results systematically prevent secondary-school graduates from going on to higher levels of study, as is the case in the traditional British and many other systems. (There are some well-known standardized tests, such as the SAT, ACT, TOEFL, and GMAT, but results on these tests are just one among several factors considered in college and university admissions decisions).

Through secondary school and sometimes post-secondary institutions as well, the American system tries to accommodate students even if their academic aspirations and aptitudes are not high, even if they have a physical and in some cases mental limitation, and even if their native language is not English. The guiding principle behind all this is that every American should be provided access to education, including higher education. Naturally, an educational system that retains as many people as the American system does is likely to enroll a broader range of students than a system that seeks to educate only the few who seem especially suited for academic work. In the American system, academic **rigor** tends to come later than in most other systems. In many instances American students do not face truly demanding educational requirements until they seek a graduate degree. In contrast, many other systems place demands on students as early as their primary years, though college may be far less demanding, as is the case in many Asian countries.

Equal Opportunity and Well-Rounded People

While the principle access to education is to make sure that no individual in America is denied the opportunity to receive education, it does not specifically stipulate that such opportunity will be made equal to all. Therefore, following the principle access to education is another equally important guiding principle in American education, that is, equal opportunity. These two are closely related to each other, with one reinforcing the other.

The key point of Equal Opportunity in education is that America should provide comparable educational programs to everyone, **regardless of** gender, race, income level, social class, or physical or mental disability. To be sure, equal opportunity in education in America is **more of** an ideal that has yet to be realized than a reality that has already been achieved. But America has gone a long way towards achieving this goal. For instance, over the past half a century, **assorted** programs have been introduced into the American educational institutions of various levels, radically transforming the character of **student bodies** at American schools and universities. At **the K-12 level**, for example, special programs have resulted in the enrollment of more and more students with physical or **cognitive** limitations.

More significantly, **prior to** World War Ⅱ, **tertiary** institutions enrolled mainly European American, upper- or middle-class, English-speaking males in their late teens or early twenties. Since the implementation of Affirmative Action in American higher education, however, all of this has changed. Not only have student bodies in institutions of higher learning become more diverse, but the percentage of their representation has grown in number as well. Such social groups as ethnic minorities, working-class children, and women had been largely denied equal opportunity in higher education. Now, they represent a significant portion of college student population in the United States. **Looking in on** classrooms at colleges and universities in the U.S., one will see countless people who are different from the "traditional" college students—people of many ethnic and racial backgrounds, people in wheelchairs or using aids for vision or **hearing impairments**, and "returning students" who are middle-aged or older. All of this demonstrates that more and more Americans, regardless of race, gender, class, health and

---

regardless of 不管、不论

more of 更大程度上的……

assorted 各种各样的

student body 学生团体

the K-12 level 美国第12级教育,即高中最后一年

cognitive 认知上的

prior to 在……之前

tertiary 第三的、(继小学和中学之后的)高等教育的

look in on 顺便看望一下

hearing impairment 听力障碍

Unit Five Education in America

age, are given more equal opportunity to receive tertiary education.

Of course, higher education is made equally accessible to all Americans not just for the sake of providing equal opportunity. The **underlying** reason to do so is to ensure universal literacy, i.e., to produce a society that is 100 percent literate. While this goal has yet to be achieved, and may never be achieved, it nevertheless remains the stated goal of the United States. More importantly, equal opportunity in education, particularly higher education, is intended to make sure that all Americans will be given the opportunity to **bring out** their potential to the fullest degree possible. It is exactly in this connection that the American educational system seeks to **turn out** "well-rounded people". By "well-rounded people", Americans mean that students should not only have specialized knowledge in one area, but more importantly, they should have a general **acquaintance** with many **disciplines**.

Specifically speaking, having passed through a system that requires them to study some mathematics, some English, some humanities, some science, and some social sciences (and perhaps a foreign language), students presumably have **an array of** interests and can understand information from many fields of study. Thus, in the American educational system, specialization comes later than in many other educational systems. In other words, American students are required to take courses that they might not be particularly interested in and that appear to have little relationship to their career aspirations. But in order to become well-rounded people, they cannot afford not to follow these requirements.

Beyond that, being well-rounded also means participating in nonacademic curricular (or extra-curricular) activities in and out of school. Secondary students are continuously reminded that they will be more attractive to college and graduate admissions officers and to **prospective** employers if they take part in

---

underlying 根本的、隐含的

bring out 发挥出来

turn out 生产、培养

acquaintance 熟悉、了解
discipline 学科

an array of 一系列、一长串

prospective 未来的

school clubs, sports, community activities, or any other form of voluntary service. For this and many other reasons, many secondary and tertiary institutions in the United States have developed "service learning" programs, in which students receive academic credit for community-service work such as volunteering in a library, **homeless shelter** or home-construction program. In some schools, participation in service learning is required for graduating.

homeless shelter 无家可归者收容所

Goals of Education

Goals of education in America have varied from one era to another throughout American history. In colonial times, for example, Puritan New England aimed at religious **indoctrination**, even making the learning of the alphabet a series of theological lessons. After the founding of the nation, U. S. Founding Fathers emphasized education as a way of nurturing virtues and discovering **merits** in its citizenry. With the opening up of the frontier, people in the west **dreamed of** education as a great **leveler** to make the country more democratic. In the wake of industrialization, the focus of education shifted from classics to applied sciences and practical training. As the United States grew increasingly diverse in its **demographic composition** in the late 20th century, multiculturalism has now become a **defining** feature in the goal of American education today.

indoctrination 灌输

merit 优点、贤才
dream of 幻想
leveler 杠杆、手段、方法

demographic composition 人口构成

defining 确立其特性的

Social Goals

In general, as mentioned previously, the goal of the American educational system is to **bestow** a broad education on every youngster. This is not an overly ambitious goal. While only a few students are expected to become intellectuals, scientists or scholars, the rest will be able to read, write, think, and deal with the issues of the day. In keeping with the democracy principle, there are no absolute turning points when a **crucial** exam **separates the sheep from the goats**. Theoretically, anyone who completes the academic course is college material. To Ameri-

bestow 把……给予

crucial 决定性的、关键的

separate the sheep from the goats 分辨好人与坏人

Unit Five Education in America

cans, a high general level of education has always been seen as a necessity in a democratic society. Only in this way, they are convinced, can American democracy maintain its vitality

Because of these social functions, education in America has traditionally served the goal of bringing people together, that is, "Americanization"—instilling fundamental American values in the minds of children, native-born or foreign-born. During every school day, thousands of millions of American youngsters of various cultural and linguistic groups, religions, and social and political backgrounds are brought together in schools or universities, where, it is hoped, they would **mingle together** and eventually build bridges across racial, ethnic, religious, social and linguistic barriers.

To this end, both American public policies and legal decisions over the past several decades have increasingly stressed special rights for underprivileged groups in the area of education. For linguistic minorities, like **Hispanics** and Asians, bilingual education has been made available in most of the states. Similarly, for ethnic minorities, certain **quotas** are set aside each year for their admission into colleges or universities. Such measures are designed to **lessen** differences in social backgrounds as well as those of ethnic or racial origin in the university setting, using education as a tool. This explains some of the special characteristics of the American system of education. One of these, for example, is the "busing" of children. The goal is to have in each school the same proportion of children from various ethnic or racial groups that exist in the city's overall population. Such an idea of **"education starts with babies"** reflects the American view that education should help to reform society. Imagine: if school children could build a good sense of ethnic or racial understanding, won't America **stand a good chance** to turn their country into a harmonious society?

In a sense, the American view of education as a vehicle for social reform can be traced to the **pragmatic theory** of John

---

mingle together 打成一片

to this end 为了实现这一目的

Hispanic 有西班牙血统、讲西班牙语的美国人

quota 名额

lessen 减少

education starts with babies 教育从娃娃抓起

stand a good chance 很有……可能

pragmatic theory 实用主义理论

Dewey, an American educator and philosopher. Dewey believed that the school's job was to enhance the natural development of the growing child, rather than to pour information in him/her. Also, Dewey believed that the school was a microcosm of society, and therefore, in the Dewey system, the child not only becomes an active **agent** in his own education, rather than a passive **receptacle** for facts, but also potentially an active member of society, ready to apply what he/she has acquired at school to solving social problems he/she **encounters** upon entering it. Consequently, American schools are very enthusiastic about teaching "life skills" or "practical skills", training students to do logical thinking, analysis, and creative problem-solving. The actual content of the lessons is secondary to the process, in which the child learns how to handle whatever life may present, including all the unknown of the future. Both American students and teachers regard pure memorization as uncreative and boring, and problem-solving and analysis more exciting and helpful. If one **stretches** John Dewey's ideas just a bit further, one may easily find that all of this is just one step away from social reform. In other words, according to Dewey, part of the goals of education is to prepare students to solve social problems. That at least partially explains why schools in America are assigned to deal with such social problems as racism, drug abuse, AIDS, **teenage pregnancy**, and **alcoholism**, to name just a few.

Individual Goals

While social goals of education are important for American society, for virtually all Americans, however, it is their individual goals of education that really matter. Generally speaking, education has been seen by most Americans as a way of "bettering oneself" or of "**rising in the world**". It is a fundamental part of the American Dream, that is, by taking full advantage of access to education and equal opportunity in education, one can "better oneself" and "rise in the world". That is why millions of

agent 行动者、行事者

receptacle 容器、储藏器

encounter 遇到

stretch 延伸、拉长

teenage pregnancy 未成年人怀孕

alcoholism 酗酒

rise in the world 崭露头角、飞黄腾达

Unit Five Education in America

immigrants around the world keep coming to the United States, often tying their hopes for a better life to a good education and, most importantly, for their children. The social and economic mobility of Americans, discussed previously, comes largely from the easy access to education that most Americans enjoy. So, in short, the first step upward, whether the ultimate goal is money, status, power, or simply knowledge, usually starts at the school door, especially for average Americans.

Specifically, Americans view their public school system as an educational **ladder**, rising from elementary school to high school and finally to college undergraduate and graduate programs. In many ways, the educational ladder concept is an almost perfect reflection of the American idea of individual success based on equality of opportunity and on "working your way to the top". In America, there are no separate educational systems with a higher level of education of the wealth and a lower level of education for the masses. Rather, there is one system that is open to all. Individuals may climb as high on the ladder as they can. The abilities of the individuals, rather than their social class background, are expected to determine how high a person can go.

Although the great majority of children attend the free public elementary and high schools, some choose to attend private schools. There are a number of private religious schools that are associated with particular churches and receive financial support from them, though parents must also pay tuition. The primary purpose of these schools is to give religious instruction to children, which cannot be done in public schools, due to the principle of separation of church and state. The most numerous of these, the Catholic schools, have students whose social class backgrounds are similar to the majority of students in public schools.

There are also some elite private schools, which serve mainly upper-class children. Students must pay such high tui-

ladder 阶梯

tion costs that only wealthier families can afford them. Parents send their children to these schools so that they all associate with other upper-class children and maintain the upper-class position held by their parents, in addition to getting a good education. But unlike private religious schools, elite private schools do conflict with the American ideal of equality. These schools often give an extra educational and social advantage to the young people whose families have the money to allow them to attend. However, because these schools are relatively small in number, they do not displace the public schools as the central educational situation in the United States. Nor does the best private school education protect young people from competition with public school graduates for admissions to the best universities in the nation.

There is another area of inequality in the American education system. Because of the way that schools are funded, the quality of education that American students receive in public schools varies greatly. More than 90 percent of the money for schools comes from the local level (cities and counties), primarily from property taxes. School districts that have middle class or wealthier families have more tax money to spend on education. Therefore, wealthier school districts have beautiful school buildings with computers and the latest science equipment, and poorer school districts have older buildings with less modern equipment. The amount of money spent on education may vary from $8,000 per child in a wealthy suburb to only $1,200 per child attending an inner-city school, or in a poor rural area. Although the amount of money spent per child is not always the best indicator of the quality of education the child receives, it certainly is an important factor.

In any event, to the average American, since the education system is just like a social ladder, what he/she needs to do is simply try to make the best use of it, **setting his/her sights on** the goals and then driving himself or herself hard toward them.

In any event 不管怎样、无论如何

set his/her sights on 定下……目标

Whether he/she eventually reaches these goals or not, it depends on, among other things, his/her will, effort, opportunity, wisdom, and maybe a bit of luck as well.

Management of Education

The United States does not have a national system of education. Education is considered to be a matter for the people of each state. Although there is a federal Department of Education, its function is merely to gather information, to advise, and to help finance certain educational programs. Education, Americans say, is "a national concern, a state responsibility and a local function". Since the U. S. Constitution does not state that education is a responsibility of the federal government, all educational matters are left to the individual states. As a result, each of the 50 state legislatures is free to determine its own system for its own public schools, setting whatever minimal requirements for teaching and teachers it judges to be appropriate.

In turn, however, state constitutions give the actual administrative control of the public schools to the local communities, where **school boards** made up of individual citizens are elected to **oversee** the schools in each district. It is the school board, not the state, that sets school policy and actually decides what is to be taught. So, overall, the public schools in the United States are very much community schools. They must have local public support, because citizens vote directly on how much they want to pay for school taxes. They must represent local wishes and educational interests, as those who administrate the schools are elected by the community. Additionally, there are a great many city or county-owned colleges and universities, and many are supported by the states. In general, colleges and universities, whether state or private, are quite free to determine their own individual standards, admissions, and graduation requirements. Both schools and universities have self-governing groups, associations or boards which **"accredit"**, that is, certify schools and universities as meeting certain minimum standards.

One major result of this unusual situation is that there is an enormous amount of variety in elementary, secondary and tertiary education in the **Uniked stakes.** In about 60 percent of the states, for example, local schools are free to choose any teaching materials or textbooks which they think are appropriate. In the remaining states, only such teaching materials may be used in public schools which have been approved by the state boards of education. Some state universities are virtually free to residents of the state, with only token fees, but others are expensive, especially for out-of-state students. Some school systems are, like their communities, extremely conservative, while others are very progressive and liberal. These and other substantial differences must always be considered when one tries to understand American schools and universities.

Another major result of the local control of the schools is that there is a great deal of flexibility in what each local community wants to do. For instance, there is much opportunity to experiment and to fit programs to local wishes and needs. Typically, local high schools will offer courses of study which they feel best reflect their students' needs. Students at the same school will commonly be taking courses in different areas. Some may be following pre-university programs, with an emphasis on those academic subjects required for college work. Others may well be taking coursework which prepares them for vocational or technical positions. Still others may enroll in a general program combining elements of the academic and vocational training. State-supported universities and colleges also to some degree **tailor** their courses of study to the needs of the states and the students. States with strong agricultural economies will often support major departments in related sciences. Likewise, states with strong technological interests, for example California and Massachusetts, will often give much support to technological and scientific research institutions.

tailor 为……定制

decentralized（权力）分散、下放的

In comparison with primary and secondary education, post-secondary level education in America is more **decentralized** in terms of management. Most colleges and universities, whether public or private, have their own board of regents or some such body that hires and fires the president (or chancellor) and provides general guidance for the institution. Sometimes all the public colleges and universities in a given state will be guided by a single board. However, the more specific policies that govern colleges and universities are determined not by these boards but by faculty and administrators at each separate institution. Faculty groups set curriculum and graduation requirements. Individual professors decide what they will include in their courses and how they will evaluate their students. At all levels of education, standards are set and maintained by regional accrediting associations that the schools subscribe to, not by the government.

Notes

No Child Left Behind—It is a short term for The No Child Left Behind Act of 2001, which, among other things, requires states to develop assessments in basic skills. It supports standards-based education reform based on the premise that setting high standards and establishing measurable goals can improve individual outcome in education.

John Dewey—John Dewey (1859—1952) was an American philosopher, psychologist, and educational reformer, whose ideas have been influential in education and social reform in the United States.

Exercises

Ⅰ. **Multiple Choices**

The following are questions or incomplete sentences. Below each sentence or question four possible answers marked A, B, C and D are provided. Choose the ONE that best completes the sentence or answers the question.

1. American schools can best be understood as a kind of _____ institutions that

reflect the basic values and fundamental principles of the United States.

    A. political   B. economic   C. educational   D. social

2. The American assumption about equalitarianism suggests that everyone in the United States has access to institutions of higher learning as long as he/she is _____.

    A. financially qualified   B. academically qualified
    C. politically qualified   D. religiously qualified

3. According to the National Conference of State Legislatures, twenty-six states require students to continue attending school at least until the age of _____.

    A. 15   B. 16   C. 17   D. 18

4. In many instances American students do not face truly demanding educational requirements until they seek a _____ degree.

    A. undergraduate   B. professional   C. high school   D. graduate

5. The key point of *Equal Opportunity* in education is that America should provide comparable educational programs to everyone, regardless of gender, race, income level, social class, or physical or mental disability.

In this sentence, what does the word "comparable" most probably mean _____?

    A. equal   B. same   C. identical   D. similar

6. In principle, the goal of the American educational system is to provide a _____ education for every youngster.

    A. basic   B. broad   C. long   D. well-tailored

7. The quota system in U.S. university admissions policy is designed to _____ differences in social backgrounds as well as those of ethnic or racial origin in the university setting.

    A. remove   B. eliminate   C. reduce   D. change

8. John Dewey believed that the school's job was to _____ the natural development of the growing child, rather than to pour information in him/her.

    A. promote   B. enforce   C. alter   D. redirect

9. Generally speaking, education has been seen by most Americans as a way of "bettering oneself".

The phrase "bettering oneself" most probably means _____.

    A. become a better person   B. find a better job
    C. live a better life   D. get a better education

10. The responsibility of US Department of Education includes all the following except _____.

A. gathering information

B. providing advice

C. helping finance certain educational programs

D. making policy for all schools and universities

II. True and False

Read the following statements carefully and then decide whether they are true or false. Put a "T" if you think the statement is true and an "F" if it is not.

1. To Americans, education does not merely function as a vehicle to pass on knowledge to children; it also serves the purpose of training students in industrial and high-tech skills.

2. The American educational system is based on the idea that all people should receive education from kindergarten to university.

3. According to the passage, if one works hard in the United States, he/she will be able to get higher education at a state university or a community college, if not at Harvard or Yale.

4. In order to make sure that all American children can actually "enjoy" *access to education*, including higher education, all fifty U. S. states have "compulsory attendance" laws, requiring young people to attend school only.

5. In the American educational system, rigorous academic training tends to be given later than that in most other countries' systems

6. Since the implementation of Affirmative Action in American higher education, however, student demographic composition in colleges and universities has changed significantly.

7. Following "well-rounded people" principle, American students are free not to take those courses that they are not interested in or that appear to have little relationship to their career aspirations.

8. Since America is a nation of immigrants, education in America has traditionally served the goal of Americanizing people from different parts of the world.

9. "Rising in the world" is a fundamental part of the American Dream.

10. The educational ladder concept is an almost perfect reflection of the American idea of social hierarchy based on birth and wealth.

III. General Questions

1. What have most stated done after the passage of No Child Left Behind?

2. Before WW II, what kinds of students did American colleges and universities mostly enroll?

3. What is the primary intention of equal opportunity in American education?

4. How do Americans view a high general level of education?

5. In America, where does the social and economic mobility largely come from?

6. In American elementary and secondary education, apart from public schools, what other kinds of schools are there?

7. How do public schools in America differ from each other in terms of funding, and why?

8. How do Americans characterize their education?

9. What are the main functions of school boards?

10. How do state universities in America differ from each other in terms of tuition?

Ⅳ. Essay Questions

1. Why do Americans believe that they have gone a long way toward the goal of equal opportunity in education?

2. Although all fifty U. S. states have "compulsory attendance" laws, and offer a free public education to every student who wants one, why is it that there are still some areas of inequality in American elementary and secondary education?

Reference Answers

Ⅰ. Multiple Choices

1. D 2. B 3. B 4. D 5. D 6. B 7. C 8. A 9. C 10. D

Ⅱ. True and False

1. F 2. F 3. T 4. F 5. T 6. T 7. F 8. T 9. T 10. F

Ⅲ. General Questions

1. Most states have developed examinations intended to prevent students from graduating from secondary school without attaining prescribed test scores.

2. Before World War II, American colleges and universities enrolled mainly European American, upper- or middle-class, English-speaking males in their late teens or early twenties.

3. Equal opportunity in American education, particularly higher education, is in-

tended to make sure that all Americans will be given the opportunity to bring out their potential to the fullest degree possible.

4. Americans view a high general level of education as a necessity in a democratic society.

5. The social and economic mobility of Americans comes largely from the easy access to education that most Americans enjoy.

6. In American elementary and secondary education, apart from public schools, there are also private religious schools and elite private schools.

7. Public schools in America differ from each other greatly in terms of funding. Those located in rich communities are far better funded than those located in poor areas, because over 90 percent of the money for public schools comes from the local residents' property taxes.

8. Americans characterize their education as "a national concern, a state responsibility, and a local function".

9. The main functions of school boards include: overseeing the schools in each district, setting school policy and deciding what is to be taught.

10. Some state universities are virtually free to residents of the state, with only token fees, but others are expensive, especially for out-of-state students.

Ⅳ. Essay Questions

1. Over the past half a century, various programs have been introduced into the American educational institutions of various levels, radically transforming the character of student bodies at American schools and universities. At the K-12 level, for example, special programs have resulted in the enrollment of more and more students with physical or cognitive limitations. More significantly, before World War Ⅱ, tertiary institutions enrolled mainly European American, upper- or middle-class, English-speaking males in their late teens or early twenties. Since the implementation of Affirmative Action in American higher education, not only have student bodies in institutions of higher learning become more diverse, but the percentage of their representation has grown in number as well. Previously excluded social groups such as ethnic minorities, working-class children, and women now represent a significant portion of college student population in the United States

2. There are basically two reasons for inequality in American elementary and secondary education. First, since public schools are primarily funded by local communities

in which they are located, it means that those public schools that are located in wealthier areas are better funded than those in poorer areas, thus causing inequality, at least, in school buildings and teaching facilities. Second, apart from public schools that offer elementary and secondary education in the U.S., there are also private religious schools and elite private schools that provide primary and high school education. As private religious schools and elite private schools, particularly the latter, are relatively better funded and offer more programs than public schools, inequality between public and private schools is almost unpreventable.

Unit Six The American Family

Focal Points

nuclear family extended family alternative family
single-parent family blended family cohabitation
civil union marriage relationship companionship
parenting child-centeredness rebellious teenager

Discussion Questions

What are the major changes in the American family?

Text

nuclear family 核心家庭

When Americans use the word family, they are typically referring to a father, a mother and their children. This is the so-called **nuclear family**. Grandparents, aunts, uncles, cousin and others who might be thought of as family in many other countries are usually called relatives. These usages reflect the fact that, for most Americans, the family has traditionally been a small group of people, not an extended network. That is why when Americans are asked to name the members of their families, married Americans adults will name their husband or wife and their children, if they have any. If they mention their father, mother, sisters or brothers, they will define them as separate units. Aunts, uncles, cousins and grandparents are considered "extended family".

The Changing Family

During the 1950s, the traditional American family included a husband, wife and their two or three children. The man went to work every morning during the week and on the weekend relaxed or did **home repairs** or **yard work**. The woman took care of the house and the children, and often socialized with other women in the neighborhood, and perhaps participated in a parent-teacher organization at the children's school or volunteered in the community. The children went to school, played with their friends after school and on weekends, and sometimes **got into mischief**. The family had dinner together every evening, chatting while they ate, and then watched a few TV programs. The children did their homework, and teenagers talked on the phone with their friends. On weekends, the family sometimes took a drive, visited grandparents, went to church, or shared some other activity. The children grew up, finished secondary school, perhaps went on to college, got married, had children of their own, and the cycle continued.

American families have changed quite significantly since the 1950s. To begin with, families have become smaller, with the average size of the American household standing at 2.54 in 2013, down from about 3.2 as recently as 1985. Secondly, there are now more single-parent families in America. **As of** September, 2013, single moms precisely accounted for one-quarter of U.S. households, and single dads made up another 6 percent. More significantly, it is increasingly common to find unmarried couples living together, unmarried women having children, and women of child-bearing age having no children (or not wanting to have). Additionally, a great many other forms of household have appeared on the American family scene. For instance, there are "blended families" composed of a man, a woman, and their children from previous marriages. Furthermore, there are grandparent-headed households; households

home repairs 家里修补杂事
yard work 庭院活,如修剪草坪等

get into mischief 卷入调皮捣蛋的事情之中

as of 截止……为止

that include an older couple and their grown children (perhaps with young children of their own) who have moved back in on account of economic or other misfortunes; gay or lesbian couples with or without children; and finally people living alone. Arrangements such as these are often called "alternative families" to distinguish them from the 1950s traditional families. According to some research findings, alternative families have already outnumbered traditional families in the United States by as much as 70 percent to 30 percent. Beyond all this, Americans are also getting married later in life. For instance, the average age at which men marry is 28, and women 26, both significantly higher than men and women of the 1950s.

Observers usually attribute changes in the American family to a variety of factors. For instance, some argue, that **following on** the "women's liberation movement", women began entering careers outside the traditional areas of teaching, nursing, and being a secretary. Others say that more and more women are going to college, so much so that women now earn more doctoral degrees than men. In the process women are preparing themselves for financial independence from any future husband and delaying marriage and childbirth. Still others believe that difficult economic times have often required both parents to earn enough to support a family, and have compelled many young people to remain in their parents' home beyond the age 18 or to return to it after leaving. Finally, most observers agree that the **stigma attached to** divorce, **cohabitation**, and homosexuality has **diminished** but not vanished.

Whatever different explanations there may be about all these changes in American living arrangements and family structure, they all seem to have one thing in common, i.e., they each **one way or another** reflect and **reinforce** American cultural values that emphasize individualism, freedom and quality. In general, American society accepts the idea that young people of both genders need to "find themselves" and "develop their potential". The journey to find one's true self may **entail** delaying or **forgoing** marriage and its **entanglement**; delaying or forgoing parenthood and its responsibilities; divorcing a **spouse** from whom one has grown apart; and living life in a way that responds to personal situations and convenience rather than to **dictates** of the traditional norms. It is generally believed in America that when people decide what living arrangements they prefer, they are "doing their own things". In short, Americans view the family as a group whose primary purpose is to advance the happiness of each individual member, rather than **the other way round**.

  These shifts in family structure and composition entail shifts in the traditional male-female relationship as well as male-female division of labor. It means, for instance, more women are working and achieving financial independence, making them less or not dependent at all on men for their livelihood. Also, in more and more cases, wives are earning more than their husbands, resulting in a growing number of men becoming stay-at-home parents. More importantly, as moms work during the day, children, regardless of their gender, are often expected to contribute to home maintenance by washing dishes, vacuuming carpets, cleaning their rooms, helping with yard work, or other such chores. All of this used to be done mostly by women when they were housewives, but now needs to be shared by all members of the family. Evidently, women as wives and mothers have significantly improved their role and position in the family as a result of all these changes.

Marriage Relationship

  In the United States, marriages are not "arranged". Young people are expected to find a husband or wife **on their own**, and their parents usually do not help them. In fact, parents are frequently not told of their children's marriage plans until the couple has decided to marry. This means that parents have little

---

entail 需要
forgo 放弃、抛弃
entanglement 纠缠、牵连、纠纷
spouse 配偶
dictates 命令、指令

the other way round 相反地

on one's own 靠自己、由自己

control, and generally not much influence, over whom their children marry. Americans believe that young people should fall in love and then decide to marry someone they can live happily with, again evidence of the importance of an individual happiness. Of course, in reality this does not always happen, but it remains the ideal that helps shape the views of **courtship** and marriage among the young people.

Over the years, the value Americans have placed on marriage itself is determined largely by how happy the husband and wife make each other. In the past when life was hard, happiness in marriage was largely defined by economic consideration. With the improvement of standards of living, particularly with the abundant supply of material comforts, marriage happiness is increasingly based on **companionship**. Nowadays, the majority of American women value companionship as the most important part of marriage. Other values, such as having economic support and the opportunity to have children, although important, are seen by many as less important.

All these changes of views on marriage happiness are closely related to the transformations of American women's position in the family and in society **at large**. In many ways, women's role and position in the family can be best understood by examining the marriage relationship between them and their husbands. Over the past half a century, as suggested previously, American women have witnessed steady progress toward equal status for themselves both in the family and in society at large. As a reflection of the family and society, changes in marriage relationship are certainly one of the best **indices** of such steady progress. According to some sociological studies, the institution of marriage in the United States has experienced four stages of development. In each stage, wives have increased the degree of equality with their husbands and have gained more power within the family.

Stage Ⅰ: *Wife as a Servant to Husband*

During the 19th century, American wives were expected to be completely **obedient** to their husbands. As late as 1850, wife beating was legal in almost all the states of the United States. Although both husbands and wives had family duties, the wife had no power in family matters other than that which her husband allowed her. Her possessions and any of her earnings belonged to her husband. During the 19th century women were not allowed to vote, a restriction that in part reflected women's status as servant to her husband.

obedient 顺从的、孝顺的

Stage Ⅱ: *Husband-Head, Wife-Helper*

During the late 19th and early 20th centuries, opportunities for women to work outside the household increased. More wives were able to support themselves, if necessary, and therefore were less likely to accept the traditional ideal that wives were servants who must obey their husbands. Even though the great majority of wives chose not to work outside the home, the fact that they might do so increased their power in the marriage. The husband could no long make family decisions alone, and the wife was freer to disagree with her husband. However, even though the wife's power increased, the husband remained the head of the family, and the wife became his full-time helper by taking care of his house and raising his children. Up till today, the husband-head, wife-helper marriage can still be found in the United States, though not typical any more.

Stage Ⅲ: *Husband-Senior Partner, Wife-Junior Partner*

During the 20th century, more and more wives took jobs outside the home. In 1900, for example, only 6 percent of married women in the United States worked outside the home. By 1940, 14 percent of married women did so; and by 1998 more than 60 percent of all married women living with their husbands held jobs outside the home. When married women take this step, their power relative to that of their husbands increases still further. The wife's income becomes important in maintaining the family's standard of living. Her power to affect the outcome of family decisions is greater than her duties were entirely in the home. Still, since the husband provides most of the family income, the wife, although a partner, is not an equal one with her husband. In the end, he ends up as the senior partner, and she the junior partner, of the family enterprise. Today, in spite of the fact that the majority of American married women are working outside the home, many marriages in America are still the husband-senior partner, wife-junior partner type, because men usually earn more than women do.

Stage IV: Husband-Wife Equal Partners

Since the late 1960s, a growing number of women have expressed a strong dissatisfaction with any marriage arrangement wherein the husband and his career are the primary considerations in the marriage. By the late 1970s, for example, only 38 percent of American women still believed that they should put their husbands and children ahead of their own careers. Nowadays, however, more and more American women have come to believe that they should be equal partners rather than junior partners in their marriage. In an equal partnership marriage, the wife pursues a full-time job or career which has equal importance to her husband's. The long-standing division of labor between husband and wife comes to an end. The husband is no longer the main provider of family income, and the wife no longer has the main responsibilities for household duties and raising children. Husband and wife share all these duties equally, and power over family decisions is also shared equally between them. At present, husband-wife equal partnership marriage is still not typical of most American marriages as yet, but it keeps growing, and will grow more rapidly in the future as American women are closer than ever to reaching their goal of "equal pay for equal job".

Parenting

Cultures, as we know, are **perpetuated, in part,** by the way children are raised. By taking a look at the way American children are raised and treated, one can have a good sense of how Americans turn out to be the way they are.

The general objective of child rearing for most American parents is to prepare their children to be independent and self-reliant individuals who will be able to manage their own lives by the time they reach age 18. For this reason, training for independence starts very early. Infants and young children are asked to make choices and to express their opinion, and they are encouraged to do things for themselves as soon as they can. Parents will praise and encourage their children as they try—"There—you see? You can do it all by yourself!"

Like parents in other countries, American parents generally expect that their children' lives will be at least as comfortable as their own, if not better. When they think about their children's futures, they think about them mainly in terms of the jobs their children will get and how much income those jobs will produce. To give their children the best possible chance to have a good life, they will, if they possibly can, invest considerable time and money in a child's improvement and instruction, which may include such things as dental care (straight teeth seem extremely important), a preschool where very young children learn to read, and lessons for learning to draw, play a sport, dance, sing or play a musical instrument.

American parents with the **means** to do so want to expose their children to as many aspects of life as possible. Parents also want their children to be happy and healthy: free of significant physical and emotional problems, reasonably well educated, able to find employment suited to their interests and talents, and hopefully reasonably prosperous. In order to turn out "well-rounded children", American parents will usually try very hard

---

perpetuate 保持、使长存、使永存

in part 部分地

means 财力、收入

Unit Six　The American Family

to keep their children's schoolwork and after-school activities in good balance. For instance, American parents will complain if their children are given too much homework when that work is seen as **infringing on** their **extracurricular activities**, friendships, or part-time jobs, which are considered as important as schoolwork in producing the ideal "well-rounded people".

Sometimes, young American children receive too much attention from their parents, **prompting** American sociologist Benjamin Spock to conclude that "what is making the parent's job most difficult is today's child-centered viewpoint". For instance, many American families tend to place more emphasis on the needs and desires of the child and less on social and family responsibilities. They play with their young children, and arrange play dates for their children with children of other families. They buy things their children want, and talk to their children as though they were simply small adults. These child-centered families are often very busy, since each child has his or her own schedule of lessons, practices and social arrangements. However, as the children get older, they spend less and less time with their parents. Whenever possible, older children go to and from school on their own and take care of their own basic needs. They may find themselves **unsupervised** between the time they get home from school and the time their parents return home from work.

As parents become a less significant part of their growing children's lives, the children's peers become more influential. Young Americans, especially during the teenage years, are often under intense "**peer pressure**" to dress and act like their friends and to engage in whatever activities their friends undertake. By then, they enter the stage of "rebellious teenage" in their growth. Americans assume that **adolescence** is inherently a period of **turmoil**. Teenagers are expected to be self-centered, uncooperative, and sometimes **moody** while trying to "**find themselves**", and to establish their own identities as individuals separate from others in the family.

---

infringe on 侵犯、侵占
extracurricular activities 课外活动

prompt 引起

unsupervised 不受监护

peer pressure 同辈人压力

adolescence 青少年
turmoil 混乱
moody 喜怒无常、情绪多变
find oneself 发现自我

Notes

Benjamin Spock(1903—1998)—was an American pediatrician, whose book *Baby and Child Care*, published in 1946, is one of the best-sellers of all time. Throughout its first 52 years, *Baby and Child Care* was the second best-selling book, next only to the *Bible*. Its message to mothers is "you know more than you think you do".

Exercises

Ⅰ. Multiple Choices

The following are questions or incomplete sentences. Below each sentence or question four possible answers marked A, B, C and D are provided. Choose the ONE that best completes the sentence or answers the question.

1. Grandparents, aunts, uncles, cousin and others are usually regarded as _____ in the United States.

   A. friends   B. family   C. relatives   D. companions

2. During the 1950s, the traditional American family included _____.

   A. a husband, wife, their children and their parents

   B. a husband, wife, their children and their sisters and brothers

   C. a husband, wife, their children and their uncles and aunts

   D. a husband, wife and their children

3. In the traditional American family, the wife would do all the following except _____.

   A. take care of the house and the children

   B. go to an evening school

   C. socialize with other women in the neighborhood

   D. participate in a parent-teacher organization at the children's school or volunteer in the community

4. The average size of the American household in 1985 stood at _____.

   A. 3.2   B. 2.54   C. 2.3   D. 4.25

5. In 2013, single moms precisely accounted for _____ of U.S. households, and single dads made up another _____ percent.

   A. one-quarter, 16   B. one-third, 6

C. one-fifth, 60   D. one-quarter, 6

6. Presently, the average age at which American men marry is _____ and American women _____.

A. 26, 28   B. 28, 26   C. 29, 27   D. 27, 29

7. Traditional careers open to American women include all the following except _____.

A. teacher   B. priest   C. nurse   D. secretary

8. American society accepts the idea that young people of both genders need to "find themselves".

The phrase "find themselves" most probably means _____.

A. find where they are   B. find who they are

C. find what they want to be   D. find where they want to go

9. Americans view the family as a group whose primary purpose is to advance the happiness of _____, rather than _____.

A. the whole family, each individual member

B. children, parents

C. parents, children

D. each individual member, the whole family

10. In cases where wives are earning more than their husbands, it is becoming more and more common for men to _____.

A. stay at home to parent their child or children

B. get a second job in order to make more money

C. quit their job and start to enjoy life

D. leave home and seek a divorce

Ⅱ. True and False

Read the following statements carefully and then decide whether they are true or false. Put a "T" if you think the statement is true and an "F" if it is not.

1. In America, parents are frequently told of their children's marriage plans before the couple decides to marry.

2. Throughout the American experience, the value placed on marriage has always been determined by how happy the husband and wife make each other.

3. Regarding marriage happiness, the majority of American women nowadays consider companionship to be more important than having economic support or the opportu-

nity to have children.

4. In each of the four stages of marriage relationship in the United States, wives have found themselves become more equal to their husbands and more powerful with the family.

5. During the 19th century, American wives were supposed to be completely submissive to their husbands.

6. During the late 19th and early 20th centuries, opportunities for women to work outside the household increased, and subsequently, a great majority of wives chose to work outside the home.

7. With the majority of married women holding jobs and making decent income, few marriages in America are now the husband-senior partner, wife-junior partner type.

8. As recently as the late 1970s, over 50 percent of American women still believed that the interests of their husbands and children should be put above theirs.

9. The general objective of child rearing for most American parents is to prepare their children to be able to manage their own lives by the time they graduate from college.

10. In order to turn out "well-rounded children", American parents will try to make sure that their children's schoolwork and after-school activities are kept in good balance.

Ⅲ. General Questions

1. When Americans use the word family, what do they refer to?

2. What do Americans mean by "extended family"?

3. What is a "blended family"?

4. What is a civil union or a domestic partnership?

5. What do "alternative families" mean?

6. What has happened to American women over the past half a century with regard to their family and social status?

7. During the 19th century, American women were not allowed to vote. What does that restriction indicate?

8. What was American women's status in Stage Ⅱ of marriage relationship?

9. What do American parents mainly think about when they think about their children's futures?

10. In what ways is the American family child-centered?

Ⅳ. Essay Questions

1. How has the American family changed since the 1950s?
2. The institution of marriage in the United States is said to have experienced four stages of development. What are they, and how are they different from each other?

Reference Answers

Ⅰ. Multiple Choices

1. C   2. D   3. B   4. A   5. D   6. B   7. B   8. C   9. D   10. A

Ⅱ. True and False

1. F   2. F   3. T   4. T   5. T   6. F   7. F   8. F   9. F   10. T

Ⅲ. General Questions

1. When Americans use the word family, they are typically referring to a father, a mother and their children, the so-called nuclear family.

2. By "extended family", Americans refer to their aunts, uncles, cousins and grandparents.

3. A "blended families" is composed of a man, a woman and their children from previous marriages.

4. A civil union or a domestic partnership refers to a gay or lesbian couple whose rights and responsibilities are not protected by U. S. federal law applied to married couples.

5. "Alternative families" refer to family arrangements that are different from the traditional family pattern in the United States, i. e., the nuclear family model.

6. Over the past half a century, American women have witnessed steady progress toward equal status for themselves both in the family and in society at large.

7. It indicates women's status as servant to her husband.

8. She was her husband's full-time helper, taking care of his house and raising his children.

9. When American parents think about their children's futures, they think about them mainly in terms of the jobs they children will get and how much income those jobs will produce.

10. For instance, many American families tend to place more emphasis on the needs

and desires of the child and less on social and family responsibilities. Parents play with their young children, arrange play dates for their children with children of other families, and buy things their children want, and talk to their children as though they were simply small adults.

Ⅳ. Essay Questions

1. Since the 1950s, the American family has changed significantly. American families. To begin with, families have become smaller, with the average size of the American household standing at 2.54 in 2013. Secondly, there are now more single-parent families in America, with single moms accounting for one-quarter of U.S. households and single dads making up another 6 percent. More significantly, it is increasingly common to find unmarried couples living together, unmarried women having children, and women of child-bearing age having no children. Additionally, a great many other forms of household have appeared on the American family scene. For instance, there are "blended families", grandparent-headed households, households that include an older couple and their grown children who have moved back in on account of economic or other misfortunes, gay or lesbian couples with or without children, and finally people living alone.

2. There have occurred altogether four stages in the development of American institution of marriage, namely Stage Ⅰ, where wife lived like a servant to her husband; Stage Ⅱ, where husband functioned as head of the family and wife his helper; Stage Ⅲ, where husband was viewed as the senior partner and wife the junior partner; and finally, Stage Ⅳ, where husband and wife have or will become equal partners. In each stage, American women kept moving upward in their status, both in the family and in society at large. Such upward movement in status on the part of American women is closely related to the degree of their economic independence. In general, the more economically independent women are, the more equal status they enjoy in their marriage relationship with their husbands.

Unit Seven Leisure Life in America

Focal Points

leisure life	organized/spectator sports	Super Bowl
sports culture	high-brow game	physical activity
weekend life	vacation	camping

Discussion Questions

What can we learn about Americans from their leisure life?

Text

work hard and play hard 拼命干、拼命玩

at one's disposal 任由自己支配

shrink 缩短、缩小
downturn 不振

As a nation that believes in **"work hard and play hard"**, Americans, on average, spend a considerable amount of time on their leisure life. This is made possible mostly by automation and more efficient production methods, leaving people with plenty of time **at their disposal**. Equally important, with the improvement of living standards, Americans, as a whole, have more money to spend for their leisure life. Finally, the goods and services that can be purchased in the United States have also increased significantly, making it possible for Americans not only to diversify their leisure life, but also to develop new interests in it. According to a Harris poll of 2014, while American leisure time is **shrinking** due largely to economic **downturn**, adult Americans, nevertheless, still enjoy a wide range of leisure activities at a varying degree of frequency. They include, among other things, individual and collective sports, a range of more passive pastimes like films and music, and other forms of participatory leisure activities, such as fishing, hunting, gardening and traveling. Given the limited space here, only a few typically American leisure activities will be described and discussed.

Sports

Sports are a mirror of American life, but they are more than just a mirror. They can be viewed as Americans' effort to construct an imaginative world. **As such**, sports have created their own myths, legends and stars. Their ethical rules and sportsmanship are often praised as examples for people in other fields to follow, though their not infrequent scandals also offer **a staple of conversation** for Americans. Furthermore, sports culture has its mechanism for helping individuals to identify with a particular group with the same favorite team or with the same hobby, providing them a sense of belonging and community. More importantly, such American values as individual success and achievement often find their fullest and most exciting expressions in athletes, particularly among those who managed to reach the top against all the **odds**. Above all, organized sports are seen by Americans as an inspiring example of equality of opportunity in action, where people of different races and social backgrounds get an equal chance to compete and excel.

Like people in other countries of the world, Americans are interested in sports not so much to participate in them as players as to watch them as spectators. While many Americans are engaged in sports of different kind, such as tennis, basketball, swimming, skiing, jogging, cycling, and bowling, it is the organized/**spectator sports** that reflect the basic values of American society. They may be viewed as attempts by the society to strengthen these values in the minds and emotions of its people, the younger generation in particular. Therefore, organized/spectator sports have a more serious social purpose than **spontaneous**, unorganized play by individuals. In the United States to-

---

as such 如所指事那样、就其本身而论

a staple of conversation 经常性的话题

odds 不利条件、不利因素

spectator sport 吸引大量观众的体育运动

spontaneous 自发性的

Unit Seven Leisure Life in America

day, the three major organized/spectator sports are football, basketball and baseball. To many social critics, Americans' interest in such spectator sports seems **excessive** and even **obsessive**. Television networks, for example, spend millions of dollars arranging telecasts of sports events. Apart from three television networks broadcasting sports news and providing commentaries, there are also some channels devoting themselves entirely to specific sports, such as golf and professional football. **Super Bowl** Sunday has become almost a national holiday.

Of all the spectator sports in the United States, football is probably the most popular game with Americans. So popular is football in America that it takes a man of **stern** stuff to resist a televised football game, and a man who says that he does not watch the Super Bowl is believed to be ready to lie about anything. Of course, the football game is not merely an entertainment for the spectators; it is also a **pageant**, using such devices as cheering teams and musical bands. Following football in terms of popularity is baseball. Like football, professional baseball teams also have enthusiastic following, and important baseball games arouse great interest, being followed on television all across the nation. Also like football and other spectator sports, baseball is a large scale commercial enterprise, bringing huge financial rewards to players and management alike. Together with football, baseball is said to be a typically American team sport. Next to them is basketball, which started as part of the 19th-century **campaign** to Americanize the immigrants. However, it was quickly taken over by **ethnics** as a way to express their national pride and compete with other immigrants. Today, like football and baseball games, professional and collegiate basketball matches in the U.S. also attract a large number of fans at home and abroad.

Of course, when it comes to sports, Americans are not merely spectators; they are also active participants. So, the

excessive 过度的
obsessive 着迷的

Super Bowl 美国橄榄球超级杯赛

stern 坚定的、不屈从的

pageant 盛会

campaign 活动、运动
ethnic 族裔

question one may raise is why are sports so popular in the United States? One reason may be that the variety and size of America as well as different climates in different regions have provided Americans a large choice of sports. With public sports facilities available in most parts of the country, Americans enjoy easy access to sports of their own choice. Another reason may be that Americans like competition, by teams or as individuals, of any type. It is generally believed that American schools and colleges follow the tradition of all English-speaking societies in using sports activities as a way of teaching social values. Among these are teamwork, sportsmanship, persistence, "never quitting", "being tough" or "**having guts**". Learning how to win in sports is believed to help develop the habits necessary to compete successfully in later life. This training, in turn, strengthens American society as a whole. Finally, it may be that Americans just like sports activities. For instance, they like to play a friendly game of **softball** at family picnics, and "touch football" (no **tackling**) can get started in parks or on beaches whenever a few young people come together. "Shooting baskets" with friends is a favorite way to pass the time, either with friends in a friend's driveway (the basket is over the garage door) or on some city or neighborhood court.

However, although sports in the United States are glorified by the majority of Americans, there are others who are especially critical of the power of sports to corrupt when certain things are **carried to excess**. An excessive desire to win in sports, critics argue for example, can corrupt rather than strengthen American values. Moreover, critics point out, many professional athletes and their coaches receive yearly salaries in the millions of dollars, misleading many young children to enter sports to strike a fortune there rather than to promote sportsmanship. Additionally, critics complain that Americans **bet** millions of dollars on the outcome of sports contests, transforming sports into gambling. Most important of all, violence in American

have guts 有胆量、有勇气

softball 垒球
tackling 橄榄球阻截队员

carry to excess 过度、过分

bet 打赌

sports has been increasingly criticized in recent years by those who approve of sports generally and who believe that violence is corrupting it. Of the biggest organized sports, for example, people are particularly critical of football for the growing number of injuries that have resulted from the excessive roughness of the game. Still, despite of all these criticisms, sports in the United States, on the whole, enjoy far more support than criticism. As a means of **instilling** basic American values into the minds of youngsters, sports, particularly organized ones, have become part of "the national religion", that is, it has become a mixture of patriotism and national pride on the one hand with ethical values and competitive spirits on the other.

Recreation

Apart from sports, leisure life in America also includes recreation. At the mention of the word recreation, people immediately start thinking about relaxing and enjoyable activities. An evening concert in the downtown, a Sunday picnic with the family, a casual walk in a shopping mall, a family party for friends, or working in the garden with kids, all are forms of recreation. They are unlike organized sports discussed above, where competition is the rule, and winning is all that matters. Rather, what is called recreation is intended to be spontaneous, leisurely, slow-paced, relaxing, and above all enjoyable, serving the individual's needs beyond the competitive world of work. Nevertheless, much can be learned about the values of Americans from a brief look at the kinds of recreation in which Americans engage.

According to a Harris poll in December, 2013, Americans are now changing their lifestyle based on "work hard and play hard" to one based on "we work before we play". This is largely due to worries over unemployment as the country is working hard to pull itself out of the financial crisis of 2008. **Subsequently**, there has occurred a 35-hour work-leisure gap, meaning Americans now spend more hours on work and fewer hours on recreation. Also according to the above-mentioned Harris poll of 2013, the top ten recreational activities among average Americans are reading, TV watching, spending time with family/friends, doing exercises like **aerobics** and weight-lifting, playing computer games, fishing, going to the movies, playing golf/tennis, walking and gardening. Following them are such recreational pursuits as church activities, hunting, shopping, traveling, playing music, entertaining friends and eating out.

aerobics 有氧健身操

What is ironic about American recreation is that while recreation is meant to be spontaneous and relaxing, Americans tend to approach it with a high degree of seriousness, planning, organization and expense. As we know, many urban professionals in America already lead a busy life during the week, and yet in order to relax themselves on the weekend, they often find themselves becoming busier when they plan to play golf with friends on Saturday. The night before, for example, they would spend plenty of time preparing for the golf trip, such as scheduling appointments with business partners or friends, making reservations at a restaurant for dinner, shopping fancy golf equipment online at the last minute, or just packing things up in the car. The next day, in order to avoid traffic jam, they would get up early in the morning and drive to a remote area to play a **tension-laden** round golf on an overcrowded course. After a day of exhaustive leisure, they return home from the golf course, feeling more tired than they do when they come home from work during the weekdays. Obviously, in such recreational life, spontaneity and fun are lost.

tension-laden 充满紧张感的

If golf is a **high-brow** game for a limited number of people, and therefore it does not fully explain all Americans' attitude toward recreation, recreational activities like jogging and aerobic exercises are certainly common enough to **shed light on** the seriousness with which average Americans approach recreation. In many other countries, for example, people who jog may discon-

high-brow 高雅的、阳春白雪的

shed light on 解释、说明

Unit Seven Leisure Life in America

tinue doing it in subzero winter weather, but most Americans will never have second thoughts about doing it when temperature drops to minus 10 degrees! To them, once a person has made up his/her mind about doing something, even in things like recreation, he/she must be persistent in doing that. It is a matter of self-discipline and a matter of will training. Partly for this reason, most Americans prefer recreation that requires a high level of physical activity, through which they can **carry over** their belief in hard work and efficiency into their world of play and recreation. For example, many Americans jog every day, or play tennis, handball, or bridge two or three times a week. Some do aerobic exercises three times weekly, **work out** in gyms up to six days a week, or engage in other regularly scheduled recreation, whether alone, with a partner or small groups of acquaintances. Also, they go on vacations, ski or canoe, or go on hiking trips, and hunting or fishing **expedition**s that require weeks of planning or organizing. In the Americans' view, all these recreational activities are worth the discomforts they may cause because they contribute to health and physical fitness and may also offer opportunities to socialize.

The high level of physical activity together with enormous amount of time spent on preparation by Americans has led to the observation that Americans have difficult **relaxing**, even in their leisure. Yet, the people who enjoy all these physically demanding recreational activities often say that they find them very relaxing mentally because such activities are so different from the kind of activity they must spend their time on in the world of work, mostly indoor office work involving mind rather than body. In this sense, Americans view their involvement in the high level of physical activity as a way of self-improvement, i. e., improving their minds by **exerting themselves**. Needless to say, such interest in self-improvement also finds expression in other forms of recreation that involve little or no physical activity. For instance, millions of Americans go to symphony con-

carry over 把……从一个活动范围领域扩大到另一个活动领域

work out 锻炼、训练

expedition 远征、探险

relax 轻松、放松

exert oneself 花力气

certs, attend live theater performances, visit museums, listen to lectures, and participate in artistic activities such as painting, performing music and dancing. Additionally, many Americans also enjoy hobbies such as weaving, needlework, candle making, wood carving and other **handicrafts**. To help Americans develop such hobbies, community education programs across the United States offer a wide range of classes for those interested in anything from "surfing the Internet" to **gourmet** cooking, self-defense, art, yoga and birdwatching.

handicraft 手工艺

gourmet 美食家

Much American recreation is highly organized, another indication of their seriousness in handling. Classes, clubs, leagues, newsletters, contests, exhibitions and conventions are centered on hundreds of different recreational activities. People interested in astronomy, bird watching, cooking, ecology, gardening, hiking or cycling can find a group of like-minded people with whom to meet, learn and practice or perform. Even if the level of participation in group recreational activities may be declining, the extent of Americans' involvement in recreational and **avocational** associations, comparatively speaking, is quite significant. Because of such a large-scale participation in recreational life on the part of Americans, recreation, like organized sports, is big business in America. Many common recreational activities require clothing, supplies, and equipment that can be quite costly. Running shoes, hiking boots, fishing and camping supplies, skiing equipment, cameras, telescopes, **gourmet cookware** and bowling balls are not inexpensive items. Beyond equipment, there is clothing. The fashion industry has successfully persuaded many an American that they must be properly dressed for jogging, playing tennis, skiing, swimming, yoga, biking and so on. Fashionable **outfits** for these and other recreational activities can be surprisingly expensive.

avocational 副业的、业余的

gourmet 美食家

cookware 炊具

outfit 全套装备、全部用品

Weekends and Vacations

While Americans' participation in sports and recreational

activities reveal a great deal Americans' leisure life, the way Americans spend their weekends and vacations can also be equally revealing about leisure life in America. After all, it is during weekends and vacations that Americans **while away** their leisure time.

Like people in other countries, much of what Americans will do on weekends and vacations depend on the number of children in the family, their ages, their hobbies, their interests, and above all, their income. Take an average-income American family with three children of school age for example. For such a family, Saturday is a time of cleaning, shopping, **mowing**, and activities for children. The mother will take care of the home and shopping, and the father will take care of the family car and clean the outside of the house. The children's activities will vary. They may spend some time in cleaning up their own rooms, or they may be involved in some school programs on Saturday. Usually, students will devote some time to their school work, though the exact time for this work varies greatly with each student.

For many Americans, Saturday evening is usually a social evening. It is the time for dances, plays, movies or parties, so they carry on immensely busy social lives. But for other Americans, Saturday is the day to be together with their families. Apart from **temperament**, personality and hobby, there are other factors that contribute to the different ways Americans spend Saturday, among which social class is a **determinant**. The upper classes, having more time and money at their disposal than most, **entertain** and visit a great deal. The lower classes, less mobile and lacking space for large parties, are more **opt** to limit their lives to church suppers, **moonlighting** or a part-time job. It is the middle classes that get headaches over entertaining. It is for them that magazines run endless articles about party food, serving, decorating and manners. Since entertaining guests or friends is a requirement of American middle class life, such arti-

---

while away 消磨、轻松地度过(时间)

mow 修剪草坪

temperament 秉性

determinant 决定因素

entertain 招待
opt 选择
moonlight 兼职、兼差

cles serve only to fuel middle-class American anxiety over being hosts or hostesses. To be sure, the affluence of America has given large numbers of people the leisure, money, and space to invite people to their homes in order to pass the time, but it does not come naturally to many of them for a variety of reasons.

Sunday is a different type of day—it is a day of rest from work. In most American homes, Sunday morning is a time of religious worship. The family will try and go to church together. After attending church services they may go for **brunch** before they return home. Sunday afternoon is given over to watching TV, reading the Sunday newspapers, or any other form of leisure. The main event on Sunday is the Sunday dinner which is the weekly big meal for the family, and all the family members try to be present for this meal. Sometimes, Sunday can also be a time for visiting relatives. Thus, at the Sunday family meal other relatives may be present. After the meal, some will return to watching TV, reading the newspapers, or more likely surfing the Internet and playing video games. Since the next day, Monday, is a work or school day, there is little social activity on Sunday evening.

Recently, there have appeared in the United States a growing number of so-called **ingenious** weekenders who approach their two or three-day **respites** from routine jobs with imagination and, in some cases, daring. Each weekend, these people lift themselves from a workday world into one that they believe can be both exciting and **reinvigorating**. For example, some people may sit in some training classes on weekend to learn how to perform **stunts** on the wings of a speeding biplane. Others may **wade** for hours with their friends in icy streams, **panning** for gold. Still others may conduct strangers on guided tours of the landmarks in their hometowns. In some dramatic cases, many Americans have developed such a strong passion for ingenious weekend activity that they find it difficult to stop doing it. For

---

brunch 早午餐

ingenious 灵巧的、巧妙的
respite 短暂的休闲期

reinvigorating 给以新的活力、恢复元气的
stunt 惊险动作、特技表演
wade 艰难地行进、蹚
pan(用淘洗盘)淘

Unit Seven Leisure Life in America

instance, many an American, particularly those living in rural areas, enjoy **chopping trees** and **sawing logs**. When they run out of **timber**, they would volunteer to help cut trees for their neighbors. To all these "ingenious weekenders", it is not the amount of time one spends on weekends that counts; but rather, it is the way that weekends are approached that really matters. In their eyes, weekends should be creatively spent, offering people a sense of feeling not obtainable during the weekdays.

Second to weekends are vacations in terms of **bulk of** time Americans have for their leisure life. Here, vacations involve, first American students, and second American employees. There are no national or even state-wide dates for school vacations. Each school district sets its own. Generally, **school's out** from around the first week in June until the last week in August. However, many school districts sponsor "summer school" for children who have fallen behind and wish to make up work, or, alternatively for pupils who want to take extra courses. Most universities and colleges in the United States also have summer semesters. During school vacations, most of senior high school students and college students usually try to get a job to earn either pocket money or tuition fees. They may work in a company or a government agency as an **intern**, or in a fast-food restaurant as a waiter and waitress. Those too young to work often stay at home during school vacations and help with their parents in a variety of **household chores**. And those from high-income families often travel around the world during this period, participating in a summer camp in Europe this year, and joining in another summer camp in Asia next year. In short, just as families of different income spend their weekends vastly differently from each other, so do children from low- and high-income families spend their school vacations considerably differently from one another.

As for the average American employee, he/she usually has three or four weeks of **paid vacations** during the summer,

---

chop trees 砍树
saw log 锯木
timber 木料、木材、树木

bulk of 大量、大段

school's out 学校放假

intern 实习生

household chores 家务

paid vacations 带薪假期

though it may vary from company to company considerably. Automobile workers who have spent several years on the job, for example, can commonly expect around five weeks of paid vacation. Quite many American families simply spend their vacations at home, that is, the time is used to work (and play) around the house. Others who own or rent a **cottage** near a lake or in the mountains may take the whole family with them and spend their vacation in serene, comfortable and picturesque surroundings. Locations where swimming, fishing, and other water activities are available are especially popular among American **vacationers**, and therefore beaches, lakes and seaside **resorts** are always full of **holiday-makers**. However, a great many Americans **take to the road** to see the beauty of their own country. It is often said that the unique contributions of the United States to those who love the **great outdoors** are the National and State Parks. They are beautifully organized and give particular thought to campers. The widely available and inexpensive camp grounds throughout the country offer younger families the chance to travel on a limited budget. Every year more than 65 million Americans visit these National and State Parks.

Of vacationing, Americans seem to like camping in particular. These camps are **scattered** throughout the country, by the sea, along the beaches, in the woods, inside the parks, and at the foot of the mountains, offering vacationers a wide range of activities. Some of the camps are owned and operated by the **Boy Scouts**, the **Girl Scouts** or various churches. Others are sponsored by the Red Cross and may teach swimming, boating and life-saving. Among the many summer camps, private or nonprofit, are music camps, computer camps, hiking and **backpacking** camps, tennis camps, and camps with farms and **ranches**. At these campsites, people can nearly always find picnic places **complete with** wooden tables and benches, and garbage cans and restrooms. For the retirees who enjoy camping life, camping in vehicles called "**campers**" offers a new way of

roam 漫游	life. They may spend half a year **roaming** the country, satisfying
craving 渴望、迫切的需求	their **craving** for the great open spaces. For the young adventurous people, camping gives them not only fun but also excitement. Riding on motorbikes they follow the smallest tracks up the mountains, across the deserts, or into the forests, exploring the beauty of nature on the one hand, and challenging their
physical stamina 体力	own **physical stamina** on the other, a reflection of American character in the form of leisure life.

Notes

Harris Poll—The Harris Poll, part of Harris Interactive Inc., is one of the longest running and most respected barometers of public opinion in the United States.

Super Bowl—The Super Bowl is the annual championship game of the National Football League, the highest level of professional football in the United States.

Boy Scouts—The Boy Scouts of America is one of the largest youth organizations in the United States, with 2.7 million youth members and over 1 million adult volunteers.

Girl Scouts—The Girl Scouts of the United States of America is a youth organizations for girls in the United States and American girls living abroad.

Exercises

Ⅰ. Multiple Choices

The following are questions or incomplete sentences. Below each sentence or question four possible answers marked A, B, C and D are provided. Choose the ONE that best completes the sentence or answers the question.

1. Americans believe in the principle of "_____".
   A. work hard and work easy   B. work hard and play easy
   C. play hard and work easy   D. work hard and play hard

2. According to a Harris poll of 2014, American leisure time is shrinking. The word "shrinking" means _____.
   A. being lost   B. being gone   C. being over   D. being reduced

3. According to the passage, sports in America have created their own _____.
   A. myths, legends and stars   B. myths, legends and stories

C. myths, legality and stars   D. mystiques, legends and stars

4. Organized sports are seen by Americans as an inspiring example of equality of _____ in action, where people of different races and social backgrounds get an equal chance to compete and excel.

   A. result   B. consequence   C. opportunity   D. income

5. Americans are interested in sports not so much to participate in them as _____ as to watch them as _____.

   A. spectators, players   B. players, spectators
   C. fans, audiences   D. audiences, fans

6. Football is so popular in America that it takes <u>a man of stern stuff</u> to resist a televised football game.

   The phrase "a man of stern stuff" most probably means _____.

   A. a man of strong determination

   B. a man of strong material

   C. a man of strong health

   D. a man of strong personality

7. What is the essence of recreation as opposed to organized sports?

   A. competition   B. winning   C. relaxation   D. rivalry

8. Americans are now changing their lifestyle based on "_____" to one based on "_____".

   A. "work hard and play hard", "we play before we work"

   B. "work easy and play hard", "we work before we play"

   C. "work hard and play easy", "we play and work at the same time"

   D. "work hard and play hard", "we work before we play"

9. According to a Harris poll of 2013, the top five recreational activities among average Americans are in the order of _____.

   A. reading, TV watching, spending time with family/friends, doing exercises like aerobics and weight-lifting, playing computer games

   B. TV watching, spending time with family/friends, reading, doing exercises like aerobics and weight-lifting, playing computer games

   C. reading, spending time with family/friends, TV watching, doing exercises like aerobics and weight-lifting, playing computer games

   D. reading, TV watching, doing exercises like aerobics and weight-lifting, playing computer games, spending time with family/friends

Unit Seven Leisure Life in America

10. Much of what Americans will do on weekends and vacations depend on all the following except _____.

  A. family size   B. hobby   C. income   D. residence

II. True and False

Read the following statements carefully and then decide whether they are true or false. Put a "T" if you think the statement is true and an "F" if it is not.

1. Automation and more efficient production methods have left Americans with plenty of time on hand to enjoy their leisure life.

2. According to a Harris poll of 2014, American leisure time is shrinking due largely to people's disinterest in leisure life.

3. Sports are a mirror of American life, partly because such American values as individual success and achievement are reflected in athletes.

4. It is the unorganized rather than organized sports that reflect the basic values of American society, according to the passage.

5. Of all the spectator sports in the United States, basketball is probably the most popular game with Americans.

6. Like other English-speaking countries, America also uses sports activities as a way of teaching social values.

7. As a result of the financial crisis of 2008, Americans now spend fewer hours on work and more hours on recreation.

8. Recreation is meant to be spontaneous and relaxing, but Americans, on the whole, tend to take it in all seriousness.

9. Recreation in America has turned into an industry, generating a large sum of money for the people involved in it.

10. Since Americans enjoy social life, there is usually a lot of social activity on Sunday evening in the United States.

III. General Questions

1. What has happened to Americans for their leisure life as a result of the improvement of living standards?

2. Why do we say that sports are more than a mirror of American life?

3. What are the three major organized/spectator sports today in America?

4. What has become Super Bowl Sunday in the United States?

5. What could be one of the reasons for Americans to participate in sports so easily?

6. What kinds of activities may be viewed as recreational activities?

7. What is the irony of American recreation?

8. Will most American joggers stop jogging when temperature drops to subzero degrees?

9. What are children of average-income American families most likely to do on Saturday?

10. What are the ingenious weekenders?

Ⅳ. Essay Questions

1. What are the leisure activities of most American adults?

2. What are the major criticisms of sports in the United States?

Reference Answers

Ⅰ. Multiple Choices

1. D   2. D   3. A   4. C   5. B   6. A   7. C   8. D   9. A   10. D

Ⅱ. True and False

1. T   2. F   3. T   4. F   5. F   6. T   7. F   8. T   9. T   10. F

Ⅲ. General Questions

1. As a result of the improvement of living standards, Americans have more money to spend for their leisure life.

2. Because sports can be viewed as Americans' efforts to construct an imaginative world in which to create myths, legends and stars.

3. In the United States today, the three major organized/spectator sports are football, basketball and baseball.

4. Super Bowl Sunday has become almost a national holiday in America.

5. One of the reasons for Americans to participate in sports so easily is that public sports facilities are available in most parts of the country.

6. An evening concert in the downtown, a Sunday picnic with the family, a casual walk in a shopping mall, a family party for friends, or working in the garden with kids, all are forms of recreation.

7. The irony of American recreation is that while recreation is meant to be spontaneous and relaxing, Americans tend to approach it with a high degree of seriousness,

planning, organization and expense, making it neither spontaneous nor relaxing.

8. No, most Americans will never have second thoughts about doing it even when temperature drops to minus 10 degrees!

9. They are most likely to spend some time in cleaning up their own rooms, or they may be involved in some school programs on Saturday.

10. The so-called ingenious weekenders are those who approach their two or three-day respites from routine jobs with imagination and in some cases daring.

IV. Essay Questions

1. Most American adults enjoy a wide range of leisure activities at a varying degree of frequency. They include, but not limited to, individual and collective sports like tennis and football, a range of more passive pastimes like films and music, and other forms of participatory leisure activities, such as fishing, hunting, camping, hiking, gardening, surfing and traveling.

2. Many criticisms have been made by social critics about sports in the United States. For instance, some critics are very critical of the power of sports to corrupt when certain things are carried to excess. An excessive desire to win in sports, they argue, can corrupt rather than strengthen American values. Critics also point out that professional athletes and their coaches receive yearly salaries in the millions of dollars, misleading young children to enter sports to strike a fortune there rather than to promote sportsmanship. Additionally, critics complain that Americans bet millions of dollars on the outcome of matches, transforming sports into gambling. Most important of all, violence in American sports has been increasingly criticized in recent years by those who approve of sports generally but believe that violence is corrupting it.

Unit Eight   Social Services

Focal Points

social security   Medicaid   welfare
health care   Medicare   public housing

Discussion Questions

Social services, by definition, are services provided to disadvantaged citizens. Can one expect highly developed social services in such an individualistic society as the Uuited States?

Text

In American culture, two images from its past stand out, reflecting Americans' views on social services. The first image is that of self-reliant frontiersman, who goes out into the wilderness alone and survives. He asks no man for help. The second historical image is that of the pioneer community, sharing food with and **rendering** help to each other when things got tough. The people in the community **sustain** themselves by relying on one another. In a sense, social services in the United States have always been torn between the concepts of the independent and self-reliant individual and the interdependent and caring community. It is not until the Great Depression of the 1930s that there emerged some degree of awareness that social services should be provided for those in need.

render 给予

sustain 维持（精力、体力等）

Public Social Services

Generally speaking, public social services in the United States are divided into two main sections. The first is the **contributory** Social Security system, through which benefits are earned and distributed. The second is the Welfare system, which provides assistance to people with financial problems. Aids of this kind are **accorded** on the basis of income, dependent family members and employment situation.

Social Security

Social Security is the largest social services program in the United States. Governmental provision for social security was slow to develop in the United States. Though there are now some elements of a comprehensive system, serious gaps and variations exist between states. As it is, social security derives from the programs contained in the 1935 Social Security Act, referring basically to three main areas: (1) The old age, survivors, disability and health insurance programs (OASDHI);

(2) Medicare; (3) Unemployment Compensation.

Social Security is financed through a tax on workers with earnings up to $117,000 a year (the maximum amount of taxable earnings for 2014; it rises each year.) The worker and the employer each pay a tax of 6.2 percent, for a total of 12.4 percent. For example, the average worker makes $34,700 a year. According to the Social Security Administration, the worker pays $2,151.40 a year, or 6.2 percent of his/her salary, and the employer pays an identical amount. Their combined taxes are $4,302.80. In return for these payments, they receive benefits from the system, including retirement pensions; medical care for the elderly and disabled under Medicare; disability payments; illness and accident provisions; and unemployment payments. The rate of the pension gives an income above the official poverty line (about a quarter of median earnings from employment), not particularly handsome, but sufficient for minimal comfort. Medicare provides virtually free treatment for the elderly, though, with an extremely complex system of admissible charges through Medicare, elderly people do not recover the full cost of some types of expensive treatments. As for unemployment benefits, they last anywhere between 26 and 39 weeks, with compensation amounting to about a quarter of the worker's earnings.

Social security is the nearly universal retirement program for Americans, with about 92 percent of people aged 65 and over receiving benefits. About 156 million Americans pay social security taxes and about 47 million collect monthly benefits. However, although the majority of workers are covered by the system, social security does not cover all bills. Critics point out, for example, while a huge amount of money is spent on social security each year, it in fact only keeps 40 percent of people over 65 out of economic difficulties. Consequently, as a measure of **precaution, provisions** for old age, illness and unemployment often have to include additional private resources for many Americans, such as savings, investments and insurance policies. Most employers and unions also provide additional retirement, unemployment, health care and life insurance services for employees. These are mainly paid by employers or unions, but can include financial contributions from workers as well. If a person is **incapacitated** through the error of another person or corporation, as defined by a court of law, the damages awarded may be very high. Such awards of damages, mostly arising from transport accidents, mean that the victims do not need to ask for social security benefits.

Welfare Program

Social welfare, as the term suggests, is meant to provide aid to the **needy** and the poor. However, while the United States had long been known as a nation of abundance, public concern about poverty did not find its way into legislation until the 1960s. After that, the welfare system started to provide a

precaution 预防措施
provision 预先采取的措施

incapacitate 失去(工作)能力

needy 贫困的

variety of programs, such as financial assistance for the needy, job training for the unemployed, **rehabilitation for drug addicts**, health care for the sick without financial provisions, housing for the homeless, and **food stamps** for people living below the official poverty line. However, while the number of welfare programs seems large, the total cost of these programs amounts to only 6 percent of the US federal budget annually. Moreover, for a great variety of reasons, many people (perhaps half) simply do not take advantage of the public benefits to which they are entitled.

On the operational level, the cost of welfare programs is shared by federal, state and local governments. Generally speaking, for most of the welfare programs, federal funds are distributed to the states, which are expected to **commit** an equal amount of funds to jointly finance them. However, due to reasons ranging from political ideologies to cultural traditions and financial capabilities, states differ from each other in the amount of money they spend on their welfare programs. Some northern states, for example, provide a great many welfare programs to help their poor citizens, but many states in the south provide only a few. Indeed, since American politics operates under the principle of federalism, each state has the right to **devise** and organize its own programs. For instance, it defines, on the basis of a balanced budget, which families or individuals qualify for assistance from the welfare programs in terms of their actual needs.

Taken as a whole, the main federal welfare programs in the USA, until 1996, consisted of Medicaid, Aid to Families with Dependent Children (AFDC), and Food Stamps. Additionally, many others under the General Assistance program have been made available as well, providing such assistance as income support, cash grants, housing aid, school meals, Supplemental Security Income (SSI) for the elderly poor, and help with other basic necessities.

All these federal welfare programs vary from each other in expenditure, among which Medicaid is the largest. It gives federal grants to states for the free health treatment of the poor and needy under 65, blind and disabled people, and families with dependent children who lack the money or insurance to pay for the services. Following that is the Aid to Families with Dependent Children program, operated by the US federal government until its abolishment in 1996. In essence, AFDC provided payments to the disabled and families with dependent children on the basis of need according to the official poverty line. Since 1996, welfare responsibility under AFDC has been passed to the states, which receive federal grants to run their own programs and determine eligibility and benefit levels. Under the new law (called Temporary Assistance for Needy Families, TANF), there is a five-year lifetime limit on welfare benefits. More importantly, as part of TANF **scheme**, "Workfare" (work plus welfare) is introduced into the federal welfare program, according to which welfare **recipients**, such as single parents, should be prepared to work (often in public service jobs), take part in job training schemes or attend educational courses. In other words, rather than merely offering welfare to the recipients, workfare programs encourage them to move off welfare and into the workforce. The third major federal welfare program derives from the 1964 Food Stamp Act. This program provides food aid for **eligible** needy people and their families who have liquid resources (cash, checking accounts, bonds, etc.) of up to $2,000 and who lack an adequate **diet**. Historically, recipients received **coupons** or stamps and then used them to buy food in approved shops at an average national rate of **approximately** one-third of its normal price. Nowadays, however, paper food stamps have been changed to Electronic Benefit Transfer (EBT) cards, and are limited to a period of three months unless the recipients are working. The Department of Agriculture annually defines an adequate low-cost diet and administrates this federal-

---

scheme 计划

recipient 接受者、收受者

eligible 符合条件的

diet 食物
coupon 食品券
approximately 接近、大约

financed program through state governments.

Voluntary Services

While government-sponsored welfare programs are essential to the needy and the poor, they are far from adequate in confronting the poverty issue. Indeed, given the poverty level in the US as well as the inability of federal and state governments to meet the needs of the poor and needy, charitable voluntary organizations still play an important role in rendering help to people in need of assistance. Oftentimes, voluntary services are put in the private sector of social services. But in view of their non-governmental and non-profit-making character, they should be seen as a complementary third sector to the private and public services sectors.

There are a wide range of voluntary social services in the United States, organized locally or nationally to provide help to the needy or campaign on behalf of the disadvantaged. Some devote themselves to just one service, such as The National Coalition for the Homeless (NCH), whose only mission is to end homelessness. Toward this end, NCH engages in public education, policy advocacy, and grassroots organizing, focusing its efforts mainly on the following four areas: housing justice, economic justice, health care justice and civil rights. In the process of carrying out all this work, NCH provides information to thousands of people each year, including practitioners, community groups, researchers, government staff, the general public and the media. Also, it publishes reports and fact sheets, answers telephone calls, and speaks at conferences and workshops around the country. In 1987, NCH played a leadership role in pushing the US Congress to pass The Homeless Assistance Act. Over the years, NCH has helped ensure that billions of dollars have been made available for Homeless Assistance Act programs, such as emergency shelter grants, health care for the homeless and education for homeless children.

While single-issue-oriented voluntary organizations provide specific services for the people in need of help, many other voluntary organizations in the US provide more diversified services to their **target groups**. Take the Child Welfare League of America (CWLA) for example; it is an association of more than 1,100 public and **not-for-profit** agencies devoted to improving the lives of more than 3.5 million at-risk children and their families. Member agencies are involved with prevention and treatment of child abuse and neglect, and they provide various services in addition to child protection, such as **kinship** care, **family foster care**, **adoption**, positive youth development programs, residential group care, child care, family-centered practice, and programs for pregnant and parenting teenagers. Other concerns of member agencies include mental health, **chemical dependency**, housing and homelessness, and HIV/AIDS. Additionally, CWLA devotes much of its energy to public policy, concentrating on the passage of child welfare legislation to protect abused and neglected children and strengthen vulnerable families.

In all these voluntary services, religious organizations and private foundations stand out most prominently. As for the former, the Catholic Campaign for Human Development (CCHD) and Covenant House are two cases in point. CCHD is the domestic anti-poverty, social justice program of the U.S. Catholic bishops. Its mission is to address the root causes of poverty in the United States through promotion and support of community-controlled, self-help organizations and through **transformative** education. Over the past thirty-plus years, CCHD has funded over 4,000 programs across the United States. These efforts **know no racial or religious boundaries**, and all are designed to help people find a way out of poverty for a lifetime. By contrast, Covenant House is probably the largest privately-funded child care agency in the United States, providing **shelter** and service to homeless and runaway youth. In addition, Covenant House provides a variety of services to homeless youth, including health care, education, vocational preparation, drug abuse treatment and prevention programs, legal services, recreation, mother/child programs, transitional living programs, **street outreach** and aftercare. As for private foundations, the Rockefeller and Ford foundations used to be most well-known. Recently, however, the Bill & Melinda Gates Foundation has become most prominent in private charity activities. With an assets of US $ 38.3 billion as of June 2013, the Gates' Foundation hands out grants of more than US $ 1billion annually. Some of the money funds scholarships and computers for disadvantaged students in the United States, but the **lion's share** goes to the fight against such diseases as **polio**, **malaria** and AIDS in and outside the U.S.A.

For many people in the United States, charity organizations, religious institutions and unpaid volunteers are most crucial, because they are the most immediate and most accessible sources of help whenever they are needed. These organizations and volunteers provide a mixture of professional and non-professional aid, supply services for the sick and the elderly, operate care centers and clinics, run retirement homes and shelters for the homeless, and visit elderly, disabled, and needy people in the community. In doing all this, they supplement the public services by offering assistance and comfort to people when public help is either unavailable or insufficient. Together, they form a network of social services to the American people.

Health Care Services

American health and medical care services are divided between the private and public sectors. Private hospitals and clinics are, in general, well-equipped and efficient, and may be run by a variety of commercial organizations or religious groups. By contrast, many of those in the public sector, financed by state and federal funds, tend to lack resources and adequate funding. Doctors in general, but those in the private sector in particular, earn incomes far above the national average, constituting an influential professional group.

Most employees and their families are normally insured for health care through private insurance plans. They may get themselves insured individually, on a family basis, or as a group. Companies and trade unions may also be involved in insurance plans as part of efforts to protect employees or union members against the rising cost of health treatments and loss of income in case workers fall ill. Insurance **premiums**, expensive even by American standards, are made by deductions from wages and salaries, or by individual contributions.

However, one health insurance policy is not enough to cover all possible **eventualities**, and therefore in order to provide adequate protection for themselves, most Americans have to **subscribe to** more than one **policy**. Even so, many of them may still end up bearing some of the costs themselves. Indeed, given the high cost of insurance premiums, a considerable number of Americans (about 46 million people as of March 2014) do not have health insurance, either because they cannot afford it, or because they do not have steady jobs. So, there exist two **ironies** in the American health care system. One is: although the United States is the richest country in the world, a sizable number of people still remain uninsured largely because of too high insurance premiums. The other is: while the US has top-quality medical facilities, gaining access to them remains a formidable barrier for a large portion of the population in the country.

In the public sector, health care is available to those who need it but lack money and insurance to pay for it. The federal **non-contributory** Medicaid program provides federal grants to states for the free treatment of the poor, the needy, the blind, the disabled and the dependent. However, due to matching-fund practices, the **scope** of Medicaid coverage varies greatly among states, with some providing far more aid than others. All in all, Medicaid covers only about 40 percent of the poor nation-

premium（保险人向保险公司支付的）保险费

eventuality 可能发生的事情、可能出现的结果

subscribe to 认购

policy 保险单

irony 具有讽刺意味的事情

non-contributory（养老金、医保等）非共酿的

scope 范围

wide.

Still, state and local governments do provide a wide range of public health services for many categories of people, from the poor to the war veterans and to the armed forces. They operate or support hospitals, mental institutions, retirement homes and maternity and child care health services. In many cases, public health services may be supplemented by voluntary organizations, universities and other institutions that provide free care for the local population. Ultimately, however, public medical and health care services in the US suffer from varying standards, inadequate coverage of the needy, and differences in the amount of money spent on them. This means that a considerable number of Americans under the age of 65 have to depend upon private medical insurance plans if they can afford them.

Over the past few decades, much criticism has been made about the health care system in the US. It is reported that in 2013 about 17.9 percent of GDP derived from the provision of US private and public health care services. However, astounding as the GDP figure is, the American public is not receiving the full benefit of such large expenditures. Much of it comes from a cluster of factors, such as the soaring prices of **prescription drugs**, the growing costs of medical equipment, the high incomes of doctors, the increasingly costly insurance policies, and the endless **malpractice** lawsuits against physicians and hospitals. In short, compared with other developed countries, the United States spends more on health care and yet provides less help to its own people.

Partly in response to public criticism, and partly in an effort to make the long overdue reform, on March 23, 2010, the Patient Protection and Affordable Care Act (commonly known as the Affordable Care Act, or "Obamacare") was signed into law by President Barack Obama, a milestone in American healthcare system. The Affordable Care Act, as the name indicates, was enacted with the goals of increasing the quality and

---

prescription drug 凭处方供应的药品

malpractice（医疗）失职行为

affordability of health insurance, lowering the uninsured rate by expanding public and private insurance coverage, and reducing the costs of healthcare for individuals and the government. By requiring all U.S. citizens and legal residents to buy insurance, the Act intends to provide health insurance for most Americans for the first time by 2019. To this end, the Act will provide subsidies for those who cannot afford insurance, give incentives to companies to provide health cover for their employees, establish health insurance exchanges to expand coverage to more people, and fine individuals, companies and insurers who do not **comply with** the Act. The Congressional Budget Office estimated that the Affordable Care Act will cost $940 billion over ten years, but will also lower future budget deficits and Medicare spending. Still, as the full implementation of the Act will take many years, the success or failure of it will not be known soon, though controversies and criticisms about it have never **abated** since its passage.

comply with 遵从、服从

abate 减弱、减退

Housing

Homes and houses are very important to many Americans and their families. They give a sense of possession, material satisfaction, personal identity and individual lifestyle. As a nation that emphasizes both physical and social mobility, the average American may change homes many times during his lifetime. Consequently, home-ownership in the US is associated not only with geographical movement, but also with social and economic mobility. So, a young family may move from an apartment to a house in the city in the early years, and then, as the family grows, move from the urban area to a suburban house.

Most Americans have the dream of owning their own house and a little piece of land, and the majority of them would prefer to live in suburban areas. This, in fact, is part of the American Dream. Given the abundant opportunities available in the United States, a great number of Americans eventually realize this dream. By and large, houses in the US are not excessively expensive in relation to their space and comfort, and in relation to income levels they look quite reasonable. So, in comparison with other countries, the home-ownership rate in the US is quite high. In 2009, for example, it stood at 67.4 percent. But after the crash of the housing market in 2008 with its **ensuing foreclosures**, the percentages have dropped sharply. By July 2014, homeownership rate fell to 64.8 percent, causing many Americans to complain that the American Dream is now becoming increasingly remote.

Approximately, two-thirds of the housing units in the private sector are "single-family dwellings", often of a **detached** type and usually having front and back yards or gardens. Other people live in apartments (whether owned or rented), and the rest live in a variety of different housings. In general, private houses or apartments are reasonably priced, although they are subject to price fluctuations in the real estate market. They are usually decently built and carefully decorated, complete with many kinds of **amenities**. When buying a home, most homeowners borrow money from the bank (a mortgage), which is secured by the value of their house as well as their family income. When the mortgage is paid off, which ranges anywhere between 15 to 30 years, the house becomes completely one's own.

As for public housing in the United States, it is largely meant to provide for the people who are either unable to buy property or cannot afford high-rent private accommodation. Historically speaking, the idea of providing public housing has never been well received in the United States. The strongest opposition to such a practice comes from the long-cherished value in the American creed, i.e., individualism. According to this notion, individuals are expected to be responsible for their own housing, rather than expecting the government to provide it for them. However, because of the existence of widespread urban slums, together with the great health and social **hazards** they pose to the public, public housing has been made available in the United States one way or the other. The creation of the Federal Housing Administration in 1934, for example, was the first step taken in that direction. The Administration provided loans to companies willing to build low-rent accommodations for needy people. Additionally, local and state governments were also engaged in the program by building public housing for the low-income groups in their cities and states. Since the founding of the Department of Housing and Urban Development (HUD) in 1965, the public housing problem has received more attention from the federal government. As a cabinet-level department of the US government, it has regular resources to develop and execute policy on housing and cities, though in recent years it has largely **scaled back** its urban development function. In 2013, the HUD budget for low-income housing stood at $44.8billion. While the sum of the money might seem to be big, only a small portion of people can actually get housing assistance from the federal government, for the number of Americans in need of affordable housing far exceeds the amount of money spent on it. Indeed, subsidized housing for the poor in the US is more like a **lottery** than an **entitlement**, for only a third of the families eligible for federal housing assistance receive any subsidies. Consequently, a significant number of low-income people, particularly minority groups in large urban areas, continue to live in barely **habitable** conditions.

> hazard 危险、危害物
>
> scale back 相应缩减
>
> lottery 抽奖、乐透
> entitlement 应得的权利
>
> habitable 可居住的、适于居住的

Notes

Medicare—Established in 1965 with the passage of the Social Security Amendments, Medicare is a national health insurance program in the United States for persons aged 65 and over, providing for a basic program of hospital insurance, under which most persons aged 65 and over are protected against major costs of hospitals and related care.

Medicaid—Established in 1965 with the passage of the Social Security Amendments, Medicaid is a national health insurance program in the United States for low-income persons. Of the various services covered under Medicaid, almost 40 percent of the funds are used to purchase in-patient hospital services; 30 percent nursing home services; 12 percent physician services, and the remaining 18 percent for drugs, laboratory services, X rays and other covered services.

Poverty line—Following the Office of Management and Budget's Statistical Policy Directive 14, the Census Bureau of the US Government uses a set of income thresholds that vary by family size and composition to determine who is living in poverty. If a family's total income is less than the family's threshold, then that family and every individual in it is considered to be living in poverty. The official poverty thresholds do not vary geographically, but they are updated for inflation using the Consumer Price Index (CPI). The official definition of poverty uses income before taxes and does not include capital gains or non-cash benefits (such as public housing, Electronic Benefit Transfer cards and Medicaid). The poverty threshold for a family of four in 2014 was $23,850, and $11,6570 for single people.

Exercises

Ⅰ. Multiple Choices

The following are questions or incomplete sentences. Below each sentence or question four possible answers marked A, B, C and D are provided. Choose the ONE that best completes the sentence or answers the question.

1. The image of American frontiersman is that of a _____ man.
   A. self-made   B. self-reliant
   C. self-important   D. self-righteous

2. According to Social Security stipulations, the worker and the employer each pay a tax of _____ percent, for a total of _____ percent.
   A. 5.2, 10.4   B. 6.2, 12.4   C. 7.2, 14.4   D. 8.2, 16.4

3. The rate of the pension gives an income _____ the official poverty line, not particularly handsome, but sufficient for minimal comfort.
   A. along   B. under   C. above   D. beyond

4. Social security is the nearly universal _____ program for Americans, with a-

bout 92 percent of people aged 65 and over receiving benefits.

 A. employment   B. compensation

 C. healthcare   D. retirement

5. Social welfare, as the term suggests, is meant to provide aid to _____.

 A. the jobless and the poor

 B. the needy and poor

 C. the poor and the single-parent family

 D. the needy and the sick

6. Until 1996, the main federal welfare programs in the USA consisted of all the following except _____.

 A. Medicaid

 B. Food Stamps

 C. Aid to Families with Dependent Children

 D. Medicare

7. With the passage of the new law (called Temporary Assistance for Needy Families, TANF), welfare recipients have a _____ lifetime limit on welfare benefits.

 A. two-year   B. three-year   C. four-year   D. five-year

8. As a voluntary services provider, the National Coalition for the Homeless (NCH) focuses its efforts mainly on the following four areas, namely _____.

 A. housing justice, economic justice, health care justice and civil rights

 B. economic justice, health care justice, housing justice and political justice

 C. civil rights, housing justice, economic justice and educational justice

 D. health care justice, housing justice, economic justice and social justice

9. American doctors, both in the public and private sectors earn incomes _____ the national average.

 A. a little bit above   B. much

 C. a great deal above   D. somewhat

10. In the United States, public housing largely refers to federal, state and local governments' efforts to provide housing for the people _____.

 A. who are either too young to buy property or too poor to rent apartments

 B. who are either unemployed or come from single-parent families

 C. who are either too sick to work or too old to take care of themselves

 D. who are able to neither buy property nor pay for high-rent apartments

II. True and False

Read the following statements carefully and then decide whether they are true or false. Put a "T" if you think the statement is true and an "F" if it is not.

1. In the United States, the Social Security system is contributory, but the Welfare system is non-contributory.

2. Unemployment benefits in America can last as long as necessary, i.e. until the jobless person gets employed.

3. American public concern about poverty did not find its way into legislation until the 1960s.

4. The total cost of U.S. welfare programs amounts to more than 6 percent of the US federal budget annually.

5. States vary from each other in the amount of money they spend on their welfare programs.

6. By "workfare", it means work plus welfare, i.e., welfare recipients are expected to work while still on welfare, or take some job training programs to prepare themselves for employment in the near future.

7. Before the introduction of Electronic Benefit Transfer (EBT) cards, food stamp recipients could use these stamps to buy food in any shop at a normal price.

8. Religious organizations and private foundations play a very prominent role in American voluntary services.

9. The greatest part of the Gates' Foundation goes to the fight against such diseases as polio, malaria and AIDS in and outside the U.S.A.

10. All American employees and their families are normally insured for health care through private insurance plans.

III. General Questions

1. What were the two key traditional attitudes of Americans towards social services?

2. When did Americans realize the importance and necessity of social services?

3. What are the main areas covered by social security?

4. How are welfare programs in the United States administered?

5. What are the main purposes of voluntary services and how do they function?

6. How much do you know about The Bill & Melinda Gates Foundation, and what do you think of the things they have been doing?

7. How do average Americans get health insurance, and how do poor Americans seek medical care?

8. Why is home-ownership so important for most Americans? What are its social and cultural implications?

9. Where do the majority of American homeowners prefer to live?

10. Where does the strongest opposition to public housing come from?

Ⅳ. Essay Questions

1. What could be the possible reasons for Americans to be so slow and so reluctant in initiating and developing their social services, particularly in comparison with other developed countries in the world?

2. Poverty is ubiquitous around the world, but it is made more poignant in the United States, for it claims to be not only a nation of wealth, but also a land of opportunity. Do you think the poverty issue in the United States has been adequately addressed? If not, what more can be done about it?

Reference Answers

Ⅰ. Multiple Choices

1. B 2. B 3. C 4. D 5. B 6. D 7. D 8. A 9. C 10. D

Ⅱ. True and False

1. T 2. F 3. T 4. F 5. T 6. T 7. F 8. T 9. T 10. F

Ⅲ. General Questions

1. The first image is that of self-reliant frontiersman, who goes out into the wilderness alone and survives. He asks no man for help. The second historical image is that of the pioneer community, sharing food with and rendering help to each other when things got tough.

2. It is not until the Great Depression of the 1930s that there emerged some measure of awareness that social services should be provided for those in need of them.

3. Social security mainly covers three areas, namely: 1) the old age, survivors, disability and health insurance program (OASDHI); 2) Medicare; 3) Unemployment Compensation.

4. On the operational level, the cost of welfare programs is shared by federal, state

and local governments. For most of the welfare programs, federal funds are distributed to the states, which are expected to commit an equal amount of funds to jointly finance them. However, since American politics operates under the principle of federalism, each state has the right to devise and organize its own programs.

5. The main purposes of voluntary services are to complement and supplement social services provided by public and private sectors. For many grass-roots Americans, voluntary services are most crucial, because they are the most immediate and most accessible sources of help when needed.

6. The Bill & Melinda Gates Foundation has already become a household name in the United States, playing a prominent in private charity activity. It is reported that in 2013 Gates' Foundation has assets of US $38.3 billion, handing out grants of more than US $1billion annually. Some of the money funds scholarships and computers for disadvantaged students in the United States, but the lion's share goes to the fight against diseases such as polio, malaria and AIDS in and outside the United States of America.

7. Most employees and their families are normally insured for health care through private insurance schemes. Companies and trade unions may also be involved in insurance schemes as part of efforts to protect employees or union members against the cost of health treatment and loss of income in case workers fall ill. For the poor, the needy, the blind, the disabled and the dependent, they can seek help from the federal non-contributory Medicaid program which provides federal grants to states for the free treatment of their illnesses.

8. Homes and houses are very important to many Americans and their families. They give a sense of possession, material satisfaction, personal identification and individual lifestyle. As a nation that emphasizes both physical and social mobility, the average American may move home many times during his lifetime. Consequently, home-ownership in the U.S. is associated not only with geographical movement, but also with social and economic mobility.

9. The majority of American homeowners prefer to live in suburban areas.

10. The strongest opposition to public housing comes from the long-cherished value in the American creed, i.e., individualism, according to which each individual is responsible for his/her housing, rather than looking to the government for help.

IV. Essay Questions

1. First, private charity organizations have been highly developed since the early

days of the settlement, making it possible for people to receive charity, including services, from private institutions rather than from government agencies. Secondly, Americans have a long tradition of self-reliance, self-help, and self-independence, believing that one should be responsible for everything he does. They hold that when one fails, it is an indication that he has not tried hard enough, and thus become a failure. Unless he is physically or mentally incapacitated, he should take care of himself, and therefore no government aid should be given to such a person. Thirdly, Americans in general do not trust government, believing government power should be limited rather than expanded. Setting up any new institution like public services is in fact delegating more power to the government. Finally, church organizations have been heavily involved in community services, providing necessary and timely help to the needy in their own community. Gradually, people tend to go to their churches for help rather than to the government for assistance.

2. No, it has not been adequately addressed. For one thing, welfare programs are far less developed in the U.S. than those in other industrialized countries. For another, not enough educational or training programs have been provided to retool the poor people to make them competitive in the job market. Government, political party, civil organizations, and the public should work together to work out some practical and enduring programs to help the poor to help themselves, providing more opportunities for them to learn how to support themselves. On the other hand, the poor should take the initiative themselves, trying to get descent education, picking up industrial skills, building good habits, and making efforts to rely more upon themselves. Above all, the society should stop discrimination against the poor, trying every possible means to create a fair and friendly social environment for the poor to live as anybody else.

Part II The Great Britain

Unit Nine The Land and the People

Focal Points

England	Wales	Scotland
Northern Ireland	the UK	Great Britain
regionalism	accent	British identity

Discussion Questions

Why is there regionalism in the UK?

Text

"Britain" is a short form of the full and official name of the United Kingdom of Great Britain and Northern Ireland (the UK). Therefore, Great Britain strictly comprises the three countries England, Scotland and Wales, whereas the UK also includes Northern Ireland. On formal occasions, "the United Kingdom" is used, but in everyday conversation, "Britain" is a widely accepted name for the nation. The United Kingdom covers a land area of just over 243,610 square kilometers (94,000 square miles) and claims a population of about 64.51 million (estimated by the end of 2014). It has London as its national capital, located on the bank of the river Thames in south-east England. The Union Flag, popularly known as the Union Jack, is the national flag and "God Save the King/Queen" is used as the national anthem.

The Land

Britain is located on the **westernmost** edge of the **continental shelf** of Europe. It consists of two large and several hundred small islands that were separated from the European continent in about 6000 BC. The mild **maritime climate** and gently **undulating** lowlands give the mainland an excellent agricultural base. The landscape becomes increasingly mountainous toward the north, rising to the **Grampian Mountains** in Scotland, the **Pennines** in northern England, and the **Cambrian Mountains** in Wales. The major rivers include the Thames in the south, the **Severn** in the west and the **River Spey** in Scotland.

England

England is the largest, most populous, and wealthiest division of the United Kingdom. It makes up 130,281 square kilometers (53.7 per cent) of the country's total area, one of the important reasons why England is mistaken for Britain abroad. However, a stronger factor for such misunderstanding is the relatively large size of England's population. It was estimated in 2014 that 53.9 million people or 83.6 percent of the total population of the UK lived in England, making this region, particularly the capital London, not only the **most densely populated**, but also the most influential, part of the country, **beaming** its television programs to the rest of the nation, for example.

With the bulk of the most fertile lowlands and six of the country's seven **conurbations**, England has a higher proportion of wealth and natural resources than the rest of the UK. London, which is the seat of government, centre of business, and the heart of arts and culture, dominates England, just as England dominates Great Britain. This English dominance is so apparent that many people use "England" to refer to the whole U-

---

westernmost 最西边

continental shelf 大陆架

maritime climate 海洋性气候

undulating 起伏的

Grampian Mountains 格兰扁山脉

Pennines 奔宁山脉

Cambrian Mountains 坎布里安山脉

Severn 塞文河

River Spey 斯佩河

most densely populated 人口最密集的

beam 广播

conurbation (连接卫星城镇和市郊的)大都市

nited Kingdom, the entire island of Great Britain, or the British Isles. This is not only incorrect but may annoy people from other parts of the UK. Not surprisingly, the English themselves feel most British and least attached to a separate English identity. However, this also means that England no longer officially exists as a nation when the other three nations of the UK can enjoy separate political status in one way or another.

England is often talked about in terms of a **north/south divide**, which is cultural, economic and political. For example, the Labor Party has far more support in the north and the Conservative Party in the south. More significantly, such a divide is **accentuated** by **discrepancies** in unemployment levels, crime rates, house prices, and standards of living, all of which have in recent decades **deteriorated** in the north. The perceived divide does not occur in the middle of the country, however, and southerners sometimes refer to a cold, industrial region that is everywhere "north of **Watford**", a town not particularly far north of London. In turn, some northerners caricature many southerners as both "soft" and unsociable. This is because people from the south-east, and particularly London, are sometimes seen as **fast-living**, career-minded and unfriendly, while they are also **more comfortably off** and enjoy better weather than those further north. Differences between north and south have evolved over the last centuries and are more cultural than simply industrial or economic. Indeed, during much of the 19th century, the north was more prosperous than the south.

Scotland

Scotland is the second largest of the four nations both in area and population. It has an area of 77,925 square kilometers (32.1 percent) with a population of 5.3 million (8.2 percent) as reported in 2014. But its population density is the lowest in the country (only about 65 persons per square kilometer), due to most part of Scotland being rugged and unsuitable for people to live. Three-quarters of the population and most of the industrial towns are in the central lowlands between the two uplands in the north and south. It is the home of Glasgow in the West and Edinburgh on the east coast, respectively the largest city and the capital of the region.

Before Scotland formally joined the Union with England in 1707, it had been a unified state independent of the UK for a long time. Today Scotland no longer has a separate legislature and executive and its economy is integrated into that of the rest of Britain. But it does have a separate administration, different legal and educational systems as well as its Presbyterian national church. Here are located some of the most important "enterprise zones" and development areas, assisted by government funding and incentives for industry.

Above all, it has retained much of its distinct cultural identity. For instance, a vigorous cultural life has as its **highlight** the annual Edinburgh International Festival, one of the world's leaning cultural events. Notable performing arts bodies are the Royal Scottish **Orchestra**, Scottish Opera, Scottish Ballet, Scottish **Chamber Orchestra**, and the BBC Scottish **Symphony** Orchestra. Scotland possesses excellent collections of the fine and **applied arts**, notably in the National **Gallery** of Scotland, the Royal Museum of Scotland, and the City of Glasgow Museum and Art Gallery.

Wales

Wales, a peninsular **jutting** from England into the Irish Sea, is the smallest among the three nations on the island of Great Britain, with an area of 20,732 square kilometers (8.5 percent). It has a population of 3.1million (4.8 percent) as reported in 2014, with a population density of 142 persons per square kilometer. Cardiff, the capital, is located in southern Wales, serving as an important seaport and industrial centre.

Due to its **adjacency to** England, Wales has been dominated by England for longer period of time than the other nations of the UK—officially since its union with England in 1536. Never-

---

highlight 最突出、最显亮部分

orchestra 管弦乐队
chamber orchestra 室内乐队
symphony 交响
applied arts 应用工艺美术
gallery 陈列馆、美术馆

jut 突出、伸出

adjacency to 邻近、靠近

theless, it retains a unique cultural, social, and economic development, notably its national language, Welsh and a **devolved** Welsh Assembly.

Welsh accent, vocabulary, and idioms of speech distinguish the Welsh from the rest of Britons. Welsh is one of the oldest languages in the British Isles. Tens of thousands of the Welsh population still speak Welsh, adult educational institutions run language courses, and since the 1970s bilingual education in Welsh has become firmly established. About a quarter of the Welsh population speak both languages, and because Welsh and English are both officially supported, it is usual to see signs written in the two languages.

Northern Ireland

Northern Ireland, often referred to as the province of **Ulster**, is part of the Island of Ireland located in its northeast corner. It is the smallest both in area and population among the four nations of the UK. It occupies an area of 13,576 square kilometers (5.7 percent of the UK and one-six of the Island of Ireland) and had a population of 1.8 million (2.8 percent) in 2014. The capital Belfast, a seaport on the east coast, is a centre of shipbuilding and linen textiles.

Ireland, in fact, is the second largest of the British Isles. However, unlike smaller islands, which are wholly British, such as the Isle of Wight and the Shetlands, Ireland is officially **partitioned**. In 1921, when an agreement was signed giving the rest of the country independence, six of the nine Irish counties that constituted the ancient province of Ulster remained part of the United Kingdom—these were the north-eastern counties that were predominantly Protestant. For this reason, Northern Island is sometimes known simply as "the six counties".

Geographically, the northern part of Ireland is separated from Scotland by a very narrow channel, which has historically subjected the region to intrusive British influences. Just under two-thirds of the population are descendants of Scots or English settlers who crossed to northeastern Ireland mainly in the 17th century, most of whom belong to the Protestant faith and support the maintenance of the union with Great Britain. The remainder, over a third, are Irish in origin and mainly Roman Catholic. Northern Island, therefore, has national and official links with the rest of Britain, but its people share deep roots with histories and traditions south of the border. Since the Anglo-Irish agreement of 1985, **the Republic of Ireland** has participated in its political and legal matters. Under an accord in 1998, a semi-autonomous government was established in mid-2000 in this region.

the Republic of Ireland 爱尔兰共和国

The People

Multicultural Britain

Politically speaking, all the peoples of the United Kingdom of Great Britain and Northern Ireland, including the English, Scots, Irish, and Welsh, those from former colonies, and the many others who have made Britain their **adopted country**, are called "British". On the other hand, it is essential to understand that the historic cultural traditions of the British, particularly the **Celtic**, **Anglo-Saxon**, **Nordic**, and **Norman French** cultures, remain at the center of the "British way of life".

Historically, **indigenous** British people were thought to be **descended from** the various ethnic groups that settled there before the 11th century: the Celts, **Romans**, Anglo-Saxons, **Norse** and the **Normans**. The ancestors of today's English are Anglo-Saxons, while the Scots, Welsh and Irish are all descendants of the Celts. Until the Second World War, Britain was a predominantly white country—most immigrants over the centuries had come from continental Europe, and later from the white dominions of the Old Commonwealth: Australia, Canada, New Zealand and South Africa. However, since 1945, but particularly over the past three decades, there have been some new patterns of migration in the UK. Among the new immigrants,

adopted country 移居的国家

Celtic 凯尔特人的
Anglo-Saxon 安格鲁-撒克逊人的
Nordic 北欧人日耳曼民族的
Norman French 讲诺曼法语的人的
indigenous 本土的、土生土长的
descend from 是…后裔
Romans 古罗马人
Norse 古斯堪的纳维亚人、古挪威人
Norman(10世纪定居于诺曼底的)斯堪的纳维亚人和法国人的后裔

for example, a large portion of them have come from British former colonies, principally from the Indian subcontinent (India, Pakistan, and Bangladesh) and the Caribbean, making Great Britain an increasingly multi-ethnic, multicultural society. According to the 2011 Censuses of the UK, of the total population of Great Britain in 2011, White Britons represented 87.17%, Asians or the Asian British 6.92%, Blacks or the Black British 3.01%, the British Mixed 1.98%, and others 0.92%.

These different racial and ethnic communities are not evenly spread across the country, creating a very mixed pattern of **integration** and **cohesion**. In such large cities as London, Leicester and Birmingham, for example, ethnic-based communities can be found everywhere. About two-thirds of all Black ethnic groups live in London, and a large number of Indians, Pakistanis and Bangladeshis reside in Birmingham, Greater Manchester, and West Yorkshire. In all these communities, people do not speak English, nor do not practice Christian relief. Indeed, in virtually every aspect, they do not appear to have anything in common with the majority "white" culture of the UK. Because of their presence, most of large cities in Britain are now largely multiracial in character, and life there is all the more colorful and **vibrant** for it.

While many Britons applaud the direction of Britain toward multiculturalism, there are some people against it. **In the main**, those in favor of it cherish and celebrate the cultural diversity that new immigrants have brought over to Britain, while critics express the worry that these new cultural groups are not able to integrate and assimilate into British society. To illustrate it by analogy, opponents of multiculturalism would like to see Britain as a **"melting-pot"**, while proponents of it insist that Britain be made a **"stir fry"**. Apparently, debate over this issue is not likely to go away, as long as new immigrants from Africa, Asia, and the Middle East keep coming to Britain. It is often said that nowadays only traditional town or village life in Britain remains more typically British, where the presence of new immigrants is neither heavy, nor concentrated.

Languages, Dialects and Accents

There is no single British language, although English is the main language spoken by British citizens, being spoken **monolingually** by over 70% of the UK population. English is, therefore, the **de facto** official language of the United Kingdom.

Modern English is a West Germanic language descended from Old English which features a large number of borrowings from Old Norse, Norman French, Greek and Latin. Thanks to the great influence of the British Empire from the 17th to the mid-20th century, the English language has spread across the world and has become the main international language of business as well as the most widely taught second language.

However, although English is widely spoken around the world, more variety is found among the regions of Britain. Among the most distinctive are the dialects of **Glasgow**, Liverpool, the West Midlands, Northern Island, **Yorkshire**, and east London. They contain many non-standard words and their intonation and distinctive pronunciation of **vowels** makes them easy to recognize. In Liverpool the dialect is known as **Scouse**, a mixture of **Lancashire**, Irish and Welsh, while the **vernacular** speech of east London is **Cockney**, a dialect known for its rhyming slang. Additionally, a different from of speech is used by some Afro-Caribbean immigrants and their descendants. This mixes dialect speech from the West Indies with an English accent of the locality, and is known as Black British English or Black English vernacular.

Both accent and dialect thus give the listener **clues** about a speaker's geographical and social background. Non-standard features are commonly present in the speech of people who have had less formal education, and who have spent most or all their lives in the same locality. As a result, in Britain, a high degree of social significance has been attached to English speech. Long

---

monolingually 单语言地
de facto 实际上的、事实上的

Glasgow 格拉斯哥
Yorkshire 约克郡

vowel 元音
Scouse 利物浦方言
Lancashire 兰开夏(郡)
vernacular 本地语的、方言的
Cockney 伦敦东区土话

clue 线索

before, for instance, some British **grammarians** recommended the speech of London and **the Court** as the most correct and desirable in an attempt to eliminate what they saw as a **cacophony** of regional accents. It was selected largely because it was spoken by the ruling class—the aristocracy and Court—and therefore carried authority. It was sometimes called "Queen's English" and later became known as "received pronunciation" (often abbreviated to RP), which everyone was expected to "receive", i.e., "understand".

The prestige and authority of RP implied the **inferiority** of regional accents and vocabulary. Dialect speakers became socially **stigmatized** as **rustic**, provincial, poor and uneducated. Linguistic differences came to be seen as linguistic errors, and socially ambitious had to modify their speech toward that of their betters. The arrival of public broadcasting in 1922 helped to extend the social prestige of RP. Although it was spoken by only 2-3 percent of the population, it was preferred by the BBC because it was widely understood and respected. Due to the dominance of RP, for many years regional speech was rarely heard on TV, radio or at the cinema, except in the roles of "character" actors.

However, greater educational opportunities for a generation of working-class and lower-middle-class children in the 1940s, more openness and authenticity in arts in the 1950s, and above all, the emergence of popular culture in the 1960s, all helped promote a wider acceptance of regional speech in the public sphere. Consequently, with changing social attitudes and greater social **convergence** and movement between the social classes, the RP has become less influential and is no longer regarded by everyone as the "best pronunciation". Indeed, the "marked" or "advanced" RP tends to mark the speaker as being old fashioned, **detached** and remote from mainstream society. Nevertheless, despite a wider acceptance of regional accents and dialects, there is evidence that some varieties may still carry negative connotations in the public sphere, and a milder "moderate" RP speech is considered the most desirable, with many people associating it with intelligence, ambition, occupational status, and even good looks!

Identity Crisis: Are Britons Becoming a Disunited Kingdom?

Historically, British identity is a relatively recent **construct**, and was gradually **superimposed on** earlier national identities of English, Scottish and Irish. For all of its relatively short history, Britain has been a multi-nation state since its beginning and a British identity has had to coexist with separate national identities. First, Wales was formally **incorporated with** England by the 1536 Act of Union. Next, came the 1707 Act of Union between England/Wales and Scotland, which is usually taken as the formal constitutional beginning of Great Britain, while the 1810 Act of Union created the United Kingdom of Great Britain and Ireland. In 1922, the twenty six counties of southern and western Ireland formed the Free State, leaving a United Kingdom composed of Great Britain and the six counties of the Province of Ulster that became known as Northern Ireland.

With Britain's decline in modern times, but particularly with a large inflow of immigrants from Asia and Africa, the old concept of England-based British identity has weakened. Not only do Welsh and Scots generally unite in defense of their respective national identity and differences from the English, but many of ethnic groups tend to see themselves as primarily some other nationality or ethnicity and "British" only secondary as well. More significantly, in recent years, there has occurred a revival of passions for England among the English—the revival of interest in English folk, English history and English geography. All of this, when combined, has raised a serious question about British identity: is it going to lead to the break-up of Britain, or is it going to create a new identity?

construct（构思的）结果、观念、概念

superimpose on 把…放在上面、加上

incorporate with 把合并、使并入

Unit Nine The Land and the People

According to a report released by the British Department of Justice, over the past thirty years, there has been a significant decline in the proportion of British citizens who feel their British identity to be their primary national identity. On the one hand, the number of English, Welsh, and Scottish residents who consider their nationality to be primarily British has fallen. On the other hand, the number describing themselves as Scottish, Welsh, or English has risen. Take the census of 2011 for example, the first ever to ask people to tick boxes for their national identity (or identities), 60% of people in England described themselves as English (not British), while 38% of people from an ethnic minority (i.e. **Bangladeshi** or **Pakistani**) said they were exclusively British, as against only 14% of white people. More **tellingly**, the Economic and Social Research Council found in its recent study that 16% of the Welsh felt "British not Welsh, **as against** 9% in 2007. Similarly, the 2010 Northern Ireland Life and Times surveys showed 37% saw themselves as British, 26% Irish, and 29% Northern Irish, with 3% choosing Ulster.

Behind all these figures emotions run deep. Is national identity in the UK purely a personal badge to be worn with pride, or could it fundamentally change the nature of British state? To be sure, there is still much shared culture in Britain, whether on pop music, clothing, fish and chips or on comedians and **Coronation Street**. But what is equally clear is that over the past thirty years, there has been a significant decline in the **prevalence** of a British national identity among British citizens. Today, when Britons talk about "Britishness" or "British cultural identities", the emphases have shifted to multiplicity and plurality, suggesting that the weakness and strength of Britain lies in the fact that many people in Britain see themselves as primarily some other nationality or ethnicity and "British" only secondarily. In short, they share the same islands, but they are not all British, the consequences of which can never be overemphasized for British society, particularly for social cohesion within the nation.

Bangladeshi 孟加拉国
Pakistani 巴基斯坦
tellingly 有力地

as against 与…相比较

Coronation Street 肥皂剧 "加冕街"
prevalence 普遍、盛行

Notes

Anglo-Irish agreement of 1985—The Anglo-Irish Agreement, signed on 15 November 1985, was an agreement between the United Kingdom and Ireland which aimed to help bring an end to the Troubles in Northern Ireland. The treaty gave the Irish government an advisory role in Northern Ireland's government while confirming that there would be no change in the constitutional position of Northern Ireland unless a majority of its people agreed to join the Republic. It also set out conditions for the establishment of a devolved consensus government in the region.

Coronation Street—*Coronation Street* is a British soap opera made by Granada Television and shown on ITV since 1960. The program centers on Coronation Street in Weatherfield, a fictional town based on Salford, its terraced houses, café, corner shop, newsagents, textile factory and The Rovers Return pub. The fictional street was built in the early 1900s and named in honor of the coronation of King Edward VII.

Exercises

Ⅰ. Multiple Choices

The following are questions or incomplete sentences. Below each sentence or question four possible answers marked A, B, C and D are provided. Choose the ONE that best completes the sentence or answers the question.

1. Strictly speaking, Great Britain comprises three countries, namely, _____.

   A. England, Scotland and Northern Ireland

   B. England, Welsh and Northern Ireland

   C. England, Scotland and Welsh

   D. Scotland, Welsh, and Northern Ireland

2. On formal occasions, _____ is used, but in everyday conversation, _____ is a widely accepted name for the nation.

   A. Great Britain/Britain   B. the United Kingdom/Britain

   C. England/Great Britain   D. the United Kingdom/England

3. The Thames is located _____.

   A. in the south   B in the north

   C. in the west   D. in the east

4. England has a higher proportion of wealth and natural resources than _____.

A. Scotland B. Welsh
C. Northern Ireland D. the rest of the UK

5. England is often talked about in terms of a _____/_____ divide, which is cultural, economic, and political.

A. east/west   B. north/south   C. west/north   D. east/south

6. Southerners are caricatured by northerners as both "soft" and unsociable, largely because _____.

A. people from the south-east are sometimes seen as fast-living, career-minded, unfriendly, and more comfortably off

B. people from the south-east are oftentimes seen as driving fast, playing around, kindly, and always busy

C. people from the south-east are occasionally seen as running fast, money-minded, approachable, and enjoying life

D. people from the south-east are always seen as drinking fast, job-minded, hanging out with friends, and having an easy time.

7. Before Scotland formally joined the Union with England in _____, it had been a unified state independent of the UK for a long time.

A. 1701   B. 1717   C. 1770   D. 1707

8. In Scotland are located some of the most important _____ and development areas.

A. trade zones B. scenic spots
C. science parks D. enterprise zones

9. Welsh retains a unique cultural, social, and economic development, notably its national _____, Welsh and a devoluted Welsh Assembly.

A. music   B. education   C. language   D. sports

10. Northern Island is sometimes known simply as "_____".

A. the six counties B. the six countries
C. the six nations D. the six states

Ⅱ. True and False

Read the following statements carefully and then decide whether they are true or false. Put a "T" if you think the statement is true and an "F" if it is not.

1. Since the 1970s, bilingual education in Welsh has become firmly established and about the half of the Welsh population speak both languages.

2. Less than two-thirds of the population in Northern Ireland are descendants of Scots or English settlers who crossed to northeastern Ireland mainly in the 17th century.

3. Regardless of all the changes brought about by waves of immigrants from around the world, the Celtic, Anglo-Saxon, Nordic, and Norman French cultures still remain at the center of the "British way of life".

4. Britain remained a predominantly white country well into the 1980s.

5. The racial and ethnic communities of the new arrivals are evenly spread across Great Britain, creating a good environment for national cohesion.

6. Most of the racial and ethnic communities in Britain do not appear to have anything in common with the majority "white" culture of the UK.

7. Racial and ethnic groups tend to be concentrated in large cities in Great Britain.

8. English is the single language spoken in the UK.

9. The fact that English has become the main international language of business as well as the most widely taught second language around the world has nothing to do with Great Britain as an empire from the 17th century to the mid-20th century.

10. There is a great variety of English spoken in the UK.

III. General Questions

1. What is the full and official name of Britain?

2. Why do many people use "England" to refer to the whole United Kingdom, the entire island of Great Britain, or the British Isles?

3. What "privileges" does Scotland enjoy as part of the United Kingdom?

4. Which is the second largest of the British Isles?

5. Where were Indigenous British people thought to be descended from?

6. Do all Britons want to see Great Britain move in the direction of multiculturalism?

7. Where can Britons still possibly maintain their traditional life and why?

8. Where is modern English descended from?

9. What do one's accent and dialect tell the listener?

10. Has British identity issue been talked about for a long time?

IV. Essay Questions

1. What is the social significance of accent and dialect in Great Britain?

2. Why do we say that there is now an identity crisis in Great Britain?

Unit Nine   The Land and the People

Reference Answers

Ⅰ. Multiple Choices

1. C   2. B   3. A   4. D   5. B   6. A   7. D   8. D   9. C   10. A

Ⅱ. True and False

1. F   2. T   3. T   4. F   5. F   6. T   7. T   8. F   9. F   10. T

Ⅲ. General Questions

1. The full and official name of Britain is the United Kingdom of Great Britain and Northern Ireland (the UK).

2. Because England dominates the United Kingdom in many areas, such as politics, business, arts, education, culture, and mass media.

3. It has a separate administration, different legal and educational systems as well as its Presbyterian national church.

4. Ireland is the second largest of the British Isles.

5. Indigenous British people were thought to be descended from the various ethnic groups that settled there before the 11th century: the Celts, Romans, Anglo-Saxons, Norse and the Normans.

6. No, some people are against it.

7. They are most likely to maintain their "British way of life" in the traditional town or village, because the presence of new immigrants there is neither heavy nor concentrated.

8. Modern English is a West Germanic language descended from Old English which features a large number of borrowings from Old Norse, Norman French, Greek and Latin.

9. The speaker's accent and dialect give the listener clues about his/her geographical and social background.

10. No, British identity is a relatively recent construct.

Ⅳ. Essay Questions

1. Since both accent and dialect thus give the listener clues about a speaker's geographical and social background, a high degree of social significance has been attached to English speech. For instance, non-standard features in speech may suggest that the

speaker has had less formal education, and that he/she may have spent most or all his/her life in the same locality. Partly for this reason, some British grammarians recommended the speech of London and the Court as the most correct and desirable in an attempt to eliminate what they saw as a cacophony of regional accents. It was selected largely because it was spoken by the ruling class—the aristocracy and Court—and therefore carried authority. Thus, dialect speakers became socially stigmatized as rustic, provincial, poor and uneducated. Although many efforts have been made to promote a wider acceptance of regional speech in the public sphere, evidence seems to suggest that some varieties may still carry negative connotations in the public sphere.

2. Many surveys suggest that Great Britain is now having an identity crisis. For instance, according to a report released by the British Department of Justice, over the past thirty years, there has been a significant decline in the proportion of British citizens who feel their British identity to be their primary national identity. On the one hand, the number of English, Welsh, and Scottish residents who consider their nationality to be primarily British has fallen. On the other hand, the number describing themselves as Scottish, Welsh, or English has risen. While there is still much shared culture in Britain, there has been a visible decline in the prevalence of a British national identity among British citizens. Today, when Britons talk about "Britishness" or "British cultural identities", the emphases have shifted to multiplicity and plurality, suggesting that the weakness and strength of Britain lies in the fact that many people in Britain see themselves as primarily some other nationality or ethnicity and "British" only secondarily. In short, they share the same islands, but they are not all British.

Unit Ten Government and Politics

Focal Points

constitutional monarchy   parliamentary democracy
representative government cabinet   citizenry
House of Lords   House of Commons

Discussion Questions

What is the key to the understanding of British politics?

Text

The United Kingdom today is a **constitutional monarchy** and a **parliamentary democracy**. Britain, which is regarded as the "**Cradle of Democracy**", can **trace** its political roots back over a thousand years. Its history of state-building process shall be better described as **evolutional** rather than revolutionary. The British political system, though often criticized, has been the model and the inspiration for many national governments worldwide.

A Bird's-Eye View of British Political History

The system of constitutional monarchy has been formed by eight centuries of evolutionary development. In this process, the seat of power has slowly passed from the non-democratic **Crown** to the aristocratic Lords and to its final resting place in

---

constitutional monarchy 君主立宪制
parliamentary democracy 议会民主制
Cradle of Democracy 民主的摇篮
trace 追溯，查考
evolutional 演进

Crown 君主、国王

the House of Commons with a powerful Prime Minister. The British Monarchy is the **supreme** illustration of the way British institutions develop. With few violent **upheavals**, this process has been largely accompanied by a gradual progress of democracy for the people. Britain's current political institutions, its political culture, and the whole **apparatus** of the political system are deeply **steeped in** its history. And the pride of the British is that although it is illogical, it works.

Magna Carta (*The mixed monarchy of the Middle Ages*)

As was discussed in the previous chapter, William of Normandy claimed the English **throne** in 1066 and invaded England, bringing dramatic changes not only to English life, but also to English politics. For the Normans brought with them a political system that had first emerged on the **Continent**—**feudalism**, a kind of contract in which lords granted **vassals** land and protection while the vassals supported the lord with military service. Power here was a two-way street, where the king depended on the nobles for political control and the nobles needed the king for political privileges.

This period of the English history was a long struggle on the part of **the nobility** to keep the king within his feudal **bounds** and from turning into an **absolute monarch**, which happened in most of Europe. The Great Charter **the barons** forced on King John at Runnymede in 1215 never mentions liberty or democracy. The barons and top churchmen simply wanted to stop the king from **encroaching on** feudal customs, rights, and law by which they **held sway** in their localities. In this sense, the Magna Carta, one of the great documents of democracy, was feudal and reactionary but did limit the monarch's power—an important first step toward democracy. The significance of the Magna Carta lies in the fact that it kept the king in balance with the nobles, preventing either **despotism** or **anarchy**. **In the long run**, therefore, this English struggle laid the foundation for limited, representative government, democracy and civil rights, even

---

supreme 最卓著的、最高超的

upheaval 动乱、剧变

apparatus 机构、组织

steep in 浸透于

Magna Carta Latin: the Great Charter: ((英国) 大宪章

throne 王位、君权

Continent 欧洲大陆
feudalism 封建制度
vassal 封臣、仆人

the nobility 贵族、阶级
bounds 界限、极限
absolute monarch 专制君主
the baron 贵族、男爵

encroach on 侵犯、侵害
hold sway 统治、支配

despotism 专制、专制统治
anarchy 混乱、无政府状态
in the long run 从长远来说

Unit Ten Government and Politics

though the participants at the time had no such intent.

The Development of Parliament

Parliament began as an extension of the king's court, but over the centuries **took on** a life of its own. **Knights** and **burghers** formed a lower house, the House of Commons, while nobles and top churchmen formed an upper house, the House of Lords. Originally, Lords was more powerful, but over time Commons pushed Lords into a weaker role. As a way of self-protection, parliamentary privileges developed to prevent the arrest of members, and a leading member of Commons became its **Speaker**, one who could speak to the king. However, Commons represented only a few locally wealthy or powerful males, and Parliament, as a whole, continued the blocking **mechanism** of the Magna Carta: it diffused power and prevented the king from getting too much.

During the ruling period of King James, Parliament felt equal with the king and even, in the area of raising **revenues**, superior, which can be illustrated by the English Civil War of 1642-1648 when Charles tried to act like a Continental absolute monarch but was successfully blocked by the English people and Parliament. Eventually, he ended up tried by Parliament and got beheaded.

Commonwealth and the "Glorious Revolution" (*Bill of Rights*)

From 1649 to 1660, England had no king; instead, it became a republic called the Commonwealth under Cromwell. After the death of Cromwell in 1658, the English monarchy was restored, with a much stronger Parliament now in place.

Unable to be an absolute monarch, Charles II tried to manipulate Parliament, but his efforts were all made in vain. His successor James II, an open Catholic, was **worse off**, **ultimately** getting **dumped** by Parliament. **Subsequent to** James II' removal, his Protestant daughter Mary and her Dutch husband, William of Orange, were invited to be England's queen and king.

Parliament, in full control of the political situation, passed, in 1689, the well-known "Bill of Rights", **spelling out** Parliament's relationship to the Crown: no laws or taxes without Parliament's assent. With most Englishmen's approval, Parliament comfortably gained the upper hand over the monarch in their political struggle. Ever since then, the British monarch has become increasingly a figurehead who "reigns but does not rule."

The Democratization of Parliament

Although Parliament was supreme by the late eighteenth century, it was by no means democratic or representative. After the American and French Revolutions, however, Parliament had to expand the electorate. People talked about democracy and the right to vote. Under the impact of the Industrial Revolution and economic growth, two powerful new social classes arose – the middle class and the working class, and together with **Whigs** and **Tories**, they demanded for the mass vote.

Gradually, Parliament passed the Reform Act of 1832 and the Second Reform Act in 1867, establishing the principle that Commons ought to the representative of and responsive to citizens, not just notables, and giving about 16 percent of adult Britons the vote. In 1884, male **suffrage** was achieved by the passing of the Third Reform Act, and in 1918 women joined men in exercising their voting right.

In spite of all these changes in suffrage, the British **electorate** grew **incrementally**, giving Parliament sufficient time to assimilate mass politics without an upheaval. It also meant that citizens started using the vote when they were ready for it. Otherwise, as it has happened in many other countries, the **universal franchise** may only result in fake democracy. At any rate, by the time the British working class got the vote, they were prepared to use it calmly rather than radically. Now, with the expanded voting population, political parties had to win over millions of voters by means of organization, programs, prom-

---

spell out 讲清楚、详细说明

Whigs 辉格党、辉格党人
Tories 托利党、保守党

suffrage 选举权

electorate(总称)选民、选举人
incrementally 逐渐地
universal franchise 普选权

ise, and continuity. Evidently, the growth of the electorate forced parties to become **vehicles for democracy**, at least in theory.

Political System

Although Great Britain is unitary in its government structure, it political power is not as highly concentrated at the central government as it is in other unitary political systems. Reforms since 1997 have further **decentralize**d the UK by setting up a Welsh Assembly in 1998, and a devolved Scottish Parliament in 1999. Northern Ireland has also had its own self-government, which was returned to it in 2000. Nevertheless, the dominant mechanisms of power in Britain still reside at the House of Parliament in Westminster in London.

Given the limited space here, attention will be given only to the central government, which loosely follows the Roman Republican model—a **bicameral** body consisting of a lower house, the House of Commons, and an upper house, the House of Lords, with the reigning monarch presiding over both. In actuality, the king/queen has zero political power, and power in Britain is primarily in the hands of the Prime Minister and the Cabinet.

The Monarch

The Monarchy is the oldest institution of government in Britain. Its history can be traced back to Egbert, King of Wessex, who united England under his rule in 829. The only interruption to it was the short-lived republic, or Commonwealth, established by Oliver Cromwell.

The Queen is arguably the most powerful person in Britain, or so it goes in theory. In legal terms, the Queen is head of the **executive** and therefore Head of State. She is not only an integral part of the government's legislature, but also head of the judiciary and commander-in-chief of all the armed forces of the Crown. Additionally, she is also "supreme governor" of the established Church. She goes on official state visits abroad, invites other world leaders to come to the UK. More importantly, she approves the appointment of Ministers and the formation of a cabinet, summons Parliament and introduces the new sessions with a speech from the Throne in which she summarizes the government's program, gives her **assent** to bills before they become laws, concludes treaties and declares war, makes appointment to all officers of State and Church, **dismiss**es Parliament when the government has been defeated or has reached the end of its term, and chooses a new Prime Minister.

Indeed, she is informed and consulted on every aspect of national life. And yet, it remains true that she has no power. Ever since the English Civil War in the 17th century, when Parliament ordered the **execution** of King Charles I, the power of the monarch has **dwindle**d. In other words, Britain is a constitutional monarchy, where the king or queen reigns but not rules. For this reason, Britain has a separate "head of state" and "chief of government". However, this does not mean that Britain is undemocratic; it just means that the head of state is a **carryover** from old days. Staying above politics, a monarch is psychological **cement** to hold a country together because he or she has no important governing role.

While the Queen is independently wealthy, much of the financial support for the Royal Family comes from the taxpayer. This has led to great controversy in recent years. Although not many Britons would exchange the monarchy for a republic, some people (including Elisabeth Queen herself) have suggested that reforms be made to cut government funds for the royal house and make female **heirs** to the throne the equal of males.

Parliament

In a parliamentary system like Britain's, voters only choose a parliament, which in turn chooses the executive branch, headed by a prime minister. In a presidential system, such as the United States, voters choose both a legislature and a chief execu-

---

assent 同意、赞成、赞同

dismiss 遣散,解散

execution 处死刑

dwindle 缩小、日渐减少

carryover 剩余物、遗留物
愤怒

cement 起团结作用的纽带

heir 继承人

tive, and the two are expected to check and balance each other. In a parliamentary system, they do not check and balance but reinforce each other.

The parliament is made up of two "houses". The less important of these is the unelected House of Lords, composed of **Lords Spiritual, hereditary and life peers**. Once immensely powerful, the House of Lords has seen its authority dramatically **curtailed** in the past century. Until 1911 the upper house actually had a veto over government legislation. Today it can only give advice on government policies. The Lords now has some 740 peers, most of them life peers nominated by the party leaders, along with 92 hereditary peers and 26 top churchmen.

The 1911 Parliament Act allows **the Lords** to delay legislation not more than 30 days on financial bills and two years (since 1949, one year) on other bills. As part of their duty, **Lords** review and amend legislation formed by **Commons** and send it back. Also, the House of Lords plays the role of safeguarding against the increasing power of government and the Prime Minister. Some people remark that Lords serve as "conscience of the nation" since every few years, the Lords **jolts** the government by forcing the Commons to take another look at bills passed too quickly. Since it is more independent from the parties than **the Commons**, the Lords is also able to debate questions too hot for elected officials – for example, abortion and homosexuality.

Presently, the composition of Lords is seen as being both sexist and elitist because the hereditary peerages are passed down through aristocratic **patrilineal lines**. Most Britons agree that the House of Lords is an **anachronism** ripe for reform but cannot agree on what to do with it. Occasionally the Commons considers making Lords fully or partially elected, like the U.S. Senate, but some fear that would **dilute** the legislative **supremacy** of the Commons and turn Lords over to party politicians.

The House of Commons holds elected members from England, Wales, Scotland and Northern Ireland. Members of Parliament (MPs) represent voters in a particular area, known as a **constituency**. In total there are 646 members of "the Commons", though this number has **fluctuated** over time because of the change of population. General elections, in which people throughout the UK vote for members of the House of Commons (though not directly for the Prime Minister), are not held on a specific schedule as they are in the US. Therefore, MPs are only allowed to sit for the lifetime of the parliament, though they can be reelected a limitless number of times.

    The primary function of the House of Commons is to pass legislation. The House sessions, which often involve questions and heated debates, are **presided over** by the Speaker. Debates are often televised and the formal divisions and votes are open to the public. When legislation is initiated by the cabinet in the form of a public bill, it is given **three separate readings**. If passed on the third reading, the bill is sent to the House of Lords, where it goes through the same procedure. If passed by the second house, the bill is sent to the monarch for the ceremonial formality of royal assent before becoming law.

    The House of Commons is elected at general elections, which can be held at any time, but can only run for a maximum period of five years. There is much less balance in this system than there is in the United States. The party with the most total seats gets both a majority in the House of Commons and the **prime ministership**, unlike the US where there can be, for example, a Democratic president and a Republican majority in Congress.

    In theory, the House of Commons can pass any law it likes, making it possible for the British political system to change over time without a systemic crisis. The negative side of it is apparent—nothing can be declared "unconstitutional." Such dominance on the part of the House of Commons in British politics has led to the accusation that British political system is

---

constituency（选举议员的）选区、选区的全体选民

fluctuate 波动

preside over 主持

three separate readings 即提出、审议、表决三读

prime ministership 首相职位

in fact "an elected dictatorship". However, this is a bit **overstated**. On the whole, the Commons is now less important than it used to be since legislatures are declining in power. More importantly, a deliberate weakening of Britain's parties might excite the Commons. After all, legislatures are invaluable for **scrutiniz**ing executive power, always holding it **accountable** under any circumstances, and ousting it whenever necessary. Indeed, to most Britons, the House of Commons is still **bulwark** of democracy.

The Cabinet

As a rule, the British cabinet is formed by the party that wins the most seats in the General Election, but in the event of a **hung parliament**, it is possible for a minority government to be formed. The cabinet consists of the elected members of the House of Commons, as well as a few members of the House of Lords, who are high up in their parties and important political figures. Most have lots of experience, first as ordinary members of Parliament (MPs), then as junior ministers, and finally as cabinet ministers. A British minister is not necessarily an expert in his or her **portfolio** but is picked by the Prime Minister for political qualifications. The leaders of both houses are in the cabinet, along with a chief secretary for the cabinet. Balancing party **factions** in the cabinet helps keep the party together in Parliament and in power.

The second most powerful party in British politics is called "Her Majesty's Official Opposition". They, and the other opposition parties, each **assemble** what is called a "**shadow cabinet**", which includes a shadow **chancellor of the exchequer**, shadow foreign secretary, shadow home secretary, and so forth for all the positions held in the regular cabinet. Shadow ministers, whose purpose is to be a spokesman for arguments **counter to** those made by the party in power, develop policies according to their party's platform and beliefs.

The Prime Minister, or PM for short, is the **linchpin** of the

British system. Because the Prime Minister picks and controls the cabinet and heads the largest party in Parliament, he or she should be able to get nearly any measure passed. British parliamentarians are well-disciplined, and **party whips**' job is to make sure that their MPs turn out for **divisions** and vote the party line. Yet prime ministers do not turn into dictators, chiefly because general elections are never more than five years away. Prime ministers are powerful, but only with the solid support of their parties in the Houses of Commons.

The British cabinet practices "**collective responsibility**," meaning ministers all stick together and, in public at least, support the Prime Minister. Occasionally, ministers resign in protest over a major controversy (but keep their parliamentary seats). Prime ministers design their cabinets; they add, drop, rename, or combine ministries, so each cabinet is different. If the government loses a crucial vote in Parliament, or if there is a **vote of no confidence** in the government, the Cabinet as a whole is expected to resign. The British cabinet **straddles** the gap between "executive" and "legislative." The **elaborate** American separation of powers does not hold in Britain. The United Kingdom has a combining or **fusion** of powers.

Political Parties and Citizenry

Political Parties

Britain is described as a two-party system, but, like many other democracies in the world, Britain is actually a "two-plus" party system, meaning some third parties are important. Currently, there are three major political parties in Britain, namely the Conservative Party, the Labor Party and the Liberal Democrats, though, in reality, the two dominant governing parties since 1918 have been the Conservatives and the Labor parties. From 1950 to 1970, for example, a **staggering** 92 percent of votes went to these two parties. As recently as May 2010, when the General Election was held in Britain, the two main

---

party whip 党派组织秘书
division (议会) 分组表决

collective responsibility 集体负责制

vote of no confidence 失去信任投票表决
straddle 跨立于、相叉于
elaborate 精心制作的、复杂的
fusion 合并、聚合、熔化

staggering 难以置信的,令人震惊的

parties had a combined vote of 65.1 per cent, with the Liberal Democrats polling 23 percent.

The Conservative Party, **colloquially known as** the Tory party, is the major right-wing party. For most of the twentieth century they were the dominant political force. Oftentimes, people tend to think of them as the British version of U.S. Republicans, with all the same talk about free trade, low taxes, a strong military, **or some such**. While they're not quite as **wrapped up in** morals as US conservatives, as religion isn't such an issue in British politics, they're still **preachy** enough that the nation smiles whenever another Tory member of Parliament is caught up in some sex scandal or other. Famous Conservative prime ministers include Winston Churchill and Maggie Thatcher.

The Labor Party was formed in the early twentieth century when working-class people became frustrated with the Liberal Party (which has evolved into today's Liberal Democrat Party). Not surprisingly, given its name, the Labor Party was **aligned with** the trade unions and **championed** such issues as education and social services. In the 1990s, Tony Blair grabbed the **steering wheel**, and "New Labor" was born. They haven't produced as many famous prime ministers as the Conservatives, expect, perhaps, Prime Minister Tony Blair (1997 - 2007), if he could be viewed so.

The Liberal Democratic Party evolved out of a 1988 **merger** between the older Liberal Party and the Social Democrats. The Liberal Democrats are the third largest party in the country, usually winning about 20 percent of the popular vote. The Liberal Democrats adhere to a basically progressive, center-left philosophy with a strong environmental stance and a platform whose issues include constitutional reform, European integration, and civil liberties. As a third largest party in Britain, it has never had a prime minister.

Citizenry

British citizens have an abundance of rights, from marriage

and **civil partnerships** to the right to protest and the right to **make a complaint** against the government--and plenty more. With these rights come an abundance of responsibilities. British citizens are expected to contribute to society in certain ways to help the country **thrive** domestically and operate smoothly. While they aren't required to do all of these things, the government sees them as duties for citizens.

Additionally, the government expects **loyalty** from its citizens in ways that can't necessarily be enforced by law, but which are still duties. For instance, British citizens are expected to **take pride in** being from and/or living in Britain, honor the Queen, and participate in and recognize national holidays and activities. This loyalty has been expected from British citizens-- in many different capacities--for hundreds of years. Moreover, citizens are required to abide by laws established by the British government and not plot against the government. All of these things are part of being a loyal British citizen.

While voting is part of civic duties British citizens are expected to fulfill, the government does not require them to vote. Nevertheless, citizens are encouraged to participate in the political process, because when citizens do not vote, election results will not be accurate, making it difficult for democracy to **find full expression**. According to British laws, all British citizens who are at least 18 years old can vote unless they are in prison.

Beyond all of this, British citizens are required to report for **jury** service when called and attend for as long as it takes to find a verdict. Being a juror gives citizens a chance to play an important and vital role in the justice system in the U. K. Since prior knowledge of the justice system is not required, citizens sitting on a jury are simply required to hear the evidence, discuss the case and decide if the defendant is guilty or not guilty. In Britain, minor criminal cases are judged without a jury in the Magistrate's Court; in middle-ranking cases, the defendant can choose jury or no jury in the Crown Court; and in serious crimi-

---

civil partnership 民事伴侣关系

make a complaint 投诉、告状

thrive 兴旺发达

loyalty 忠诚

take pride in 为……感到自豪/骄傲

find full expression 得到充分表达

jury (小)陪审团

nal cases, the jury has to decide the sentence in the Crown Court. Citizens' involvement in the jury system, therefore, is not only a process of self-education, but also a way of rendering services to the public.

Notes

Civil partnerships—Civil Partnerships in the UK, granted under the Civil Partnership Act 2004, allow same-sex couples to obtain essentially the same rights and responsibilities as civil marriage. For instance, civil partners are entitled to the same property rights as married opposite-sex couples, the same exemption as married couples on inheritance tax, social security and pension benefits, and also the ability to get parental responsibility for a partner's children, as well as responsibility for reasonable maintenance of one's partner and their children, tenancy rights, full life insurance recognition, next to kin rights in hospitals, and others. There is a formal process for dissolving partnerships akin to divorce.

Common Law—One of England's lasting contributions is the Common Law, the legal system now also practiced in the United States (except in Louisiana), Canada, Australia, and many other countries once administered by Britain. It developed on the basis of precedent set by earlier decisions and thus has been called "judge-made law." Common Law is based heavily on case law and differs from code law, which is used by most of the Continent (and Scotland) and of the world, and which emphasizes fixed legal codes rather than precedent and case study. Compared with code law, Common Law is flexible and adapts gradually with new cases.

Vote of No Confidence—A vote of no confidence is also called "a motion of no confidence", "a censure motion", or "a confidence motion." It is a parliamentary motion which when passed would demonstrate to the head of state that the elected parliament no longer has confidence in the appointed government. Typically, when a vote of no confidence passes parliament, the government official must either resign or seek a parliamentary dissolution or general election.

Exercises

Ⅰ. **Multiple Choices**

The following are questions or incomplete sentences. Below each sentence or question four possible answers marked A, B, C and D are provided. Choose the ONE that best completes the sentence or answers the question.

1. Which of the following is not right to describe the Prime Minister?

   A. the head of the country   B. the leader of Cabinet

   C. the leader of the Party in power   D. a member of parliament

2. The party that has the majority of seats in _____ will form the government.

   A. the House of Commons   B. the Cabinet

   C. the House of Lords   D. the Royal Family

3. The current Prime Minister (2015) of the UK is _____.

   A. Tony Blair   B. Benjamin Disraeli

   C. Maggie Thatcher   D. David Cameron

4. Under whose reign was the Bill of Rights passed?

   A. James II   B. William of Orange

   C. George I   D. Oliver Cromwell

5. By whom is a "vote of no confidence" decided?

   A. the House of Commons   B. the House of Lords

   C. the Prime Minister   D. the Queen

6. Which of the following is TRUE about life peers?

   A. They are not from aristocratic families.

   B. Their children can inherit their title

   C. They sit in the House of Commons

   D. They can be removed

7. Which of the following is NOT a true description of the Queen's role?

   A. The Queen is the temporal head of the Church of England

   B. The Queen selects the Prime Minister and the Cabinet

   C. The Queen is the Head of the Armed Force

   D. The Queen symbolizes the tradition and unity of the British state

8. The policies of the Conservative Party are characterized by pragmatism and _____.

A. nationalization of enterprises

B. social reform

C. a belief in individualism

D. government intervention

9. The Labor Party affected the British society greatly in that it _____.

A. set up the National Health Service

B. abolished the old tax system

C. enhanced the economic development

D. improved public transportation

10. In Britain, the general election is held at least every _____ years.

A. Three   B. Four   C. Five   D. Six

Ⅱ. True and False

Read the following statements carefully and then decide whether they are true or false. Put a "T" if you think the statement is true and an "F" if it is not.

1. Britain, like the U. S., has a written constitution.

2. Common laws are laws which have been established through common practices in the courts.

3. The three major parties in Britain are: the Conservative Party, the Social Democratic Party and the Labor Party.

4. The UK Parliament can call an election sooner than five years.

5. The Liberal Democratic Party evolved out of its predecessor, the Liberal Party.

6. Britain is a two-party system, because the two major parties control the government by turn.

7. The oldest institution of government in Britain is the Monarchy.

8. British citizens don't have to fulfill their jury service as long as they don't want to.

9. Strictly speaking, the Queen is part of the Parliament.

10. The Parliament of the UK has no power to change the terms of the Constitution.

Ⅲ. General Questions

1. What's the Queen's role as monarch?

2. How is the House of Lords composed of?

3. What are the characteristics of the British Constitution?

4. What's the most important function of the UK Parliament?

5. Strictly speaking, what does the UK Parliament consist of?

6. Is the official head of state the same person as the head of government in Britain?

7. What documents did Parliament pass to ensure that its right would never be ignored by the monarch?

8. How does a new government come into being?

9. Normally, how long can a government stay in power?

10. Under what circumstances does the government have to resign?

Ⅳ. Essay Questions:

1. What kind of roles does the Queen play for her country? What kind of powers does the Queen enjoy?

2. Discuss the key elements of the British parliament democracy.

Reference Answers

Ⅰ. Multiple Choice

1. A   2. A   3. D   4. B   5. A   6. A   7. A   8. C   9. A   10. C

Ⅱ. True and False

1. F   2. T   3. F   4. T   5. F   6. F   7. T   8. F   9. T   10. F

Ⅲ. General Questions

1. In theory, the monarch has enormous powers; but in reality, she is supposed to reign but not rule. In a nutshell, the Queen's role as monarch is basically a figure head.

2. The House of Lords consists of the Lords Spiritual, who are the Archbishops and most prominent bishops of the Church of England; and the Lords Temporal, which refers to those lords who either have inherited the seat from their forefathers or have been appointed.

3. Britain has no written Constitution. The foundations of the British state are laid out in statute laws, passed by Parliament, common laws, established through common practices in the courts, and finally conventions.

4. The most important function of the UK Parliament is to pass laws.

5. The UK Parliament today consists of the Queen, the House of Lords and the House of Commons.

Unit Ten Government and Politics

6. No, officially speaking, the Queen is the head of state, but in reality she does not rule. Instead, the Prime Minister is the most powerful person in Britain.

7. In 1689, Parliament passed the Bill of Rights which ensured that no laws could be made or tax bills passed without Parliament's assent.

8. Generally speaking, the party that wins the majority seats in Parliament forms the government and its party leader becomes the Prime Minister. However, in the event of a hung parliament, it is possible for a minority government to be formed.

9. A government can be in power for five years, and then it has to resign and hold a general election.

10. If a government loses a vote of no confidence in the House of Commons, it has to resign.

Ⅳ. Essay Questions:

1. Constitutional monarchy is the characteristic of the British government. It is a political system that has been practiced in Britain since the Glorious Revolution of 1688. According to this system, the Constitution is superior to the Monarch. In law, the Monarch has many supreme powers, but in practice, the real power of the Monarch has been greatly reduced and today the Queen acts solely on the advice of her ministers. The Queen plays the following roles for her country: as Head of State, the Queen goes on official state visits abroad. She also invites other world leaders to come to the UK. She is also Head of the Armed Forces, meaning she is the only person who can declare when the country is at war and when war is over, although she must take advice from her government first. Moreover, the Queen is Head of the Church of England. She appoints archbishops and bishops on the advice of the Prime Minister. In addition, the Queen has to fulfill many government duties, which mainly involve reading and signing government documents. However, she reigns but not rule. The real power lies in the Parliament, or to be exact, in the House of Commons.

2. The British democratic parliamentary system of government is used, or was once used, in the national legislatures and subnational legislatures of most Commonwealth and ex-Commonwealth nations.

Important features of the Westminster system include the following:

(1) A sovereign or head of state (the monarch) who is the nominal or theoretical holder of executive power, holding numerous reserve powers, but mostly performing the role of a ceremonial figurehead.

(2) A head of government (the Prime Minister), who is officially appointed by the Monarch, but actually functions as the leader of the country.

(3) A de facto executive branch usually made up of members of Parliament, with senior members of the executive in a cabinet led by the Prime Minister.

(4) Parliamentary opposition (a multi-party system)

(5) A bicameral legislature, in which at least one house is elected; legislative members are usually elected by district in first-past-the-post elections

(6) A lower house of Parliament with the ability to dismiss a government by "withholding (or blocking) Supply" (rejecting a budget), passing a motion of no confidence, or defeating a confidence motion.

(7) A parliament which can be dissolved and elections called at any time.

Unit Eleven British Values and Assumptions

Focal Points

sense of irony	sense of humor	fair play
trust	compromise	reserve
politeness	class consciousness	class system
work ethic	keep order	love of alcohol

Discussion Questions

Of all the British values and assumptions, which one do you believe to be most typically British?

Text

Like any other country in the world, Great Britain has also developed its own values and assumptions in its long course of national growth. **Derived from** their national experience, such values and assumptions not only **embody** Britain's national spirit, but also represent the norms and customs by which Britons **go about** their life. In this sense, to understand these values and assumptions is, in fact, to understand the national character of the British people.

Given the great diversity of the British people, it is important to keep in mind that there is no such a thing as a **uniform** "British culture", and hence there are no uniform values or assumptions in Britain. They could be English, Scottish, Welsh, Irish, or indeed, Asian British or African British values and as-

---

derive from 源于、形成于
embody 体现、包含

go about 着手干、做、忙于

uniform 统一的、一致的、一样的

sumptions. The English, however, are by far the largest of these islands' people, and are culturally dominant. The main part of this chapter, therefore, and much that follows, describes largely English characteristics, although there will be many that apply to all.

Senses of Irony and Humor

Britons in general, English in particular, attach great importance to a sense of irony and a sense of humor. Anyone without a sense of irony or a sense of humor is often viewed as being a boring person, unable to **make good company**. A British newspaper columnist once wrote that, after having been abroad for an extended period of time, it was an enormous **relief** to be back home in Britain and "**on the same wavelength**" as everyone else again. He put this down to reconnecting with the British sense of irony, one of the **arteries** of everyday communication.

It is true that much of what the British say is not quite what they mean. This is self-evident to the native listener, but with others it can cause misunderstandings. This particular aspect of the British character does not seem to travel well, for foreigners are never quite sure whether the British are being serious or not. It exists partly because Britons dislike **gushing** emotions and mistrust people who "**wear their hearts on their sleeves**", and partly because British people value negative politeness—the idea that one must not give too much away and people's privacy must be respected.

Irony has to do with **self-deprecation**, **banter**, and understatement, with the "**buzz**" that comes from a tendency to laugh at oneself and one's situation, and an **anticipation** of constant, gentle amusement. Irony is a **trigger** for laughter, which the British see as a form of free medication for body, mind, and spirit. "An ability to laugh at oneself" and "not taking oneself seriously" are characteristics which are highly valued in the U. K. Not surprisingly, the

make good company 成为有趣的伙伴

relief 解脱、缓解

on the same wavelength 有同感、相互理解

artery 渠道、干线

gushing 装腔作势的、过分动感情的

wear their hearts on their sleeves 流露自己的感情、公开自己的私事

self-deprecation 自我贬低

banter 戏谑

buzz 陶醉感、兴奋

anticipation 预期、预料、期望

trigger 引起/触发反应的行为

Unit Eleven British Values and Assumptions

British are not routinely polite to each other-a habit that can be oppressive in other cultures; and they don't **suffer** fools gladly. They are good "**on parade**," when they have to be, though they might **grumble**; but later they **make merry**, and usually make a good job of doing that too. Chaucer, a great British poet, read the English character very well, and used irony, among other things, to great effect throughout the **Canterbury Tales**.

Likewise, humor is also highly valued by the British in their inter-personal relationship. In Great Britain, humor **pervades** conversations, covers many kinds of emotional responses, and is common to all classes. On stage, it is a popular form of entertainment, ranging from **stand-up** comedy to the "**theater of the absurd**"; from "other people's misfortunes" (slipping on a banana peel or walking into a lamppost), to "**knock- about**" or "**slapstick**" (with comics and clowns); from **satire** to **parody**; from self-mockery to the **scatological**; from **farce** to irony.

There is humor in **cross-dressing**—once a requirement for all drama in Shakespeare's time, but today found particularly in **pantomime**, where the classic children's shows, such as **Cinderella**, require that the "leading boy" (the hero) is played by a pretty girl and the "wicked stepmother" (the comic character) is played by a **bulky**, middle-aged man — the "pantomime **dame**."

On television, comedy programs run across a similar range of humor, with the addition of **sitcoms**. Nowadays these include several highly popular American imports, such as Friends, Sex and the City. Cartoons such as The Simpsons also **appeal to** the Britons — and not only children. Most recently, Mr. Bean has properly been the biggest hit in British entertainment business, and its actor, Rowan Atkinson, is by far the most popular comedian in the country, demonstrating again British fondness for humor.

---

suffer 容忍
on parade 炫耀自己、示众
grumble 抱怨
make merry 尽情欢乐、寻欢作乐

Canterbury Tales 坎特伯雷特故事集
pervade 弥漫于、遍及于
stand-up 单人喜剧、单口相声
theater of the absurd 荒诞派戏剧
knock- about 闹剧演员（演出）
slapstick 打闹剧
satire 讽刺作品
parody 滑稽模仿
scatological 诲淫文学
farce 闹剧、滑稽戏
cross-dressing 女扮男装、男扮女装
pantomime 哑剧
Cinderella 灰姑娘
bulky 肥胖的、又大又笨的
dame 爵妇
sitcom 情景喜剧
appeal to 对……有吸引力

Fair Play, Trust and Compromise

While Britons cherish irony and humor, it does not mean that they lack seriousness or self-responsibility in their job or life. In Great Britain, there is an old saying that "An Englishman's word is his **bond**." In other words, English society, which is not governed by a written constitution or a bill of rights, conducted itself on the basis of mutual trust and a sense of "fair play." For some, this is best expressed in the national game of cricket. Although incomprehensible to most of the rest of the world (except the few other countries that play it), cricket demands great skill and judgment, particularly on the part of the **umpire**, who must make key decisions on every ball bowled. It is all a matter of "fair play", and in fact the word "cricket," used in the sentence "**it's not cricket**," itself sums up the English idea of fairness.

Indeed, a traditional English criticism of unsportsmanlike or unethical behavior is "it's not cricket". This is because the game of cricket is supposed to **epitomize** everything that is moral and **upstanding** in an English gentleman's behavior. The notion of fair play pervades British notions of acceptable and ethical behavior. To cheat or to act in bad faith is one of the worst things one can be accused of. In the late 1990s, the famous English cricket umpire Dickie Bird, now retired, was asked "What is Englishness?" He replied with the following key words: "beer, honesty, **bulldog-type** virtues, royal family, cricket, the weather, and not giving up when things get tough." Here, the word cricket symbolizes "fair play", meaning observing the rule of the game.

To a great extent, fairness is dependent upon mutual trust, for **in the absence of** mutual trust, fairness can hardly be achieved, **much less** sustained. In his book Trust, American political scientist Francis Fukuyama wrote of cultures that vary in fortune because of the levels of trust they enjoy and sustain. He

bond 契约、保证金

umpire（棒球、板球）裁判员
"it's not cricket" 不公正、不光明磊落

epitomize 象征、作为……缩影
upstanding 诚实的、正直的

bulldog-type 斗牛犬式的

in the absence of 在…缺席下
much less 更别说

cites Britain and Japan as high trust cultures, where mutual trust is virtually taken for granted. Anyone who repeatedly commits "breaches of faith" is likely to be **shunned** by people around him.

It is quite true that trust is implicit in the way the British manage their affairs, within local and central government, in their approach to law and order, including the principle that policing is done "with the consent of the people," in the way their judiciary system operates, and so on. It is no surprise, therefore, that the degree of trust extended to each other in daily life is also remarkable, even though it is being seriously undermined by a rising tide of materialism and selfishness. The tradition of the "gentlemen's agreement" epitomized this philosophy of life and continues to be cherished, especially by the older generations committed to traditional values.

Coupled with fairness and trust are tolerance and an instinct for compromise. These four values or assumptions are said to be the fundamental qualities of the British character, along with a strong sense of justice, which **draws on** all of these and remains an **abiding** passion. For these and many other reasons, there are an enormous number of charities in Great Britain, and the great amount of volunteer work done in the community, all of which reflect and at the same time contribute to the strengthening of these long-held values among the British people. In more recent times, however, the consensus has shifted from a sense of obligation to a new focus on individual rights and self-interest, and the concern for fairness that traditionally informed individual and group behavior is less apparent.

The English Reserve and Politeness

To people from outside Great Britain, the best known quality of the British, and in particular of the English, is "reserve". A reserved person is one who does not talk very much to strangers, does not show much emotion, and seldom gets excited. It is difficult to get to know a reserved person: he/she never tells you anything about himself or herself, and you may work with him/her for years without ever knowing where he/she lives, how many children he/she has, and what his/her interests are. English people tend to be like that. If they are making a journey by bus, they will do their best to find an empty seat, and if by train, an empty compartment. If they have to share the compartment with a stranger, they may travel many miles without starting a conversation. If a conversation does start, personal questions like "How old are you?" or even "What is your name?" are not easily asked, and it is quite possible for two people to know each other casually for years without ever knowing each other's name. Questions like "where did you buy your car?" or "What is your salary?" are almost impossible. Similarly, conversation in Britain is in general quiet and restrained and loud speech is considered ill-bred.

This reluctance to communicate with others is an unfortunate quality in some ways, as it tends to give the impression of coldness. While the English are not noted for their generosity and hospitality, they, on the other hand, are perfectly human behind their barrier of reserve, and may be quite pleased when a friendly stranger or foreigner succeeds for a time in breaking the barrier down. We may also mention at this point that the people of the North and West, especially the Welsh, are much less reserved than those of the South and East.

Just as the English reserve is not properly appreciated, so is the English form of politeness not sufficiently understood. Being polite in a formal context, such as in an office, may involve joining in and appearing to have a good time at a big social event organized by a company, or at a private dinner arranged by one of the directors. This is considered good manners; but for many English people, that's all it is. Likewise, if two strangers strike up a friendly conversation on a train, for example, this is usually purely good manners, and the relationship is un-

Unit Eleven British Values and Assumptions

likely to develop further. Such occasions can, of course, be the beginning of a real friendship, but don't be hurt or surprised if the relationship stops there.

British habits of politeness are on the whole very informal. There are no complicated greetings, for instance: a simple "good morning" or a cheery wave of the hand across the street is quite satisfactory. Handshakes are only exchanged on a first introduction, or on special occasions, or as a token of agreement or congratulation. All politeness is based on the elementary rule of showing consideration for others, and fitly acknowledging the consideration they show to you. "Excuse me" is used as an advance apology for troubling somebody, as when passing in front of him or interrupting his conversation, or when putting a question to a stranger. "Sorry" expresses regret for an accidental disturbance or **breach** of manners. It also takes the place of "no" when you cannot **accede** to a request or an implied request like "May I borrow your pen?" or "Do you know the time?" "Pardon?" is the polite way of asking somebody to repeat what he has said. In Britain, except at school, "please" is no longer used in asking permission to speak, and the phrase "No, please", so common abroad, would sound most unusual in Britain itself. "Yes, please" is the commonest use of the word, and is the opposite of "No, thank you" when replying to an offer. When a request is granted, and at any time when you are receiving something, however obviously you are entitled to it, you are always expected to say "Thank you".

British people do not readily ask each other to do anything which would involve real inconvenience: they prefer to wait for such service to be offered, rather than ask for it. If they do ask, then the request is accompanied by an implied apology like, "I don't really like asking you, but…" or "I know the trouble I'm causing you, but would you mind…?" and so on. Similarly it is often polite to refuse an offer of service by means of such a reply as, "Oh! Please don't bother", followed by an explanation of

breach 违反
accede 同意

why you can do without it. In fact, without being conscious of it, British people sometimes make offers purely out of politeness, not really expecting them to be accepted, and offers of this kind are refused with corresponding politeness.

Politeness towards women is less observed today than it used to be. It is still considered polite to give up one's seat to a woman who is standing, to open doors for her, help her **alight** from the bus, carry things for her, to protect her from the traffic, and so on; and the maxim "Lady first" is well known; but now that women are the equals of men, having the vote, taking paid employment and receiving higher education, they receive much less consideration than formerly, for the whole basis of politeness towards women is the feeling that they need protection.

> alight 从（飞机或车上）下来

The same principle applies to old people. If they are respected in Britain, it is because they are felt to be in need of protection and support. Old age and seniority alone do not command authority among the British: in fact modern life has been developing so fast that old people often appear tiresome and out of date. Thus, "We need some young blood" is often heard in organizations where the energy and modern methods of younger men are felt to be more likely to succeed than the long but partly irrelevant experience of older ones. They either make an effort to remain young in heart and keep pace with the times or else they let younger men take their places.

Class Consciousness

Unlike Americans, the British are far more class conscious. Despite all the changes to the social, economic, and legal landscape in the late twentieth and early twenty-first centuries, it remains true to say that to understand England and English ways (as opposed to Scottish, Welsh, or Northern Irish ways), one needs to understand the class system. There are three main class divisions in England, which may also apply in Scotland,

Unit Eleven　British Values and Assumptions

but perhaps less so in Wales: upper class, middle class, and lower or working class.

The upper class generally refers to the aristocracy and its offshoots, and was traditionally the "ruling class," although this is no longer absolutely the case in today's fluid social mix. It largely consists of people with inherited wealth, and includes some of the oldest families in the land, many of them titled. Along with land, wealth, titles, and privileges came certain obligations and responsibilities, not the least of which was the duty to behave as **befitted one's rank**. This is still the case among those who are genuinely "upper class"—good manners are of the utmost importance.

The upper class is defined first and foremost by the families that belong to it. To be from one of the "old" families is virtually a prerequisite of being upper class. Other **pointers** are education (at good private schools such as Eton or Harrow, followed by university – Oxford or Cambridge); wealth (often in the form of land or property rather than cash); and, to a certain extent, occupation and pastimes, which include the traditional country sports of hunting, shooting, and fishing. Many upper-class people keep horses, and ride for pleasure, as well as taking an interest in racing.

The upper class generally manages to keep itself to itself, minding its own business at all times. In an attempt to maintain its exclusiveness, many marriages in the upper class continue to be "arranged" by a process of carefully managed introductions. Additionally, members of the upper class often have a distinctive, mannered accent, which is delivered in a very precise manner. A more slowly delivered version of this is known as "an upper-class drawl." Increasingly, however, the younger generation is inclined to avoid such mannerisms of speech in order not to appear too upper class!

The Middle Class refers to those whose wealth or occupations put them somewhere between the aristocracy and the peas-

befit one's rank 适合……身份地位

pointer 指示物、标记

ants. Landowners and professional people – "gentlemen" – were later joined by those who made money during or after the Industrial Revolution. The middle class is broadly based, and even divides itself into lower-middle and upper-middle class, according to wealth, level of education, and perceived standing within the community. This refinement of class distinction could be invented only by a society obsessed with status and the pursuit of minutiae.

The middle class these days encompasses the professional, managerial, and so-called "upwardly mobile" sections of society (as well, perhaps, as a "downwardly mobile" section from the upper class), and is seen to represent the greater part of the population as a whole, certainly in the southern half of England. It is generally less **rigid** in its behavior and in matters of **etiquette** than the upper class.

Middle-class values formed the backbone of society and provided the skilled professionals and administrators who ran the Empire. Education is important for the middle classes, at a private or good state school, preferably followed by university. Pastimes are not so well defined, but sports that call for expensive equipment, special clothing, or extensive training and practice, such as golf and tennis, are regarded as a middle-class preserve.

Although they tend to approach life in a more relaxed way, like the upper class, the middle classes also enjoy **pomp and circumstance** of the **Establishment**, such as the Opening of Parliament by the Queen, or the **pageantry** associated with **Royal Jubilees**. Formal social occasions, such as wedding or a ball for a daughter who is "coming out," that is, making her formal **debut** in society, are held in great style. Once an upper-class tradition, launching one's daughter in society in this way, in the hope that she will find a suitable husband, has now been taken up by the "new rich".

Below the middle class is the working class, often referred

---

rigid 僵硬的

etiquette 礼节礼仪

pomp and circumstance 大场面

Establishment 权势集团、国家权力机构

pageantry 盛况

Royal Jubilee 皇室纪念大庆

debut(青年女子)首次进入社交界

Unit Eleven British Values and Assumptions

to as "working-class Britain" by socialists and trade unionists. It was coined in the context of the exploitation and social inequality that resulted from the rise of nineteenth-century capitalism. Its use today continues to reinforce the historic class divisions of Great Britain, and of England in particular.

The working class has its own rituals and etiquette that inform behavior and determine what is expected of its members. Working-class culture is projected and played out every week through the TV "soaps," principally Coronation Street (the longest-running), which reflects the way of life in the northeast of England, and **Eastenders**, which reflects life in and around London's East End. These soaps, of course, attract viewers from across the cultural spectrum.

Like the soaps, working-class life has traditionally revolved around the local pub, working men's clubs (women were, traditionally, never admitted, but political correctness has forced changes in recent times), soccer (known as football) – with at time almost tribal loyalty-**betting shops**, **bingo** halls and **brass bands**, especially in the north. In its own way, it is a culture that also breeds its own form of **snobbishness**, which would quickly **find fault with** anyone who was thought to be **stepping out of line**, such as showing aspirations to rise "above his station," or class.

For example, there could be consequences within the community if somebody were seen joining the local fox hunt (which is considered upper class) or a smart local health clinic (which is seen as middle class) or supporting Rugby Union (which is seen as working class.) And one definitely wouldn't dare think of ordering anything but beer (or a soft drink) in a working men's club – never wine!

The most telling indicators of an English person's class are his or her accent and behavior – on this matter the English can generally sum each other up within moments of meeting. In practice, however, class is no longer a barrier to either casual

---

Eastender 伦敦东区居民

betting shop 彩票经理部
bingo 赌博游戏
brass band 铜管乐队、军乐队
snobbishness 势利行为
find fault with 找…岔子、挑剔
step out of line 出格、举止不当

social mixing or genuine friendship; but people often feel more comfortable associating with others from the same background. A working-class person might feel uncomfortable at a "society" wedding, for example, as might an aristocrat in a certain kind of pub, but this is a generalization, and a certain amount of self-confidence would **carry the day** for both.

Until quite recently, everybody's perceived sense of "self" and their interpersonal relationships were informed by their view of their status within this class structure. The royal family is essential to the survival of the class system, because it defines one's position in society. Without royalty there can be no new titles, therefore no acquiring of status, or public confirmation of one's place in society.

Keeping Order, Work Ethic and Drink

Apart from class consciousness, the British are also known for their good habit in keeping order in public places. The English expression that "there is a time and a place for everything," suggests a need for order. This can be seen in the way people stand in line for public transport and other services; the order in the way the British conduct their civic and daily life; the requirement for "orderly conduct" at all times at public events – reinforced daily by the Speaker of the House of Commons", who calls (and sometimes shouts) "Order!" to silence over-excited Members of Parliament. Not surprisingly, this desire for order is reflected in the way the British have traditionally dressed. They still have a love of uniforms, especially those connected with the **pomp** and pageantry of a grand public occasion.

However, while Britons' desire for order is strong, their enthusiasm for work is not. Traditionally, the British were not known for applying themselves over-conscientiously in the workplace: most worked simply to earn the money to live. "Devotion to duty," and the very idea of "hard work" (with honorable exceptions, no doubt) are not phrases that readily come to

carry the day 得胜、占上风、取得成功

pomp 壮丽景观

mind. Not surprisingly, given the cruel exploitation of labor during the Industrial Revolution, it was the British who established the world's first trade union movement to protect the rights of organized labor. In today's climate of economic rationalization and "perceived value for money," this attitude has also spread to the **Civil Service**, once a model of efficiency, and the **public sector** as a whole.

Part of the problem, according to social critics, has been the love of alcohol – mostly in the form of beer, with wine now making huge advances. In fact, up to the middle of the twentieth century, England had more bars (known as "public houses," or "**pubs**") than any other country in the world. It was said that there was one on every street corner in every town in the land. Partly for this reason, historians argued, not jokingly, that the Industrial Revolution in Britain was "**lubricated**" with alcohol. The great national projects, like the building of the railways and the **docks** of London and Liverpool, could not have been completed without it. Today, drinking continues to be part of the English way of life. Some country pubs have suffered because of drinking and driving laws, but the pub continues to be at the heart of local communities. But, as always, some excess is inevitable, with unfortunate outcomes such as **vandalism** and **football hooliganism**. In addition, surveys provide worrying signs that the drinking habit is now affecting more people at a younger age, especially teenage girls and young women.

Civil Service 文职部门
public sector 公共行政部门

pub 酒吧、酒店

lubricated 润滑

dock 码头、港口

vandalism 故意毁坏公共财产行为
football hooliganism 足球流氓行为

Notes

Canterbury Tales— *The Canterbury Tales* is a collection of over 20 stories written in Middle English by Geoffrey Chaucer at the end of the 14th century, during the time of the Hundred Years' War. The tales (mostly written in verse, although some are in prose) are presented as part of a story-telling contest by a group of pilgrims as they travel together on a journey from Southwark to the shrine of Saint Thomas Becket at

Canterbury Cathedral.

Francis Fukuyama—(born October 27, 1952) is an American political scientist, political economist, and author. Fukuyama is known for his book *The End of History and the Last Man* (1992), which argued that the worldwide spread of liberal democracies and free market capitalism of the West and its lifestyle may signal the end point of humanity's socio-cultural evolution and become the final form of human government. However, his subsequent book *Trust: Social Virtues and Creation of Prosperity* (1995) modified his earlier position to acknowledge that culture cannot be cleanly separated from economics.

Exercises

I. Multiple Choices

The following are questions or incomplete sentences. Below each sentence or question four possible answers marked A, B, C and D are provided. Choose the ONE that best completes the sentence or answers the question.

1. In Great Britain, anyone without a sense of irony or a sense of humor is often viewed as being a boring person, unable to _____.

   A. make a company good   B. make friends
   C. establish a good company   D. enjoy company life

2. The phrase "on the same wavelength" means _____.

   A. use the same wavelength
   B. share the same wavelength
   C. have the same points of view
   D. receive radio on the same wavelength

3. The British see irony as a form of free _____ for body, mind and spirit.

   A. expression   B. display   C. outlet   D. medication

4. The British value humor quite a lot, particularly in their _____.

   A. private life   B. political life
   C. religious life   D. inter-personal relationship

5. The old English saying "An Englishman's word is his bond" means _____.

   A. Once a promise is made, an Englishman is expected to keep his word.
   B. Once a promise is made, an Englishman's word is like his bond.
   C. Once a promise is made, an Englishman regards his word as his bond.

Unit Eleven British Values and Assumptions

D. Once a promise is made, an Englishman treats his word like his bond.

6. For some Britons, the spirit of "fair play" can be best expressed in the national game of _____.

A. football   B. rugby   C. cricket   D. baseball

7. According to the passage, trust is implicit in all the following, except _____.

A. in the way the British manage their affairs.

B. in their approach to law and order, including the principle that policing is done "with the consent of the people"

C. in the way their judiciary system operates.

D. in the way they do their household chores.

8. According to the passage, there are at least five fundamental qualities of the British character. Specifically speaking, they are _____.

A. fairness, trust, tolerance, compromise and justice

B. tolerance, compromise, trust, diligence, and fairness

C. fairness, friendliness, justice, compromise, and tolerance

D. trust, tolerance, compromise, justice, and candidness

9. In more recent times, the consensus has shifted from _____ to a new focus on _____.

A. a sense of egoism/collective rights and community interests

B. a sense of duty/minority rights and national interests

C. a sense of nationalism/personal privacy and family well-beings

D. a sense of obligation/individual rights and self-interest

10. According to the passage, to people from outside Great Britain, the best known quality of the British, and in particular of the English, is "_____".

A. shyness   B. reserve   C. frankness   D. talkativeness

Ⅱ. True and False

Read the following statements carefully and then decide whether they are true or false. Put a "T" if you think the statement is true and an "F" if it is not.

1. In a sense, fairness is dependent upon trust, and trust, in turn, is based on fairness.

2. American political scientist Francis Fukuyama regards Britain and Japan as low trust cultures.

3. When English people are making a journey by bus, they will do their best to find

an empty seat, and if by train, an empty compartment.

4. In Britain, it is considered good manners to join in and appear to have a good time at a big social event organized by a company where one works.

5. The English do not think that a simple "good morning" or a cheery wave of the hand across the street is enough to show one's politeness to other people.

6. In Britain, politeness towards women is as much observed today as it was in the past.

7. Thanks to the enormous changes to the social, economic, and legal landscape in the late twentieth and early twenty-first centuries, the British are now far less class conscious than before.

8. England, Scotland, and Wales are very much the same in their class divisions.

9. One of the obligations and responsibilities of the upper class in Britain was the duty to behave in conformity with one's rank.

10. For those who are genuinely "upper class", good manners are of the utmost importance.

III. General Questions

1. What are the key pointers of the upper class in Britain?
2. What kind of accent do members of the upper class have?
3. What kind of people are now put in the middle class in Britain?
4. What kind of sports do middle-class Britons play?
5. What did British socialists and unionists mean when they coined the term "working-class Britain"?
6. How is working class culture projected in Britain?
7. Why is it said that the royal family is essential to the survival of the class system in Britain?
8. What does the English expression that "there is a time and a place for everything" mean?
9. How did the British view their work?
10. Why did historians argue that the Industrial Revolution in Britain was "lubricated" with alcohol?

IV. Essay Questions

1. British habits of politeness are said to be very informal. How informal are they?
2. How important is alcohol in British life?

Unit Eleven British Values and Assumptions

Reference Answers

Ⅰ. Multiple Choices

1. B 2. C 3. D 4. D 5. A 6. C 7. D 8. A 9. D 10. B

Ⅱ. True and False

1. T 2. F 3. T 4. T 5. F 6. F 7. F 8. F 9. T 10. T

Ⅲ. General Questions

1. They include, but not limited to, being one of the "old" families; having education at good private schools such as Eton or Harrow, followed by university—Oxford or Cambridge); possessing wealth (often in the form of land or property rather than cash); holding prestigious occupation; and, enjoying such pastimes as hunting, shooting and fishing.

2. Members of the upper class often have a distinctive, mannered accent, which is delivered in a very precise manner.

3. In Britain, the middle class these days encompasses the professional, managerial, and so-called "upwardly mobile" sections of society, as well as a "downwardly mobile" section from the upper class.

4. The sports that middle-class Britons play usually call for expensive equipment, special clothing, or extensive training and practice, such as golf and tennis.

5. They coined the term "working-class Britain" to suggest the exploitation and social inequality that resulted from the rise of nineteenth-century capitalism. Its use today continues to reinforce the historic class divisions of Great Britain, and of England in particular.

6. Working-class culture in Britain is mostly projected through the TV "soaps," which, in fact, are viewed by people from across the cultural spectrum.

7. The royal family is essential to the survival of the class system, because it defines one's position in society. Without royalty there can be no new titles, therefore no acquiring of status, or public confirmation of one's place in society.

8. The English expression that "there is a time and a place for everything" suggests a need for order.

9. Most Britons worked simply to earn the money to live.

10. Because the British have the love of alcohol, particularly the working class. The

great national projects, like the building of the railways and the docks of London and Liverpool, could not have been completed without it.

Ⅳ. Essay Questions

1. British habits of politeness are on the whole very informal. Take greetings for instance: a simple "good morning" or a cheery wave of the hand across the street is quite satisfactory. Handshakes are only exchanged on a first introduction, or on special occasions, or as a token of agreement or congratulation. All politeness is based on the elementary rule of showing consideration for others, and fitly acknowledging the consideration they show to you. For example, "Excuse me" is used as an advance apology for troubling somebody, as when passing in front of him or interrupting his conversation, or when putting a question to a stranger. "Sorry" expresses regret for an accidental disturbance or breach of manners. It also takes the place of "no" when you cannot accede to a request or an implied request like "May I borrow your pen?" or "Do you know the time?"

2. Alcohol is very important in British life, for the British have the love of alcohol. In fact, up to the middle of the twentieth century, England had more bars than any other country in the world. It was said that there was one on every street corner in every town in the land. In part for this reason, scholars suggested, not jokingly, that the Industrial Revolution in Britain was "lubricated" with alcohol. The great national projects, like the building of the railways and the docks of London and Liverpool, could not have been completed without it. Today, drinking continues to be part of the English way of life. Some country pubs have suffered because of drinking and driving laws, but the pub continues to be at the heart of local community.

Unit Twelve   Religion in British Life

Focal Points

the Reformation
established church
Free Churches
Jews

Protestantism
Muslim
Lord Spiritual

Catholicism
the Church of England
denominations

Discussion Questions

What role does religion play in British political and public life?

Text

Sikh 锡克教信徒
Hindu 印度教徒
Baha'i 巴哈派教徒
Jain 耆那教教徒
Zoroastrian 琐罗亚斯德教徒

Lord's prayer 主祷文

Britain has one of the most religiously diverse populations in the European Union, providing people full freedom to choose and follow their own religious beliefs. Although Christianity is the main religion, there are also large communities of Muslims, **Sikhs**, **Hindus** and Jews, and smaller communities of **Baha'is**, Buddhists, **Jains** and **Zoroastrians**. When in 2001 a voluntary question on religious affiliation was included for the first time on the census form, 72 percent of respondents described themselves as Christians.

Yet, despite the official uniformity provided by an established church, and the shared heritage of, for example, religious music and the **Lord's prayer**, the religious experiences available in contemporary Britain form a complex and remarkably varied picture. The fact that Britain is commonly assumed to be a Christian country is **undermined** by a number of factors. They include, for instance, the rapidly declining levels of people's involvement with the churches to which they **nominally** belong, the sharp decline in the value which young people attach to Christianity, and the presence of large Hindu, Sikh and Muslim communities as a result of post-war immigration. All of these changes and developments have resulted in considerable differences between the religious identity of the **segments** of society and of different generations.

A Bird's Eye View of Religious History

Religion in the United Kingdom and in the countries that preceded it has been dominated, for over 1,400 years, by various forms of Christianity. According to the national census, a majority of British citizens identify as Christians, although regular church attendance has fallen dramatically since the middle of the twentieth century. However, while Christianity has weakened among Britons, immigration and **demographic** change have contributed to the growth of other faiths. More interestingly, with regular church attendance **on the decline**, religious tourism for recreation is **gaining popularity**, taking the place that **pilgrimage** for a spiritual purpose held for previous ages.

Pre-Roman forms of religion in Britain included various forms of ancestor worship and **paganism**. Little is known about the details of such religions. Forms of Christianity have dominated religious life in what is now the United Kingdom for over 1,400 years. It was introduced by the Romans to what is now England, Wales, and Southern Scotland.

The word Christ, in English, means Jesus. The main branches of the Christian religion are Catholic, Protestant and Orthodox. Throughout the **Middle Ages**, Roman Catholicism remained the dominant form of Christianity, and Protestant Christianity arose as a reaction to corruption and immorality in the Catholic Church. In response to **the Reformation**, England

Unit Twelve Religion in British Life

and Scotland separated from the Roman Catholic Church for political as well as religious reasons in the 16th century. Henry VIII founded the Church of England in 1536 when the Pope wouldn't let him divorce his first wife, and made himself the head of the Church. His daughter, Elizabeth I, consolidated it in 1569. Ever since then, this branch of the Church has been considered to be quintessentially English, and the British monarch is its Supreme Governor.

The traditional distinction between **Anglicanism** and Roman Catholicism was that the former emphasized the primacy of the individual conscience while the latter stressed the need for the observance of authority. Generally speaking, most English and Scots gradually became Protestants from the 16th century onwards, while most people in Ireland remained Catholic, and Catholics became a persecuted minority in Britain for 300 years. In Scotland, the Presbyterian Church of Scotland, established in a separate Scottish Reformation in the sixteenth century, is recognized as the national church. It is not subject to state control, and the British monarch is an ordinary member, required to swear an oath to "maintain and preserve the Protestant Religion and Presbyterian Church Government" upon his or her accession.

The adherence to Roman Catholicism continued at various levels in different parts of Britain and most strongly in Ireland. From the time of the Industrial Revolution of the early 19th century, the Catholic population has increased again in Britain because of migration from Ireland and Southern and Eastern Europe.

Although Britain has been predominantly Christian since Saxon times, following the Reformation in the sixteenth century many different Christian denominations have existed. Particularly from the mid-seventeenth century, forms of Protestant nonconformity, including Congregationalists, Baptists, Quakers, and later, Methodists, grew outside of the established church. The

Anglicanism 基督教圣公会教义

(Anglican) Church in Wales was disestablished in 1920 and, as the (Anglican) Church of Ireland was disestablished in 1870 before the partition of Ireland, there is no established church in Northern Ireland.

The Jews in England were **expulsed** in 1290 and only **emancipated** in the 19th century. British Jews had numbered fewer than 10,000 in 1800, but after 1881, around 120,000 Russian Jews settled permanently in Britain.

The substantial immigration to the United Kingdom since the 1920s has contributed to the growth of foreign faiths. Immigration has resulted in large Muslim communities from Pakistan, **Somalia** and Bangladesh, and mosques and people who are readily identifiable as religious Muslims can be seen all over Britain. Islam, Hinduism and Sikhism, Buddhism in the United Kingdom experienced growth partly due to immigration and partly due to **conversion** (especially when including Secular Buddhism). As elsewhere in the western world, religious demographics have become part of the **discourse** on multiculturalism, with Britain variously described as a post-Christian society, as "multi-faith", or as secularized.

expulse 驱逐、把…赶出去
emancipate 解放

Somalia 索马里

conversion 皈依、转换

discourse 话语、交谈

Christianity and Other World Religions

The three main branches of the Christian church found in Britain today are the Anglican, or Church of England, the Roman Catholic Church, and the several Protestant denominations, for example the **Methodists** and **Congregationalists**. Though they share the same origins and have many common beliefs, historically they developed different forms of rituals and doctrines which have led to some major differences between the churches.

The Church of England

The Church of England occupies both a political role and a spiritual one. The organization is referred to as "the Church of England" when considering its place in the constitution or life of

Methodist 循道宗教徒

Congregationalist 公理会教徒

Unit Twelve Religion in British Life

the nation, and as "the Anglican church" when its spiritual or **theological** identity is **at issue**. Because it is the body chosen by and connected to the British political system of government, the Church of England is the **established church** (it differs, however, from the Church of Scotland). It is thus formally tied to both Parliament and to the Monarchy.

In the 1990s there were, nominally, 27 million Anglicans in Britain. That is, almost two-thirds of the adult population claimed to belong to the Church of England. However, at the same time the Anglican Church had less than two million **registered** members. Membership signifies active involvement with the Church, for example in attending services and offering financial contributions. Between 1960 and 1985 the Church of England's registered membership halved, while the number who thought of themselves as belonging to the Church barely changed. This apparent contradiction between those who choose to think of themselves as Anglicans and those who are actively committed to Anglicanism is perhaps the single most important feature of British Christian life. In 2008 self-claimed Anglicans numbered 13.4 million.

The presence of the established Church is evident in numerous ways in British life. British coins bear the head of the Monarch plus the Latin initials "F. D.", signifying that the Monarch is Defender of the Faith, a title given to Henry VIII by Pope Leo X in 1521. In 1995, Prince Charles caused some controversy among traditionalists by suggesting that at his coronation he would like to be known as Defender of Faiths (plural) in recognition that Britain was no longer an exclusively Christian country. He again caused controversy in 1996 when he suggested that money from the "millennium fund" (a fund of money from the National Lottery which is intended to finance projects to enhance Britain's cultural life and national prestige) should in part be spent on mosques. Despite many moves towards multiculturalism in Britain, sections of the **tabloid** press reacted with hostility to

---

theological 神学的
at issue 争议中的
established church 国教

registered 注册的

tabloid 通俗小报的

this suggestion, seeing **mosques** as a symbol of a foreign and minority religion despite the fact that British Muslims now outnumber **adherents** of most British Protestant denominations. Meanwhile, even government reforms to the House of Lords in 2001 did not include giving a formal place in the Lords for religions outside the Church of England.

The Church of Scotland

Founded in 1560 by John Knox, the Church of Scotland is the established church in Scotland and is known informally by its Scots language name, the Kirk. Although it is the national church, the Kirk, dissimilar to the Church of England (the established church in England), is not a "state church". Under its constitution (recognized by acts of Parliament), the Kirk enjoys complete independence from the state in spiritual matters, which means when in Scotland, the British monarch simply attends church, as opposed to her role in the English Church as Supreme Governor. The Monarch's accession oath includes a promise to "defend the security" of the Kirk. The Church of Scotland is a Presbyterian Church, decisively shaped by the Scottish Reformation. According to the 2001 national census, 42% of the Scottish population claim some form of allegiance to it.

The Roman Catholic Church

After Britain cut off ties with the Roman Catholic Church, the early years of the UK were difficult for English adherents of the Roman Catholic Church. The civil rights of adherents to Roman Catholicism were severely curtailed, and there was no longer, as once in **Stuart times**, any Catholic presence at court, in public life, in the military or professions. It was not until the late 18th and early 19th century that most restrictions on Catholic participation in public life were relaxed. Recently, the rights of Catholics were restored even further with the permission of the spouses of **Royals** to be Catholic, as well as Catholics to be Members of Parliament. According to a poll in 2009, there were

---

mosque 清真寺

adherent 追随者、信徒

Stuart times 斯图尔特时代

Royals 王室成员

about 5.2 million Catholics in England and Wales, 9.6% of the population, making the Roman Catholic Church the second largest denomination of Christianity in the UK.

The Church has an extensive formal structure in the UK made up of provinces, **dioceses** and local parishes. From the 1960s till recent times religious issues in Northern Ireland have been overshadowed by "the Troubles"—the continuing violence generated by the unresolved political issue of whether Northern Ireland should form part of the UK or of a united Ireland. The religious differences between Protestants and Catholics have thus been exacerbated, as Nationalists want Northern Ireland to be part of a Catholic country (with the South) while Unionists want the province to belong to a Protestant country—that is, the UK. It is often implied by British people that "the Troubles" are based on religion, but it is probably more accurate to see the conflict as political, or even tribal, at root, a **stand-off** in which the communities have both looked to their differing churches for support.

Free Churches

A number of Protestant denominations are called Free Churches whose members embrace **non-conformism**, a form of Protestantism comparatively extreme in comparison with the Church of England. The Methodist Church is the largest of these, followed by the Baptist Union of Great Britain, the United Reformed Church, and the Salvation Army, which emphasizes saving souls through a practical Christianity and social concern.

The influences of Free Churches are more evident in Wales than in any other region in the U.K. Compared with the rest of the U.K., Wales has a separate religious tradition in which Methodism and the Congregational Church have traditionally played an important part, both churches laying an emphasis on individual devotion and strict adherence to **puritanical** rules of **abstention** from worldly behavior, such as drinking and **fornication**. Welsh chapels are plain and **unadorned**, and Welsh non-conformist Christianity has traditionally had no concept of the minister as priest (one with unique spiritual powers and authority to administer **sacraments** such as **Holy Communion**), but has a strong sense of the **prophetic** tradition (preachers inspired directly by God). There has been no established church in Wales since 1920 – the Anglican Church in Wales is known as "the Church in Wales".

Other World Religions

Britain has approximately 2,869,000 Muslims, the majority of whom were born in the UK. Others have arrived from the Indian sub-continent or from African countries. Since the bombing on the London Underground in July 2005, the British government has been **apprehensive** about relations between Christian and Muslim groups, **sparing no efforts** to seek **mediation** and compromise. Its endeavor can be best **illustrated** by the fact that whereas in the 1980s only a fifth of the Muslims in Britain claimed to actively practice their religion, in 1990s that figure rose to half.

Although the history of the presence of other faiths and peoples, and their role in public life in Britain, is not widely known, there is a long cultural heritage of Asian people and faiths in the UK. This was well demonstrated in 1995 by the opening of the largest Hindu temple outside India, in London. There are now Hindu temples across the UK in major cities and towns.

The Sikh community is also well represented in Britain and is concentrated in particular areas – for example, in **Southall** and **Gravesend** in Greater London. At the beginning, they held religious meetings at home, often in all-male households, but soon set up Sikh temples for Sunday services.

Aside from religions from Asia, Britain has the second largest Jewish population in Europe. Most Jews live in London, but there are several hundred Jewish congregations in the UK, many Jewish schools and synagogues serving both the **Orthodox** faith and the minority Reform group. Fears have been voiced

---

sacrament 圣事、圣礼
Holy Communion 圣餐
prophetic 预言的、先知的

apprehensive 担忧的、疑惧的
spare no efforts 不余遗力地
mediation 调解
illustrate 表明、显示

Southall 索夏尔（伦敦西部郊区）
Gravesend 格雷夫森德（英格兰肯特郡古镇）

Orthodox 正统的、正宗的

that nowadays half of Jewish men are marrying non-Jewish women, and this will lead to a decline in faith and religious observance.

Finally, the **Rastafarian** religion has had a sizable cultural influence in Britain. Rastafarian's philosophy of life was originally based on their adaptation of Christianity they experienced in the colonial West Indies. They see themselves as **Israelites** displaced from their homeland, and **Babylon** is the collective name for all countries of **exile** outside Africa. Rastafarians have been influential in many cultural ways in Britain, for example their "**dreadlocks**" hairstyle; and they were probably influential in promoting a climate of tolerance towards soft drugs, a major aspect of their religion, in the 1980s.

Religion and Society

A peculiarly British phenomenon is the presence of established churches such as the Church of England. These churches have an official constitutional status within the legal and political framework of Britain, and in day-to-day life Britain's churches are very involved in its culture, especially the Christian religion which is to some degree woven into every level of British life: government, education, architecture, the arts, broadcasting and many other areas. In Northern Ireland, religion has had the extra political significance of marking the line between Catholic and Protestant paramilitary factions.

At a personal level, Christianity may have been **encountered** in the form of prayers or **hymns** that were taught at school, or personal acquaintance with a local **vicar** or a **chaplain** at a hospital. A lot of British people accept the fact that there is a role for churches to play in society, and they feel in some way **reassured** by the background presence of this religion, though they themselves may not be believers and do not wish to become actively involved with it.

The following discussion takes a brief look at the influence of religion on politics, education and people in Britain. Let's, first of all, examine the relationship between politics and religion. With the monarch being its supreme head, the Church of England is a state church. However, it is also not a state church in the strict sense, since it receives no financial aid from the state besides salaries for **non-clerical** positions and help with church schools. Although the state has shown less interest in the affairs of the Church of England, the connection is still very real. For instance, the Church of England is represented in the UK Parliament by 26 bishops (the Lords Spiritual), who have seats in the House of Lords and debate government policies affecting the whole of the United Kingdom. The Church of England also has the right to draft legislative measures (related to religious administration) through the General **Synod** that can then be passed into law by Parliament.

non-clerical 非神职人员的

Synod 教会会议

Also, though the main political parties are secular, the Church of England has sometimes been nicknamed "the Conservative Party at prayer" because of its safe and establishment image, though it has less to do with any identification with the political policies of Conservative governments than with its role as a guardian of the past. It is, as British people will say, conservative with a small "c". In the past, the Church of England tended to avoid controversial issues about social and political issues. However, in recent years, the Church has been more willing to enter into controversial arguments, such as the living condition of people in the inner cities, and has been critical of government policies. But, to most Britons, the Church, like the Monarchy, should not involve itself in such issues. In modern UK, Northern Ireland is an exceptional place where religion is deeply **entwined** with politics.

entwine 缠绕、纠缠在一起

Secondly, a look at the relationship between religion and education will further illustrate the importance of religion in British life. Until 1944 there was no requirement for state schools to provide religious education or worship, although

Unit Twelve Religion in British Life

most did so. **By virtue of clauses** 69 and 70 of the School Standards and Framework Act 1998, Religious Education and Collective Worship have become compulsory in many state schools in England and Wales, though more than three-quarters of schools fail to meet this requirement. This is particularly so in areas with large ethnic communities. Clause 71 of the Act gives parents the right to withdraw their children from Religious Education and Collective Worship and parents should be informed of their right in accordance with guidelines published by the Department for Education.

In Scotland, the majority of schools are **non-denominational**, but separate Roman Catholic schools, with an element of control by the Roman Catholic Church, are provided within the state system. The Education (Scotland) Act 1980 imposes a **statutory** duty on all local authorities to provide religious education and religious observance in Scottish schools. These are currently defined by the Scottish Government's **Curriculum** for Excellence (2005).

Northern Ireland has a highly segregated education system. 95% of pupils attend either maintained (Catholic) schools or controlled schools, which are open to children of all faiths and none, though in practice most pupils are from the Protestant community.

In England and Wales, a significant number of state funded schools are faith schools with the vast majority being Christian (mainly either of Church of England or Roman Catholic), though there are also Jewish, Muslim and Sikh faith schools. Faith schools follow the same national curriculum as state schools, though with the added **ethos** of the host religion. Although these schools sometimes produce better-than-average results, there have been criticisms centering around them. For one thing, 64 percent of the public, according to a poll in August 2005, believed that "the government should not be funding faith schools of any kind". For another, many people argue that

---

by virtue of 由于、因为
clause 条款

non-denominational 非宗派的

statutory 法规的、法令的

curriculum 课程

ethos 特质、气质

by accepting fewer poor and disadvantaged students, faith schools tend to create the segregation that increases racial and religious **sectarian** tensions. Along this line of thought, demands have been made that faith schools be abolished.

> sectarian 派别的、宗派的

Finally, let's move on to the relationship between religion and people. On the whole, British people's **stance** on belief can be described as "half belief" or "passive belief". While membership of all Christian churches in Britain and churchgoing are in decline, active Christianity in Britain is not being replaced by **atheism**, but rather by a less **taxing**, but **harder-to-define** "passive Christianity", meaning a vague belief in God/Christ, but a strong adherence to the idea of being Christian. As suggested earlier, the contradiction at the heart of Christianity in Britain is that while most of the population believe themselves to be in some sense Christian, they have no commitment to, little knowledge of or belief in things that the Church regards as central to Christianity. Winston Churchill **reputedly** said: "I'm not a **pillar** of the Church, I'm a **buttress**. I support it from outside." There is in many quarters of the non-churchgoing-population an assumption that being English automatically qualifies one for membership of the Church of England and hence confers the right to be considered a Christian.

> stance 立场
>
> atheism 无神论
> taxing 费劲的
> harder-to-define 更难界定的
>
> reputedly 据说、据一般认为
> pillar 支柱
> buttress 扶壁

In a nutshell, most British people, it can be said, live in a state of "popular religion", which, while loosely based on Christianity, would not be recognized as faith by most priests. In moments of crisis, it is the Christian God in some form to whom they will turn in private prayer. Such religion requires no active participation, but may be satisfied, for example, by listening to radio or TV broadcasts.

Notes

The Reformation—also known as the Protestant Reformation, was the schism within Western Christianity initiated by Martin Luther, John Calvin, and other early Protestant Reformers. As one of the greatest events of the past 1000 years in the West, it began on October 31, 1517, when German monk Saint Martin Luther nailed his 95 Theses to the Castle Church door in Wittenberg, Germany.

Henry VIII (1491—1547)— was King of England from 21 April 1509 until his death. He was Lord, and later assumed the Kingship of Ireland, and continued the nominal claim by English monarchs to the Kingdom of France. Henry was the second monarch of the Tudor dynasty, succeeding his father, Henry VII.

Exercises

Ⅰ. **Multiple Choices**

The following are questions or incomplete sentences. Below each sentence or question four possible answers marked A, B, C and D are provided. Choose the ONE that best completes the sentence or answers the question.

1. Britain has one of the most religiously diverse populations in _____.

   A. the world   B. the European Union
   B. Europe   D. the English-speaking world

2. When in 2001 a voluntary question on religious affiliation was included for the first time on the census form, _____ percent of British respondents described themselves as Christians.

   A. 75   B. 73   C. 72   D. 74

3. The fact that Britain is commonly assumed to be a Christian country is undermined by a number of factors. They include _____.

   A. the rapidly declining levels of people's involvement with the churches to which they nominally belong

   B. the sharp decline in the value which young people attach to Christianity

   C. the presence of large Hindu, Sikh and Muslim communities as a result of postwar immigration

   D. all above combined

4. Regular church attendance in Britain has fallen dramatically since the _____ of the twentieth century.

   A. beginning   B. first half   C. middle   D. end

5. Christianity was introduced to England, Wales, and Southern Scotland by the _____.

  A. Romans B. Anglo-Saxons C. Celts D. Danes

  6. England and Scotland separated from the Roman Catholic Church for _____ as well as _____ reasons in the 16th century.

  A. political/financial   B. political/cultural

  C. political/territorial   D. political/religious

  7. From the time of the Industrial Revolution of the early 19th century, the Catholic population has increased again in Britain because of _____.

  A. greater tolerance of Britons toward the Catholics

  B. greater power gained by the Catholics

  C. migration from Ireland and Southern and Eastern Europe

  D. increased births in Catholic community in Britain

  8. The Jews in England were _____ in 1290 and only emancipated in the 19th century.

  A. expelled   B. exiled

  C. executed   D. excommunicated

  9. According to the passage, all the following expressions can be used to describe British society, except _____.

  A. a post-Christian society   B. a "multi-faith" society

  C. a secularized society   D. an atheist society

  10. The vast majority of the people of the UK are _____.

  A. Roman Catholics   B. Presbyterians

  C. Anglicans   D. Methodists

  Ⅱ. True and False

Read the following statements carefully and then decide whether they are True or False. Put a "T" if you think the statement is true and an "F" if it is not.

  1. From the passage, it can be inferred that there is no established church either in Wales or in Northern Ireland.

  2. In Britain, there are more Anglicans than Methodists, Congregationalists or Presbyterians.

  3. The Church of England has a spiritual role to play only.

  4. Those Britons who think of themselves as Anglicans would normally register

their membership with the Church of England.

5. Prince Charles' remarks about his coronation and the "millennium fund" suggest that he is in favor of multiculturalism.

6. The Church of Scotland is similar to the Church of England in that it is also a state church.

7. In Scotland, close to half of the Scottish population claim some form of allegiance to it.

8. It was not until the late 19th and early 20th century that most restrictions on Catholic participation in public life were relaxed.

9. Many Protestant denominations in Britain are called Free Churches, because their adherents embrace a comparatively extreme form of Protestantism in comparison with the Church of England.

10. Before 1920, there used to be an established Anglican church in Wales.

Ⅲ. General Questions

1. Where do Muslims in Britain come from?

2. In what ways has the Rastafarian religion been so influential in Britain?

3. What is a particularly British phenomenon in religion?

4. What is the extra political significance of religion in Northern Ireland?

5. What is the general attitude of Britons toward religion?

6. Why is it said that the Church of England is not a state church in the strict sense?

7. Why has the Church of England sometimes been nicknamed "the Conservative Party at prayer"?

8. According to Clauses 69 and 70 of the School Standards and Framework Act 1998, what are state schools in England and Wales supposed to do?

9. What does the Education (Scotland) Act 1980 ask local authorities to do in Scottish schools?

10. What does it mean when we say that British people's stance on belief can be described as "half belief" or "passive belief"?

Ⅳ. Essay Questions

1. How did England become Protestant, and the Church of England the established church?

2. How do British Christians feel about Christianity at their personal level?

Reference Answers

I. Multiple Choices

1. B 2. C 3. D 4. C 5. A 6. D 7. C 8. A 9. D 10. C

II. True and False

1. T 2. T 3. F 4. F 5. T 6. F 7. T 8. F 9. T 10. T

III. General Questions

1. The majority of Muslims were born in the UK, and the rest have come from either the Indian sub-continent or African countries.

2. The Rastafarian religion has been influential in many cultural ways in Britain, for example their "dreadlocks" hairstyle; and they were probably influential in promoting a climate of tolerance towards soft drugs in the 1980s as well.

3. A peculiarly British phenomenon is the presence of established churches such as the Church of England.

4. The extra political significance of religion in Northern Ireland is that it marks the line between Catholic and Protestant paramilitary factions.

5. A lot of British people accept the fact that there is a role for churches to play in society, and they feel in some way reassured by the background presence of this religion, though they themselves may not be believers and do not wish to become actively involved with it.

6. The Church of England is not a state church in the strict sense, since it receives no financial aid from the state besides salaries for non-clerical positions and help with church schools.

7. The Church of England has sometimes been nicknamed "the Conservative Party at prayer" because of its safe and establishment image, as well as its role as a guardian of the past.

8. According to clauses 69 and 70 of the School Standards and Framework Act 1998, state schools in England and Wales should provide Religious Education and Collective Worship.

9. The Education (Scotland) Act 1980 imposes a statutory duty on all local authorities to provide religious education and religious observance in Scottish schools.

10. By "half belief" or "passive belief", it means that most of Britons have a vague

belief in God/Christ, but a strong adherence to the idea of being Christian.

IV. Essay Questions

1. England became Protestant as a result of its response to the Reformation of the 16th century, separating itself from the Roman Catholic Church for political as well as religious reasons. Henry VIII founded the Church of England in 1536 when the Pope wouldn't let him divorce his first wife, and made himself the head of the Church. His daughter, Elizabeth I, consolidated it in 1569. Ever since then, this branch of the Church has been considered to be quintessentially English. With the British monarch as its Supreme Governor, the Church of England thus became and remains till today the established church.

2. At their personal level, British Christians may feel Christianity on daily basis. For instance, they may encounter it in the form of prayers or hymns that were taught at school, or personal acquaintance with a local vicar or a chaplain at a hospital. A lot of British people accept the fact that there is a role for churches to play in society, and they feel in some way reassured by the background presence of this religion, though they themselves may not be believers and do not wish to become actively involved with it.

Unit Thirteen British Education

Focal Points

Oxbridge   "Redbrick" universities   the Open University
grammar school   public school   state school
faith school   vocational school   moderns comprehensives
the Education Act 1944 the Education Reform Act 1988

Discussion Questions

What are the main characteristics of the secondary education in Britain?

Text

The history of education in England can be traced back to the Anglo-Saxons' settlement of England, or even back to the Roman occupation. School for the most **privileged** of British people started in 600 AD, through **royal patronage**. The oldest is King's School, Canterbury, which was founded in 597. Two universities were established later: the University of Oxford in 1249, followed by the University of Cambridge in 1284. Many independent schools were **charitable foundations**. A group of these charity schools, much later, **invoked** the name "public school" to indicate that they were open to the public regardless of religious beliefs. At that time, education belonged to the Catholic Church which was committed to teaching the principles of Christianity. A reformed system of "free grammar schools" was established **in the reign** of Edward VI. Schooling for the

---

privileged 特权的

royal patronage 皇室恩赐

charitable foundation（靠基金建立）的学校或医院等机构

invoke 启用、行使

in the reign 在…统治时期

rest came only in the eighteenth and nineteenth centuries with the Education Act passed in 1902, bringing **state secondary education** onto the stage. Towards the end of the 19th century and around the beginning of the 20th century, the **"Redbrick" universities** were founded. With its full range of subjects and complete structure, British education has been ranked among the world's best on the ground of its **renowned** scientific research, education quality as well as the quality of its graduates.

Schools

There are about 27,000 schools in Britain, with 8,600,000 pupils and 610,000 teachers. Full-time education is **mandatory** for all children in the UK between ages five and sixteen. At the end of the school year during which a student turns sixteen, they are free to leave – those who do so at this point are referred to as "**school-leavers**". Under the present law, the school leaving age is 16, and suggestions have been made time and again to raise it to eighteen, largely in an effort to produce a better-trained workforce and address the persistent 10 percent of sixteen-to eighteen-year-old NEETs (Not in education, employment, or training).

The State System: Grammar Schools, Comps, and Secondary Moderns

The state offers "primary" (for ages 5-11) and "secondary" (for ages 11-18) schooling. There are a very few "middle" schools for children aged 10-13 and some "specialist" schools for children with learning difficulties. From the 1940s until the 1970s, all children in the Welsh, English, and Northern Irish state education system took the eleven-plus exam at approximately age eleven. Depending on their exam results—there was no official pass or fail—students entered a **grammar school**, a technical school, or a secondary **modern**. Grammar schools were the most **prestigious**, taking roughly the top quarter of children. Technical schools, or "techs", were **few and far between** but intended for those who showed an **aptitude** for science and technical subjects. Secondary moderns took the **ungifted** majority. These are the main state schools, although there are others in, for example, hospitals and youth **custody** centers.

England, Scotland and Wales have respectively 3,446, 372 and 222 state secondary schools. Of the English schools, 1,300 are **academies** and 6,955 are **faith schools**. Most are Christian, with 36 Jewish, 6 Muslim, 2 Sikh, 1 Hindu, 1 Greek Orthodox and 1 **Seventh Day Adventist**. There are a few hundred faith schools in Scotland and Wales. Additionally and separately there are 790 independent schools and 164 grammar schools. Children are **allocated** places by the Local Education Authority in the schools nearest to them. The government has encouraged the exercise of parental choice by promoting competition among schools and adopting a policy of **incentives** for "good" schools and a **laissez-faire** attitude to the closure of those that are becoming less popular.

Children who **made it** into the grammar schools received a first-rate learning experience and an open road to a professional career. The other branches were left to **wither**, providing the majority of children with a substandard education. Opposition to the system came from **both ends of the spectrum**: the working-class opposed a system that created **an elite** at the expense of the majority; the middle-class opposed it once they realized the grammar schools weren't **reserving spaces** for their children.

Under the Labor government of the mid-1970s, the eleven-plus exams and the **elective system** were **phased out**, and the schools of the **tripartite** system were reinvented as **comprehensives**, so-called because they were intended to provide a comprehensive education for all. Though grammar schools **have hung on** in some regions, nowadays about 90 percent of children attend comprehensives, or "comps", as they're **abbreviated**. The grammar schools that do remain **trounce** the comprehensives in exam results.

---

aptitude 天资、才能
ungifted 无天资的、无才华的
custody 监护、监管、拘留

academy 即 academy school：中等学校
faith school 教会学校
Seventh Day Adventist 基督复临安息日会教友
allocate 分派、分配

incentive 刺激、奖励
laissez-faire 自由放任的

make it 办成、做到

wither 枯萎、消失

both ends of the spectrum 教育体系的两端

reserve space 保留位置

elective system 选修课制度
phase out 逐步淘汰
tripartite 三部分的
comprehensives 综合性学校
hang on 持续、坚持
abbreviate 缩写
trounce 彻底打败、击溃

On the whole, the British school system has a reputation for quality. However, a number of factors—continual reforms, the **over-prescriptive National Curriculum**, inspections without **feedback**—have produced low **morale** among teachers, many of whom leave the profession. The government is trying to address these problems through various **initiatives** to improve educational opportunities for children.

In these circumstances, unsurprisingly, the independent schools sector has continued to flourish – partly because of their comparative stability and their high academic standards.

The Private System: Putting the "Private" in Public Schools

When children reach the **tender** age of eight years old, the sons of the upper-classes, as a rule, are **shipped out** to **boarding school** in the country. Daughters are sometimes **packed off**, too, but usually that occurs a few years later. These **preparatory schools**, or "prep schools" as they are called, **ready** children for secondary school. Children attend prep school, whether they are boarding or day students, generally from the age of eight to thirteen. At thirteen, they take (or, in British **parlance**, they "sit") the common entrance exams, which are used by independent secondary schools, sometimes called **colleges**, to determine admission and scholarships..

After prep school, the next stop for **affluent** teens is **public school**, a type of secondary school. Confusingly, famous private schools like Eton and Harrow, Winchester or Stonyhurst are known as "public schools". It should be said **right off the bat** that "public school" is a complete **misnomer** There is, actually, nothing public about them: for boarders, fees can run over £20,000 a year. The term derives from the fact that the schools were public – open to anyone who could pay the fees – in contrast to the private tutors hired by some families. The system of education is now, as Chambers dictionary put it, "for such as can afford it". Of course, the term "public school" is now **synonymous with posh** and privileged. That students at

Eton still wear **tails** to class doesn't do much to **dispel** this image. Most of the top public schools were single-sex until fairly recently; many are now **coed**.

The independent school sector is **disproportionately** important in British life for a variety of reasons. Although only 7 percent of British children attend independent schools, their **alumni figure** much more significantly as **entrants** to the universities, particularly Oxbridge (Oxford and Cambridge), and figure **prominently** in the higher **echelons** of British society. For instance, both the Prime Minister David Cameron and the Mayor of London Boris Johnson went to Eton and Oxford.

In the past, the Labor Party always **made a great fuss about** the public schools, but that sort of thing is not heard much anymore. Today, most **griping** is targeted at the schools' use of merit rather than **means** to determine scholarships. Top schools like Eton spend only a few percent of their **revenue** on needs-based scholarships, a tiny sum when compared with the top American prep schools.

Colleges and Universities

University education is generally less **contentious** for the general public and in recent years Britain has had in Europe the highest percentage (over a third) of 21-year-old graduating from university. There are 116 universities in the UK: 89 in England, 14 in Scotland, 11 in Wales and 2 in Northern Ireland. Oxford and Cambridge (known collectively as "Oxbridge") are the oldest universities in Britain. Though much expanded, their student numbers (in 2010, for example, Oxford had 11,225 students, and Cambridge, 11,515) are still small, compared with student numbers in big universities in the United States. Other old universities are Durham and St Andrews, and they are distinguished from the so-called "Redbrick" universities (for example, Birmingham, Liverpool, Manchester) through their emphasis on traditional subjects. "New" universities created in

---

tail 辫子
dispel 消除、驱散
coed 男女同校的
disproportionately 不成比例地
alumni(男)校友、毕业生
figure 出现、露头角
entrant 进入者、新学员
prominently 显赫地
echelon 阶层

made a great fuss about 对……大声喧嚷
gripe 牢骚、抱怨
means 收入、财力
revenue 收入、收益

contentious 有争议的

the 1960s include Lancaster, York, Keele and Sussex. In 1992 all the former **polytechnics** changed their names and joined the existing 44 universities. Apart from all these institutions of higher learning, Britain has two other main universities. The Open University (250,000 part-time students in 2010) offers a wide range of degree programs delivered formerly by TV and radio, now also by DVDs and **podcasts**, especially for people already engaged in full-time work. The University for Industry is a public-private partnership that offers basic and technological skills, 80 percent of which are taught online.

Further or continuing education in Britain is also known as **post-compulsory** education, providing learning opportunities for people over sixteen. The forms of further education usually include general further and tertiary colleges, certain specialist colleges, adult education institutes and work based learning. Normally the courses run in most further education colleges are similar to those in higher education colleges, but often students could **enroll in** the short-term training program. **Vocational** and **foundation courses** are also available in the further education sector. Some colleges also offer degree-level courses. Teachers in further education must gain professional status.

The British university experience is very different from the American. Take university admissions for example, in Britain, candidates for university will declare what subject they want to "**read**", interview at a couple of universities, and then receive conditional "offers," **provided that** their A-level grades meet requirements. Oxford and Cambridge will generally make offers **contingent on** A-level results of "AAA", or A's in three A-level exams. The interviewers are looking for academic **prowess**; they don't care much whether the **prospective** student was the captain of a high school football team, or whether he/she spent a lot of time providing community services at weekends. Along these lines of thinking, sports are pretty **inconsequential** at the university level.

Academically speaking, the biggest difference among college students is the level of specialization. A freshman, or "fresher" in British parlance, who **embarks on** an English literature degree will study nothing but English literature for the three years of their undergraduate career (four years in Scotland). The standard length of undergraduates study for "vocational" degrees (ones linked to a specific job), like medicine, **dentistry, veterinary science** or architecture is seven years. As a result, British graduates in these **fields of study** will have a base of knowledge in their subject comparable to an American with a master's degree, though an American college graduate from a comparable institution will have a broader foundation. Students on Master's courses study for at least one year and those doing Doctorates for **upwards of** three years.

With the British system's emphasis on exams there is not really anything like the US **grade point average**. Students take quizzes and write essays, but these generally don't count toward their final grades. While it varies from course to course, students will submit a **dissertation** and **sit exams** on their final year of courses, and these grades are the ones that count heaviest in determining the quality of degree received.

Those who excel will receive a first-class degree, called a "first"; next is an upper-second degree, or "two-two", sometimes affectionately known as a "Desmond" in a **rhyming** slang reference to **Nobel laureate** Desmond Tutu; at the bottom are third-class degrees or ordinary degrees; anything below that is a failure for which no degree is **awarded**.

Scotland is a little less narrow in its focus. There, university courses generally run for four years instead of three. The first two include studies ranging a little beyond just the subject that the student is reading. Due to the extra year, some Scottish universities award a master's degree to graduates who excel at their exams.

More than twenty years ago, less than 20 percent of British

embark on 从事于、开始工作

dentistry 牙科学
veterinary science 兽医学
field of study 学科领域

upwards of 以上、多于

grade point average 平均积分点

dissertation 论文
sit exam 参加考试

rhyme 押韵
Nobel laureate 诺贝尔奖获得者
award 授予

students graduated from schools of higher education, which includes both universities and the less prestigious polytechnics, which have since been absorbed into the university system. Back then, for those lucky enough to attend, education was free, and students received both **housing grants** and **living stipends** from the government. Nowadays, higher education has a 40 percent participation rate, a figure higher than even the US, but **the free ride** is gone and there is a **gender imbalance** with more young women entering university than young men. Hence, today, students experience real financial hardship. Only those whose parents can afford to **subsidize** them are without money worries. The percentage of working-class children attending university is declining as **tuition fees** have risen over the course of fifteen years from virtually nothing to in most cases £9,000 a year (the most expensive in the world after the United States and South Korea). Fortunately, even without the enormous **endowments** and **alumni generosity** of American universities, Britain's institutions of higher education have managed to **retain** their world-class reputations.

Despite the expense, attending university is becoming an increasingly important requirement to succeed in both the UK and global economics. More jobs than ever advertise now for "graduates." However, participation in higher education is still largely determined by the class one happens to be born into. There are deep divisions in education as in society. For example, five schools (four independent and one state sixth form college, namely Eton, Westminster, St Paul's Boys and St Paul's Girls and a Cambridge state community college) accounted for more Oxbridge places over three years than 2,000 comprehensives, according to a study published by Sutton Trust in 2011. Moreover, in Britain as a whole, currently 80 percent of children from professional middle-class families study at university, compared with 17 percent from the poorest families in the country.

Changes and Trends in Education

Over the past several decades, Britain has made some major changes in its educational system, among which the following stand out more notably: the **imposition** of a national curriculum, the introduction of pre-**GCSE** examinations, and the publication of **league tables** of schools' performances.

Historically, the Education Act 1944 laid a major **framework** for education for decades until another **radical** movement was made in the enactment of the Education Reform Act 1988. This new legislation has several features. First, the introduction of a national curriculum for pupils aged 5-16, according to which the responsibility of deciding what to teach would be shifted from individual teachers to the central government. Second, the establishment of compulsory national tests, whose results would be published annually to allow schools to compete for pupils and to be compared directly with one another. Third, considerable freedom and **flexibility** in management would be given to individual schools to run their own **budgets**. Fourth, a new type of school, city technology college, would be set up in inner city areas, offering courses in the fields of technology, arts, mathematics and sciences. Fifth, a series of standards in education would be set up to ensure a greater degree of uniformity in education quality.

The turn of the century saw greater changes continue to take place in Britain. With the slogan "education, education and education" for the 1997 general election, the Labor Party came into power, bringing with it a series of reforms in education. Attention was shifted from the former comprehensive system to caring for each child's ability. Specific measures included: 1) a higher percentage of GDP was spent on education; 2) more special schools were created (the number of such schools grew from 196 in 1997 to 1000 by 2002). Though the results were mixed, the positive effect remains visible. For instance, school-leavers decreased and nearly half of them went on to higher education. .

In 2007, in response to criticisms about the British educational system, the central government decided to move further in its education reform. Subsequently, it adopted **a "one size fits all" approach**, asking all schools to be more child centered. Specifically speaking, children should be allowed to **proceed** at their own pace in response to teaching tailored towards them individually. This aim was very worthy but had huge resource implications and contributed further to the destabilizing process of constant change within education.

Why do the British keep reforming their educational system? One key reason is that schools matter to people. To Britons, education is not just about the delivery of **syllabuses**. And primary schools in particular are believed to be the sites for the transmission from one generation to the next of shared culture. The culture is not only of the classroom, but also of the playground, where children socialize. In choosing a school for their children, British parents are concerned with such things as potential academic progress, the **prevalence** of **bullying**, the development of life skills and the kind of social, cultural and spiritual experience offered by the school. Furthermore, because schools are so important in the formation of shared cultural identity, the British are interested in the way in which **prominent public figures** choose to educate their children. For example, Prince Charles was the first member of the royal family not to be educated by palace tutors. He was sent to Gordonstoun in Scotland, and his own sons William and Harry were sent to Eton.

Of course, not all British parents can afford to do so. But **parents with means** do send their children to public schools, either because they can afford, or because of the **availability** of an **"Old School Tie"** network. so, they may help their child to get a good job and develop socially useful life-long friendships. Traditionally, Britain works on a system of contacts among people

---

a "one size fits all" approach 适合所有人的标准之做法
proceed 进行、开始做

syllabuse 教学大纲、课程大纲

prevalence 流行、盛行
bullying 威胁、欺负行为

prominent public figure 社会名流、社会显赫人物

parent with means 有财力的家长
availability 可利用性
Old School Tie 学校老关系

whose business, professional, sporting and social lives produce a shared cultural **milieu**. What is interesting to note is that pupils from single-sex schools like Eton have performed better than those at mixed ones—without the distractions of the opposite sex, so the argument goes. In the 2011 GCSE tables, for example, the ten top schools nationally were single-sex. Recently, moreover, the trend in school and university education is that girls seem to be performing much better than boys.

  More recently, with many children in school feeling bored by the GCSEs they are doing, the British government has encouraged a shift from education to training, in an attempt to enable the students to embark on **apprenticeships** two days a week at 14 years of age. People's response to this initiative is mixed. Those against it argue that similar programs in the past had failed amid complaints that firms had exploited students on work-experience as unpaid labor. Those concerned with social equality see this leading to a divisive **two-tier** education system where some children are denied quality education and others, with a privileged background, are enabled to flourish. And those in favor of it suggest that publicly funded education should be **pragmatic** and indeed have a duty to satisfy society's need for skilled labor. In short, in order to make Great Britain competitive, most of the British believe that their educational system should be made competitive as well.

milieu 环境

apprenticeship 学徒资格、学徒期

two-tier 两个等级的

pragmatic 实用的、实际的

Notes

  Redbrick Universities—The term "red brick" or "redbrick" was first coined by a professor of Spanish at the University of Liverpool to describe six civic universities founded in the major industrial cities of England. His reference was inspired by the fact that The Victoria Building at the University of Liverpool was built from a distinctive red pressed brick. Nowadays, the term is used more broadly to refer to British universities founded in the late 19th and early 20th centuries in major cities. All of the six original redbrick institutions gained university status before WWI.

Unit Thirteen British Education

Eton—Eton College, often informally referred to simply as Eton, is an English single-sex boys' independent boarding school located in Eton, Berkshire, near Windsor. Founded in 1440 by King Henry VI, Eton is one of nine English independent schools, commonly referred to as public schools, included in the original Public Schools Act 1868. It educates over 1,300 pupils, aged 13 to 18 years.

Harrow—Harrow School, commonly referred to as "Harrow", is an English independent school for boys situated in the town of Harrow in north-west London. There is some evidence that there has been a school on the site since 1243, but the Harrow School of today was formally founded in 1572 by John Lyon under a Royal Charter of Elizabeth I. Harrow is one of the original nine public schools that were regulated by the Public Schools Act 1868. The School has an enrolment of 814 boys spread across twelve boarding houses, all of whom board full-time.

Winchester—Winchester College is an independent school for boys in the British public school tradition, situated in Winchester, Hampshire, England. It has existed in its present location for over 600 years and claims the longest unbroken history of any school in England. It is the oldest of the original nine English public schools defined by the Public Schools Act 1868, and is one of four remaining full boarding independent schools, meaning all pupils are boarders, in the United Kingdom.

Stonyhurst—Stonyhurst College is a coeducational Roman Catholic independent school, adhering to the Jesuit tradition. It is located near the village of Hurst Green in the Ribble Valley area of Lancashire, England. Founded in 1593, the school has been fully co-educational since 1999, providing currently boarding and day education to approximately 450 boys and girls aged 13—18. Under the motto *Quant Je Puis*, "All that I can", the school combines an academic curriculum with extra-curricular pursuits. Roman Catholicism plays a central role in college life, with emphasis on both prayer and service in an effort to create "Men and Women for Others".

Desmond Tutu—(born 7 October 1931) is a South African social rights activist and retired Anglican bishop who rose to worldwide fame during the 1980s as an opponent of apartheid. Admirers see him as a man who since the demise of apartheid has been active in the defense of human rights and uses his high profile to campaign for the oppressed. He received the Nobel Peace Prize in 1984; the Albert Schweitzer Prize for Humanitarianism in 1986; the Pacem in Terris Award in 1987; the Sydney Peace Prize in 1999; the Gandhi Peace Prize in 2007; and the Presidential Medal of Freedom in 2009.

Specialist schools—are state secondary schools that aim to be local centers of excellence in their chosen specialism, encouraging secondary schools in England to specialize in certain areas of the curriculum to boost achievement.

Specialist colleges—They are a small but important part of the Further Education and skills sector in Britain, known as a person-centered education, educating young people between the ages of 19 and 25 who have learning difficulties and/or disabilities.

Exercises

Ⅰ. **Multiple Choices**

The following are questions or incomplete sentences. Below each question or sentence four possible answers marked A, B, C and D are provided. Choose the ONE that best completes the sentence or answers the question.

1. The University of Oxford was founded in _____, followed by the University of Cambridge in _____.

    A. 1249/1284   B. 1248/1249   C. 1249/1294   D. 1248/1284

2. Charity schools invoked the name "public school" to indicate that they were open to the public regardless of _____.

    A. political beliefs   B. social beliefs

    C. educational beliefs   D. religious beliefs

3. British education has been ranked among the world's best on the ground of its renowned _____.

    A. long history, classic study, and English language

    B. scientific research, literature program, and outstanding faculty

    C. education quality, the quality of its graduates, and scientific research

    D. the number of Nobel Prize winners, long history, and creative teaching methods

4. Full-time education is compulsory for all children in the UK between ages _____.

    A. five and fifteen   B. six and sixteen

    C. five and sixteen   D. six and seventh

5. Among the main state schools in Britain, the most prestigious ones are _____.

    A. technical schools

    B. grammar schools

    C. modern schools

D. schools in hospitals or youth custody centers

6. Though grammar schools still exist in some regions in Britain, nowadays about _____ of children attend _____.

A. 90%/technical schools
B. 90%/modern schools
C. 90%/vocational schools
D. 90%/comprehensives

7. "Prep schools" in Britain are designed to prepare children for _____.

A. university education
B. professional education
C. special education
D. secondary education

8. In Britain, public schools are _____.

A. state-funded
B. government-sponsored
C. private-run
D. public-owned

9. Public schools in Britain are largely for all the following, except _____.

A. children from affluent families
B. children with gifts but without means
C. children from the royal family
D. children whose parents have an "Old School Tie"

10. In the past, the _____ Party always made a great fuss about abolishing the public schools.

A. Conservative   B. Green   C. Liberty   D. Labor

Ⅱ. True and False

Read the following statements carefully and then decide whether they are True or False. Put a "T" if you think the statement is true and an "F" if it is not.

1. The history of education in England can be traced back to the Anglo-Saxons' occupation.

2. Under the present law in Great Britain, the school leaving age is 18.

3. In comparison with primary and secondary education, university education in Great Britain is less contentious for the general public.

4. There are more universities in England that those combined in Scotland, Wales, and Northern Ireland.

5. Other old universities such as Durham and St Andrews are distinguished from the so-called "Redbrick" universities in that they place emphasis on traditional subjects.

6. The University for Industry is a public institution that offers basic and technological skills, 90 percent of which are taught online.

7. Further or continuing education in Britain is also known as post-college education.

8. In general, British universities do not take extra-curriculum activities into serious consideration when determining admission of new students.

9. At a British university, an English literature major will study nothing other than English literature during his/her three or four years of undergraduate career.

10. On their final year of courses at university, British students only have to submit a dissertation to earn their degrees.

Ⅲ. General Questions

1. What will those who excel both in dissertation and exams receive upon graduation?

2. What happened to British polytechnics more than twenty years ago?

3. Why do British working-class children find it increasingly difficult to attend university?

4. What is the key determiner of one's opportunity to attend university in Britain?

5. What are some of the major changes in British educational system over the past several decades?

6. What happened to British education when the Labor Party came into power in the late 1990s?

7. What is meant by a "one size fits all" approach in school education in Britain?

8. How do the British view education?

9. What are British parents concerned with when choosing a school for their children?

10. What has the British government done recently in response to school children feeling bored by the GCSEs they are doing?

Ⅳ. Essay Questions

1. Why do we say that the independent school sector is disproportionately important in British life?

2. What are the main features of the Education Reform Act 1988?

Unit Thirteen British Education

Reference Answers

Ⅰ. Multiple Choices

1. A 2. D 3. C 4. C 5. B 6. D 7. D 8. C 9. B 10. D

Ⅱ. True and False

1. F 2. F 3. T 4. T 5. T 6. F 7. F 8. T 9. T 10. F

Ⅲ. General Questions

1. They will receive a first-class degree upon graduation.

2. They were absorbed into the university system.

3. Because tuition fees charged by most of British universities have risen over the course of fifteen years from virtually nothing to £9,000 a year.

4. The key determiner is the class one happens to be born into.

5. Over the past several decades, some of the major changes in British educational system include the imposition of a national curriculum, the introduction of pre-GCSE examinations, and the publication of league tables of schools' performances.

6. After the Labor Party came into power in the late 1990s, attention was shifted from the former comprehensive system to caring for each child's ability. Not only was a higher percentage of GDP spent on education, but also more specialist schools were created.

7. By a "one size fits all" approach, it means that all schools should be more child-centered. Specifically speaking, it means that children should be allowed to proceed at their own pace in response to teaching tailored towards them individually.

8. To Britons, education is not just about the delivery of syllabus. And primary schools in particular are believed to be the sites for the transmission from one generation to the next of shared culture.

9. In choosing a school for their children, British parents are concerned with such things as potential academic progress, the prevalence of bullying, the development of life skills and the kind of social, cultural and spiritual experience offered by the school.

10. In response to school children feeling bored by the GCSEs they are doing, the British government has encouraged a shift from education to training, in an attempt to enable the students to embark on apprenticeships two days a week at 14 years of age.

IV. Essay Questions

1. The independent school sector is disproportionately important in British life for a variety of reasons. First, although only 7 percent of British children attend independent schools, their alumni figure much more significantly as entrants to the universities, particularly Oxbridge (Oxford and Cambridge). Secondly, once they graduate from university, they figure prominently in the higher echelons of British society. For instance, both the Prime Minister David Cameron and the Mayor of London Boris Johnson both went to Eton and Oxford.

2. The Education Reform Act 1988 has several features. First, the introduction of a national curriculum for pupils aged 5-16, according to which the responsibility of deciding what to teach would be shifted from individual teachers to the central government. Second, the establishment of compulsory national tests, whose results would be published annually to allow schools to compete for pupils and to be compared directly with one another. Third, considerable freedom and flexibility in management would be given to individual schools to run their own budgets. Fourth, a new type of school, city technology college, would be set up in inner city areas, offering courses in the fields of technology, the arts, mathematics and sciences. Fifth, a series of standards in education would be set up to ensure a greater degree of uniformity in education quality.

Unit Fourteen The British Family

Focal Points

extended family   nuclear family step family   blended family cohabitation
marriage relationship   traditional family   modern family
hands-on fathers   child centric

Discussion Questions

In what way(s) does the traditional family differ from the modern family in Great Britain?

Text

As the basic component of society, the family holds special importance in different cultures across the world, reflecting the ethical values of a society, its cultural characteristics as well as the unique features of a particular nation. This is true of all countries, including Great Britain. Throughout British history, many reforms have been made in the form of legislation concerning sexual discrimination, abortion, divorce and sexual practice, which have affected, and in turn been affected by, social attitudes and cultural activities. Indeed, as a central institution of modern British society, the family often serves as a **barometer** of social and cultural changes of Great Britain.

barometer 晴雨表、变化的标志

The Changing Family

There are a variety of family patterns in modern Britain. Until the mid-twentieth century, the dominant form of family structure was extended rather than nuclear, with parents and even grandparents, uncles and aunts living **in close proximity to** their grown-up children. Due to the increased geographical and social mobility of the population, this often romanticized family unit has gradually disappeared and is now found mainly in **soap operas** based in traditional working-class communities, although there is some indication that rising house prices and childcare costs are reintroducing some aspects of extended family, as many young people cannot afford to buy **property** until they have worked for a considerable number of years. Couples with young children struggle to afford childcare, and many adults are becoming increasingly dependent on their relatively prosperous '**baby boomer**' parents for **accommodation** in young adulthood for free childcare when they start their own families. **Ethnicity** is also an important factor in **accounting for** different British family structures. For example, many Vietnamese and Bengali families **retain** an extended family structure, while a higher than average **proportion** of Afro-Caribbean families are mother-led.

Traditionally, a typical British family usually was made of a young happily-married couple, neither of whom had been married before, in their mid-thirties, and had two or three children. The husband worked full-time as the bread-winner; while the wife worked as the housekeeper. However, the popular image of a British family has changed. Perhaps one of the most significant shifts over the last thirty years has been in attitudes towards marriage, which, though still popular (around 75 per cent of people marry at least once), is less so than at any previous time in British history. According to the Office of National Statistics there were a total of 231,490 marriages in 2009 (the lowest total since 1895), down from 232,990 in 2008,

in close proximity to 在附近

soap opera 肥皂剧

property 地产、房地产

baby boomer 生育高峰期出生的人
accommodation 住宿
ethnicity 族裔
account for 对……做出解释
retain 保留、保持
proportion 部分、比例

continuing a downward trend since the peak of 426,241 in England and Wales in 1972. The decline in registered marriage has also been mirrored in increases in marital breakdown over the last few decades. Although divorce figures in Britain have fallen slightly every year since 2003, UK divorce rates still rank among the highest in Europe. Take 2009 for example, divorces per thousand marriages were at an average figure of 10.5.

As a result of these changes, the number of single parent families (90 percent of which are headed by women) has risen significantly, comprising in 2009 one in four of all family units. In a long line of perceived threats to the fabric of British life, such a dramatic increase in single parent family is believed to have generated the latest and the most worrisome one. It is feared by some social observers that this number is likely to go up as childbirth out of wedlock rises. Besides, the percentage of new mothers aged under 20 (over 26 per 1,000 women in England and Wales in 2010) has also given risen to concern, causing many sociologists to warn a sharp increase in the number of teen-age mothers in Great Britain.

Additionally, while the average **lifespan** has increased in the UK, the British **fertility rate**—the expected number of children born per woman in her child-bearing years—has been steadily declining since the **population boom** of the immediate post-war years. A higher number of couples do not have children and those that do generally have smaller families. There are mainly three reasons for Britain's declining fertility rate. First of all, improvements in female education and career prospects tend to discourage women from having more than one or two babies. According to the most recent statistics, the average age of a first-time mother in Britain is now 29, and 32 for first-time fathers. The majority of British women now work outside of the home both before and after having children, regardless of **marital status**. Secondly, compared with the past when there were higher **mortality rates** and children were much needed to

---

lifespan 寿命、预期生命期
fertility rate 生育率

population boom 人口激增

marital status 婚姻状况
mortality rate 死亡率

work the land for the family, there is far less social pressure for women to have children in today's Britain. Thirdly, having a child in Britain nowadays has become an expensive thing. To feed, clothe, house, educate and take care of the health of a child is now **a major financial commitment**. Consequently, the traditional twentieth-century average British family with 2.4 children has now **dwindled** to 1.8: a trend which reflects the overall decline in the proportion of 'conventional' family units. The number of British households which fall into the 'two adults plus dependent children' nuclear model is only around 36 per cent and this figure includes not only married couples, but an increasing number of long-term **cohabitees**.

Since the Industrial Revolution, rapidly changing employment patterns coupled with **demographic** and social movements have challenged the beliefs, laws and customs **governing** notions of family. Such challenges, on the one hand, were the results of progressive social movements like labor and feminist movements. On the other hand, they came in the form of protective legislation, such as the 1848 Factory Act, which, by limiting women and children to a ten-hour working day, countered the exploitation of women workers in the newly developing manufacturing industries to ensure their **allegiance to** motherhood and wifely duties. During the past forty years, however, 'permissive' legislation such as the legalization of abortion, the introduction of the **no-fault divorce** and the **decriminalization** of homosexuality has **reversed** this trend, reflecting the higher **priority** awarded to personal choice and freedom **as opposed to** public morality and duty.

However, the relatively low proportion of 'normal' or 'typical' British families does not indicate the loss of the symbolic or ideological importance of the conventional family unit, which, despite its minority status, still remains extremely strong. Of all families in Great Britain, the British royal family certainly stands out as the symbol of the ideal British family,

---

a major financial commitment 一大笔财经投入

dwindle 逐渐减少

cohabitee (未婚) 同居者

demographic 人口的
govern 制约、支配

allegiance to 忠诚于

no-fault divorce 无过错离婚
decriminalization 使（原先非法的）合法化
reverse 逆转、倒转
priority 优先
as opposed to 相比较于

though it is more of a **cosmopolitan dynasty** than a **cosy** nuclear group. Even today, the Queen is sometimes referred to as 'the mother of the commonwealth'. Indeed, the ideological importance of the royal family **goes a long way towards explaining** why the wedding of Prince William to the **commoner** Kate Middleton in 2011 was not only socially significant for many people, but symbolically important for the status of marriage—the two-parent, patriarchal family continues to be regarded by many Britons as the most important of all social institutions, **bearing the brunt of responsibility** for producing well-adjusted, **law-abiding** citizens.

Marriage Relationship

Until the mid-twentieth century, it was considered normal for women and men to inhabit quite different worlds in terms of both work and social activities. The different activities and responsibilities of husband and wife are called **conjugal** roles, which can be divided into two general categories: joint and segregated ones. Since the 1950s, the division line separating the husband's world from that of the wife has become increasingly **blurred**, leading to not only a greater sharing of household tasks and decision making between the husband and the wife, but also more and more women participating in public life.

Traditional Family

Traditional marriage **imposed** an **obligation** of the wife to be **obedient to** her husband and an obligation of the husband to provide material/financial support for the wife. In early modern Britain, the legal and social status of the couple was unequal. Take property and **inheritance** rights for example. When a woman got married, all her property (called "fortune") and expected inheritances belonged to her husband.

After the Industrial Revolution, people in Britain moved to towns and cities in great numbers, where men worked in factories. Owing to the ban on children's working in factories, women had to stay at home and look after them, thereby starting to play the role of housewife. At that time, there was a clear-cut division of labor between the husband and the wife in the household. In the view of **feminism**, such opposite-sex marriage **rooted in patriarchy** promotes male superiority and power over women, with men **labeled as** "the providers operating in the public sphere" and women as "the caregivers operating within the private sphere". However, feminist demands for a wife's control over her own property were not fully met in Britain until laws were passed in the late 19th century, and their demands for women's participation in the public sphere were not seriously addressed until the early 20th century.

Modern Family

With increased opportunities for women's education and employment, female aspirations have been raised. Meanwhile, there has also occurred greater acceptance of the idea that married women, even mothers, might choose to work because they wish to be financially independent or seek to contribute to society and find fulfillment in activities that aren't confined to the traditional feminine sphere of home and family. Furthermore, modern social developments, particularly **accelerated** process of industrialization and urbanization, together with the greater **mobility** made possible by modern **means of transport**, have introduced very radical changes into the family life.

Such changes have in many ways brought improvement into the conditions, character and conduct of family life. For one thing, these changes have led to the improvement of social standards. The rise in status of the young wife and of children is, for instance, one of the great transformations of modern time. For another, these changes have produced significant influence on a better **conception** of marriage—one that emphasizes the husband-wife **bond**. Sociologists label such marriage as partnership marriage, in which both power and household work are shared between the **spouses**. In other words, in modern

British families, major decisions are discussed and made jointly, while household chores, though still not equally shared between men and women, are nevertheless performed by both men and women. With women on more equal **footing** with men, such **marriage pattern** now seems to be spreading throughout British society.

Along with changes in husband-and-wife relationship, families in Britain are now generally smaller than they were. Rather than having three generations living under the same roof or close to each other, more families are separately housed. More importantly, improved standards of living and better **provision** for physical and material needs have introduced into family life a new degree of security. Husbands not only do more to aid their wives in emergencies; they also spend less on themselves and more on their families. Also, for the first time in modern British history, the working-class home, as well as the middle class home, has become a pleasant place to live in: it is warm, comfortable, and able to provide its own **fireside entertainment**. Perhaps more significantly, the modern husband spends his evenings and his weekends not with his workmates but at home with his family, enjoying common fireside relaxations with them, or else "**pottering**" round the house maintaining or improving its comfort and physical appearance.

All of this indicates that married and family life has improved dramatically in Great Britain, and seems to promise even a brighter future. However, it should to be pointed out that although the majority of women in Britain now work outside of the home, their **engagement in** workforce is still **disapproved of** by many, who accuse them of **greedily** wanting to 'have it all' rather than choosing between a career and a family. More significantly, as women have to work better than men in order to be successful at work, and as women still have to do most of the household chores at home, British women are apparently far from being equal to men.

Parenting

It is generally believed that family really starts to become an **all-consuming** affair with the arrival of children. Children, of course, have always been the pride and joy of their parents. But never before were they put at the very center of family life in Britain. In traditional families, children were supposed to be raised to be "seen and not heard". Many parents, perhaps **despairing of** their children's rebelliousness, tended to be very strict with their children, who, as a result, usually held an **unspoken** respect for their parents, never guestioning anything. At that time, children were certainly not at the top of the family **pecking order**. Yet by the end of the twentieth century, a **domestic revolution** seemed to be **brewing** and many of the British families had **turned the family hierarch on its head**. By the last decade of the 20th century, children had become the main focus of British family's hopes and fears, the decade in which children came to dominate every aspect of British family lives Just like Chinese parents, parents in Britain are becoming increasingly **child centric**.

What has brought all these changes? And, what does it mean to British families?

First and foremost, there has been a rejection of the often harsh **child-rearing** methods favored in the UK a century ago. Secondly, more and more attention (perhaps too much) has been given to children. Indeed, for quite a few years, **emotional and physical wellbeing** of children has been a constant source of political and media concern in Great Britain. A recently published study has shown that back in 1975, children spent **on average** about 25 minutes a day being **cared for** by their parents because **well into the 1970s** most mothers were still housewives. Wash, cook, clean was their daily routine. By 2001, however, that figure had risen to 99 minutes a day. In today's new domestic order, time with kids is meant to be quality time,

---

all-consuming 令人全神贯注的、令人废寝忘食的

despair of 对…绝望

unspoken 缄默的、无言的

pecking order 权势等级
domestic revolution 家庭革命
brew 酝酿
turn the family hierarch on its head 把家庭等级秩序颠倒过来

child centric 以孩子为中心的

child-rearing 养育孩子

emotional and physical wellbeing 身心健康

on average 平均
care for 照顾
well into the 1970s 进入70年代一段时间后

and the parents have surrendered to their children much more power.

Despite all this, a **UNICEF** survey in 2011 found British children to be the least happy in the developed world. This was largely related to the economic pressures placed on parents and the culture of long working hours in the UK. Additionally, in the past, childhood in Britain as well as in many other countries in the world was an adventure where children could discover their independence by doing things of their own choice and carrying them out all alone by themselves. But today, even the simplest freedoms, such as those things that children of the previous generation took for granted, have been **throttled** in this safety-first culture. For instance, in the early 1970s, eight out of ten children aged seven or eight used to walk to school on their own. But that is a figure that has altered dramatically. Now, for school kids aged 11, only 50% of them are allowed to walk to school alone. Apparently, such a trend towards '**micromanaging**' children's lives, with little independent outdoor play and much pressure on parents to provide a full program of **extra-curricular exercises**, together with the **disintegration** of the extended family, also seems a likely causal factor for the unhappiness of British children.

In recent years, the structure of the typical British family has been undergoing some dramatic changes. In 21st-century Britain, starting a family, for most of the people, has now become a choice rather than an obligation. Recently, this choice has been extended to gay couples, too. It seems that more same sex couples are becoming parents, though the numbers are still very small. Also **noteworthy** is the fact that it wasn't so long ago that almost every child was brought up by married mummy and daddy, and this little **idyll** dominated popular culture at every age. However, the hard reality of today is: over a third of children in England and Wales are not being brought up by their married parents. It is estimated that these days, at least 10% of all British children are part of **a step family**, or **a blended family**. While the end of one relationship doesn't necessarily mean the end of a family life, it's equally clear that these families **are far from** smooth and, for the children, often the situation is very difficult to **swallow**. Today about 30% of all 15-year-olds of single or separated parents have lost contact with their biological father.

Ironically, while single mothers are **stereotyped** in a number of **unflattering** ways, the few men who take the primary care of their children are regarded with intense admiration. On the whole, fathers today are far more **hands-on** than their dads ever were. For most of the twentieth century, Britons at least had the comfort of knowing who did what. In the past, marriage for most people meant **commuter husbands** travelling to work every day, while the wives stayed at home to look after the children, the housework and the social life. Now, being an enthusiastic hands-on dad has become **the norm**, and sharing the job of bringing up the kids really matters. It's only since 2003 that all new fathers in Britain have had the right in law to two weeks' paid time off. These days, **juggling a family and a career** isn't just something that worries women; the public has higher expectations of fatherhood as well.

a blended family 混合性家庭
be far from 远不
swallow 忍受

ironically 具有讽刺意味的
stereotyped 被有成见地描述
unflattering 出丑的、不恭敬的
hands-on 亲身实践的、亲身动手的
commuter husband 往返两地工作的丈夫
the norm 常态

juggle a family and a career 既照管家庭又发展事业

Notes

The Office of National Statistics(ONS)—is the executive office of the UK Statistics Authority, a non-ministerial department which reports directly to the Parliament of the United Kingdom. It is charged with the collection and publication of statistics related to the economy, population and society of England and Wales at national, regional and local levels.

UNICEF—The United Nations Children's Fund (UNICEF;) is a United Nations Program headquartered in New York City that provides long-term humanitarian and developmental assistance to children and mothers in developing countries. It is one of the members of the United Nations Development Group and its Executive Committee.

UNICEF was created by the United Nations General Assembly on December 11, 1946, to provide emergency food and healthcare to children in countries that had been devastated by World War II.

Exercises

I. Multiple Choices

The following are questions or incomplete sentences. Below each question or sentence four possible answers marked A, B, C and D are provided. Choose the ONE that best completes the sentence or answers the question.

1. The family in Great Britain often serves as a _____ of social and cultural changes.

　　A. direction　　　　B. barometer　　　　C. prediction　　　　D. yardstick

2. Until _____, the dominant form of family structure in Great Britain was extended rather than nuclear, with parents and even grandparents, uncles and aunts living in close proximity to their grown-up children.

　　A. the early twentieth century　　　　B. the late twentieth

　　C. the mid-twentieth century　　　　D. the late nineteenth century

3. Some aspects of extended family are coming back in Britain, because _____.

　　A. the British miss extended family lifestyle

　　B. the British find the nuclear family too boring

　　C. the British want to recover their traditional family values

　　D. many young Britons are not able to buy property or pay childcare when they get married

4. In a typical traditional British family, family members were usually composed of _____.

　　A. husband, wife, three or four children

　　B. grandparents, husband, wife, two or three children

　　C. husband, wife, two or three children

　　D. aunts or uncles, husband, wife, one or two children

5. In present-day Britain, the number of single parent families has risen significantly, comprising in 2009 _____ of all family units.

　　A. one in two　　　　　　　　　　B. one in three

　　C. one in four　　　　　　　　　　D. on in five

6. A higher number of couples _____ and those that do generally have _____.

A. have few children/ smaller families

B. have no children/larger families

C. have no children/bigger families

D. have no children/smaller families

7. The 1848 Factory Act, by limiting women to a ten-hour working day, was designed to _____.

A. help women keep fit

B. protect women from overwork

C. make sure that women would have enough time left to perform their motherly and wifely duties.

D. maintain efficiency in their work

8. _____, the symbolic or ideological importance of the conventional family unit in Britain still remains extremely strong.

A. Despite its minority status

B. As more and more Britons marry young

C. Although family in Britain now comes in many forms

D. In spite of the strong influence of modern marriage

9. The British Queen is sometimes referred to as "_____".

A. the mother of England

B. the mother of Scotland

C. the mother of Wales

D. the mother of the commonwealth

10. The two-parent, patriarchal family continues to be regarded by many Britons as _____.

A. the least important of all social institutions

B. the most necessary of all social institutions

C. the least necessary of all social institutions

D. the most important of all social institutions

Ⅱ. True and False

Read the following statements carefully and then decide whether they are True or False. Put a "T" if you think the statement is true and an "F" if it is not.

1. Great Britain enjoyed population boom in the immediate years of post-WWI.

Unit Fourteen   The British Family

2. In Great Britain, it was not until the mid-twentieth century that the notion that men and women should live in different worlds in terms of work and public activities was challenged.

3. Since the 1950s, a growing number of British women have found themselves in the workforce.

4. In early modern Britain, women were equal to men in their legal and social status.

5. According to the passage, it was not until the Industrial Revolution when men began to work in factories that women in Britain started to play the role of housewife.

6. To the feminist, when men were labeled as "the providers operating in the public sphere" and women as "the caregivers operating within the private sphere," women were already put in an inferior and subordinate position.

7. Although opportunities for women's education and employment have become more and more abundant, most British women have no aspirations to work outside of the home to achieve economic independence for themselves.

8. In modern British families, household chores are equally shared between men and women.

9. Generally speaking, families in Britain nowadays have become not only smaller, but also more secure.

10. Regardless of all the changes in modern families, the husband still tends to spend most of his evenings and weekends with his workmates rather than with his family members.

General questions

1. What changes are there in the British attitude toward marriage?
2. What is the general view of the British on family and children?
3. How were children viewed in British traditional families?
4. What does "domestic revolution" in this passage mean?
5. What was the daily routine of most of the British women before the 1970s?
6. What did the UNICEF survey of 2011 find about British children?
7. What does family mean to Britons in the 21st century?
8. Among other things, what do same sex couples want?
9. How many British children are now growing up in step or blended families?
10. How about being a father nowadays in Great Britain?

Ⅳ. Essay Questions

1. What could be the possible reasons for the declining fertility rate in Britain?

2. Why is it that British children still feel the least happy in the developed world when they have already become the main focus of their families?

Reference Answers

Ⅰ. Multiple Choice

1. B   2. C   3. D   4. C   5. C   6. D   7. C   8. A   9. D   10. D

Ⅱ. True and False

1. F   2. T   3. T   4. F   5. T   6. T   7. F   8. F   9. T   10. F

Ⅲ. General Questions

1. There are many changes in the British attitude toward marriage. For one thing, there has been a continuous decline in registered marriage in recent years. For another, there has been a steady increase in marital breakdown over the last few decades. For still another, single-parent families are now growing in number. Beyond all this, there are more and more long-term cohabitees in Britain.

2. It is generally believed that family really starts to become an all-consuming affair with the arrival of children.

3. In British traditional families, children were supposed to be raised to be "seen and not heard".

4. In this passage, "domestic revolution" largely refers to the change of children's position in the British family, i. e., from "to be seen and not heard" to the main focus of the family.

5. Wash, cook, clean was the daily routine of most of the British women before the 1970s. .

6. The UNICEF survey of 2011 found British children to be the least happy in the developed world.

7. In the 21st century, starting a family, for most of the British, has become a choice rather than an obligation.

8. Same sex couples in Britain want to be parents as well.

9. It is estimated that at least 10% of all British children are now part of a step

family, or a blended family.

10. Being a father in Britain nowadays means that he needs to be far more hands-on than his dad ever was.

IV. Essay Questions

1. There are mainly three reasons for Britain's declining fertility rate. First of all, improvements in female education and career prospects tend to discourage women from having more than one or two babies. Secondly, compared with the past when there were higher mortality rates and children were much needed to work the land for the family, there is far less social pressure for women to have children in today's Britain. Thirdly, having a child in Britain nowadays has become an expensive thing. To feed, clothe, house, educate and take care of the health of a child is now a major financial commitment. Consequently, the traditional twentieth-century average British family with 2.4 children has now dwindled to 1.8, a trend which reflects the overall decline in the proportion of 'conventional' family units.

2. According to a UNICEF survey in 2011, British children felt the least happy in the developed world. This was, first of all, related to the economic pressures placed on parents and the culture of long working hours in the UK. Secondly, in the past, childhood in Britain was an adventure where children could discover their independence by doing things in their own way and out of their own choice. But today, everything they do is under their parents' close watch. As a result, many of the simplest freedoms, such as walking to school by themselves, have been lost in this safety-first culture. Furthermore, British parents are under a lot of pressure to provide a full program of extra-curricular exercises for their children, leaving them little time to do what they really want to do themselves. Finally, the disintegration of the extended family also contributes to the unhappiness of British children.

Unit Fifteen   Leisure Life in Britain

Focal Points

leisure life	television	gentleman vs. player
pub culture	pantomime	personal and group identity
weekend life	vacation	National Lottery

Discussion Questions

What can we learn about Britons from their leisure life?

Text

British people enjoy various kinds of entertainment activities and they now have more free time and holidays than they did twenty years ago. They work the longest hours in Western Europe and attempt to express their real selves through leisure activities, both in private space of home and outside it. For example, they love to spend weekends together with the family, visiting relatives and friends, dining out at a **fancy** restaurant, watching a drama or doing shopping. Most British people enjoy traveling during their longer holidays. They love to visit warmer places due to lack of sunshine in their own country.

In dealing with leisure we are concerned not just with how people occupy themselves but with the cultural significance of their hobbies and practices. This applies to group and individual activities. The leisure pursuits British people engage in can be divided into private and public. These are **crude designations**,

fancy 价格昂贵的

crude 粗略的；简略的
designation 标示、说明

but they do offer a way into understanding how leisure affects cultural consciousness and identity.

Leisure around the Home

Television

The dominant **medium** for cultural exchange in Britain is television, though for teenagers the Web is **taking over**. It is difficult to **pinpoint** the moment at which TV became a significant part of the national cultural consciousness, but many oral histories of older people refer to the **novelty** of watching the June 1953 **Coronation** of Queen Elizabeth II on TV. This they did **in company with** friends, relatives and neighbors. Particularly since the 1960s, daily consumption of TV has risen as broadcasting expanded from evenings only, to daytime, and even to the mornings. TV watching is now available 24 hours a day, especially with numerous **cable and satellite stations**. The average time spent watching TV is more than three hours a day. The young and the old watch more, and the middle-aged a lot less.

Television's place is very much in the home. So, for example, when pubs introduced large-screen TVs for specific sports events in order to attract more customers, their success was limited, because pubs are places more for social interaction than for "watching the box". Many people prefer to go out and attend football matches than watch them on television.

However, in a country with all sorts of signs of social breakdown, from child murder and **random** knife attacks in the cities to rural suicides and **abduction**, it is electronic expressions of community that people **cling to**. They watch their own society through TV dramas which offer excitement **set in** an everyday context, or soap operas which invoke an idealized rural past. Characters in these programs supply viewers with topics of conversation which provide the potential **glue** for their own social community.

In a word, TV is a powerful social **adhesive** in Britain. Following stories on TV provides people with topics of conversation, allows them to get to know one another's tastes and preferences, and enables them to explore the current social and cultural **preoccupations** that TV directs them towards. Workmates and friends are bonded together by their responses to the news, sitcoms, dramas or soaps that they have seen on TV.

Hobby

Besides television and the ever-growing use of the Internet, the major leisure activity of many British people is their hobby. The hobbies or minority interests pursued by Britons are numerous, wide-ranging and passionately **indulged in**. They are part of the people's identities. Such minority activities include **philately**, **train-spotting**, **ferret-keeping**, fishing, bird-watching, **scouting**, swimming, cycling, **fell-running**—just counting along **a scale of physical activity**. Most of these hobbies will have magazines to accompany them, or at the very least a newsletter. The number of **browser**s in **high-street** newsagent evidences the range and diversity of Britain's leisure interests and perspectives.

Reading, and the Web

Reading of books has held up well. Book buying, ironically, is **stimulated** by television. For example, **Pride and Prejudice**(1813) sold many times more copies after their TV series than they ever did previously. E-readers may also stimulate the purchase of books. According to the statistics of 2008 National Year of Reading in the UK, the top five **reads** to impress a man are: Current affaires websites, Shakespeare, Song lyrics, Cookery books and Poetry; while the top five reads to impress a woman are: Nelson Mandela autobiography Long Walk to Freedom, Shakespeare, Cookery books, Poetry and Song lyrics. Apparently, the books people buy for themselves are divided along gender lines.

Of course much time previously devoted to reading is now

---

adhesive 黏合剂、粘着剂

preoccupation 全神贯注的事情

indulge in 沉溺于

philately 集邮
train-spotting(作为爱好的)记录机车的机车号码
ferret-keeping 养雪貂
scouting 侦察
fell-running 越野路跑
a scale of physical activity 一长串等级或范围不同的体育活动
browser 浏览者
high-street 市或镇主要商业街
stimulate 刺激
Pride and Prejudice《傲慢与偏见》
read 读物

spent, particularly by the young, on social networking. A survey conducted by UKOM (United Kingdom Online Measurement Company) reveals that the percentage of time spent online in April 2007 (536 million hours) had jumped to 884 million hours in April 2010. The Web is part of young people's **psyche**. Facebook, Twitter and Google+ are the current UK favorites. Such **virtual** "communities" are efficient and satisfying now. The future will decide whether people will miss social networking beyond the need for such tools mentioned above to stay in contact, or whether it will be their fellow participants they are missing.

Public Entertainment

Sport

Sport is part of mass culture, and an estimated 3 million people in Britain take part in some sort of sporting activity every week. Watching sport, listening to it and reading about it are also major leisure time activities. Throughout the nineteenth and into the twentieth century most sports were played by narrowly defined social groups. Horse racing and fox-hunting, for example, were the **preserve** of aristocrats and wealthy landowners, while the origins of football and **rugby** lie in the English public schools such as Eton and Harrow. But the latter half of the twentieth century saw a greater openness and democratization in British society, and many sports were transformed from the narrow preserve of affluent white males into a mass leisure and entertainment industry for urban consumers. Accordingly, women, black, Asian and disabled sportspeople have also risen sharply.

For many **spectators** sport is not just leisure—it is a way of expressing personal and group identity, through supporting a team, **chant**ing the club songs, wearing club colors and clothing, as well as bearing tattoos, face paint, flags and other **adornment**s. Habitual attendance and taking part in its rituals provide many fans with a sense of community, with the most

fanatical choosing to get married in their club's ground, and even to have their **ashes scattered** there.

The main sports practiced in Britain are rugby and football (soccer). Rugby is controlled by the Rugby Union, soccer by Football Association. The traditional division between lower-social-status professional soccer players (who need to be paid) and higher-social-status rugby players (gifted amateurs) has been **erode**d by the Union's decision in 1995 to relax its rules to allow professional rugby clubs. Soccer is known as "a gentlemen's game for **rough**s" and rugby as "a rough's" game for gentlemen". In other words, rugby is the great sport of the British middle-class, while football is for the working-class. One of the many **paradox**es of British society is that although most of the public (that is private) schools in Britain play the middle-class game of rugby as their main sport, both Eton and Harrow, Britain's most **prestigious** schools, still **field** more soccer than rugby teams.

In summer, the game of cricket is played widely on village greens, as well as the professional level and is a genuinely popular "**grassroots**" game. This game is about observance of rules, fairness and **a pitting of wits and talent** between equally matched teams. Again, there are class associations to all British sports and in the case of cricket, it is just about **cuts across class lines** and over the years **encounter**s have taken place between "gentlemen and players". This, again, **underlines** the British distinction between the upper classes (gentlemen), who are leisured and admirable, and the lower (players), who work and are **disparaged**.

There are many other outdoor sporting events in Britain, particularly in the summer, which attract national and international interest. However, although globalization has raised awareness of American sports in the UK, the local opinions are still colored by native comparisons. To most British people, for example, baseball looks to be grown men playing a **variant** of

---

fanatical 狂热的
ashes 骨灰
scatter 撒

erode 逐渐丧失、削弱

rough 粗野的

paradox 自相矛盾、有矛盾特点的情况

prestigious 受尊敬的、有声望的
field 使…出场、让…参加比赛
grassroots 基层群众、草根
a pitting of wits and talent 斗智、斗才
cut across class lines 穿越阶级界线、把……各个阶级界线之人群都包括在内
encounter 比赛
underline 表明、强调
disparage 轻视、贬低

variant 变体、变种

Unit Fifteen Leisure Life in Britain

the children's game **rounder**s (from which baseball is thought to de**scend**ed). Likewise, views on the manliness of basketball might be prejudiced by its similarity to the schoolgirls' game **netball**. Surprisingly, Britain is a country where **darts** is a televised professional sport with an actual following.

Impressionistically, the degree of health consciousness, fitness and **dietary** awareness is higher among the British young than the Americans. Most exercise takes place indoors for women and increasingly for men. Health and fitness clubs or gyms have become very popular throughout the country in recent years (**cynic**s say because they are dating agencies) and a large number of people regularly attend **aerobics** or step dance classes. In a study published by the Office for National Statistics, the following sports were most popular among the four-fifths of men: walking (48%), **snooker** (18%), cycling (15%), and swimming (13%).

Pubs

The **principal** place of entertainment outside the home that people automatically think of in relation to Britain is the public house, or "pub". The writings of Samuel Pepys describe the pub as the heart of England. It seems that the English think it rather **indecent** for people to drink alcoholic drinks in any place where they can be seen from outside; therefore, traditionally the windows of town pubs were of smoked or **frosted** glass but from the 1990s onwards, there has been a move towards clear glass, in keeping with brighter interior **décor**s.

Pubs often have interesting old names that in some way reflect their history. For example, the Tabard in Southwark, London, was mentioned by Chaucer in The Canterbury Tales six hundred years ago. Another example is Ye Olde Cheshire Cheese, in Fleet Street, London, a pub **frequented** by some England's **literary giants**, including Samuel Johnson, Oliver Goldsmith and Charles Dickens.

In the past, pubs performed different social functions. Tra-

---

rounder 圆场棒球
descend 起源、演变

netball 无挡板篮球（一种流行于英国等国家的女子篮球）
darts 掷镖游戏
dietary 饮食的

cynic 认为世人皆自私的人、愤世嫉俗者

snooker 彩色台球

indecent 不适当的、不得体的
frosted（玻璃）磨砂的、毛面的
décor 装修、装潢

frequent（客人）光顾
literary giant 文学巨匠

ditionally they were male preserve and seemed to be a more welcoming place for a man than his home. By the end of the 18th century, a new room in the pub was established: the saloon, which was more of a middle-class room—carpets on the floor, cushions on the seats, and expensive drinks; while the public bar remained working class with bare boards, hard bench seats, and cheap beer. Some city center pubs specified "men only" and many **covertly** discouraged single women. Today they are much more welcoming to people of both sexes. Many pubs today continue to be divided into public bar and **saloon bar**. There is sometimes a smaller room called a **"snug"**, a very private room with access to the bar that had a frosted glass **external** window, set above head height. A higher price was paid for beer in the snug and nobody could look in and see the drinkers. It was not only the wealthy visitors who would use these rooms. The snug was for **patron**s who preferred not to be seen in the public bar. Ladies would often enjoy a private drink in the snug at a time when it was **frowned upon** for women to be in a pub.

covert 隐蔽地、不公开地

saloon bar 雅座酒吧
snug 雅室
external 外面的、外部的

patron 顾客、老主顾

frown upon 不赞同、不悦

The minimum age for drinking alcohol in Britain is eighteen, and the minimum age for entering a public bar (for consuming nonalcoholic drinks) is fourteen, but only accompanied by an adult. The government continues to **review** licensing laws. **Publican**s are free to stay open all day and night if they wish. While Britons mostly drink beer, wine is increasingly drunk, though it normally goes with the food. Today, pubs are struggling with the percentage of men and women who never drink alcohol at 15 and 20 respectively. In 2009, 52 pubs a week were closing. According to the statistics, there were 48,000 pubs in 2013, compared to 67,800 in 1982 and 60,100 in 2002. This number has been declining every year, so that nearly half of the smaller villages no longer have a local pub. However, with the churches in Britain in decline, some pubs are finding a new role, filling the social **vacuum** created by religious decline and performing the function of community meeting place. In

review 检查、审查、审核

publican 酒馆老板

vacuum 空位、空缺、空白

short, they are still, in the new century, very much central to British life.

Cinema, Pantomimes and Theatre

Among "outside" entertainment, cinemas have been through periods of **boom and bust** in British social life. Cinema attendance in Britain reached its peak in 1946 with 1.6 billion cinema visits. It **bottom**ed in 1984 with 54 million. Over the last five years it has **plateau**ed above 150 million. There were more than 140 million cinema attendances in 2002, despite the competition of television. However, the majority of all cinema-going is still done by under 5% of the total population and the range of films **on offer** has not widened. So cinema attendance, as a cultural practice, has yet to regain its 1960s popularity, but its importance should not be **underestimate**d as a **cohesive** social force, particularly for young people.

Cinema appears to be **resilient** at the moment because it is a **communal** activity. The community wants to share collective entertainments, whether through street **carnival**, **clubbing**, or attendance at football matches. Cinema is a good **illustration** of such communal activity. **Iconic** popular films that have **coincided with** previous editions of their books are Harry Potter series and The Lord of the Rings series. All of these activities deal with **ceremonial** or **ritual** events or practices. They are about public shared experience and are chosen in their **recreation** time by people who view them not in "privacy" of the DVD or on the iPad, but in the collective experience of cinema. So, going out to the cinema is still a **staple** part of British life.

Pantomimes form an important aspect of British cultural experience especially during Christmas for children. Unknown on the Continent, they are staged in theatres, village halls and community centers of all sorts. The actors and actress can be either **amateur**s or professionals. In pantomimes, lively, colorful stories are told with music, singing and dancing. Fairy stories and **Oriental** tales are among the most common. Traditional titles such as **Aladdin**, **Cinderella** and **Snow White** are also often involved, where the badly treated individual gets justice and their rightful place in the world. Well-known TV **personalities** or even politicians often appear in them as guest stars. Parents attend with children and in a controlled dramatic environment pantomimes offer a "safe" form of initiation into the adult world.

Theatre, ballet and opera give Britain a high cultural **profile** particularly with overseas tourists, though they may remain minority pursuits in Britain. There are approximately 300 theatres in Britain, one-third of which are located in London. London **West End** theatre productions such as Andrew Lloyd Webber's Cats have always attracted a large number of tourists. In 2010 there were 14.1 million attendances at London theaters and they tend to be seen as "elitist". Indeed, theatre-goers usually are older, well-to-do people. However, plays are also performed in many different places. Settings vary from the **intimacy** of a small room above a village pub to the formality of London's Royal National Theater, whose company of actors and staff is among the most prestigious in the country. In addition, there are an estimated 1,300 youth theatres **catering for** 65,000 participants.

Holidays, Festivals and Museums

Leisure was originally the **preserve** of the upper classes. Only they had the time and money to do so. So when leisure became available to ordinary people through decreased working hours and paid annual leave, it gave social status to those benefiting from it. This soon changes, as catering for larger numbers of leisured people on a year round basis turned into an industry. Treatment of holiday-makers became more **systematic**, more professional, less **deferential** and less status-aware.

Whenever possible, Britons are more likely to spend their two-week annual holiday abroad. Of the tourist destinations, the British tend to **congregate** in places they used to own, such

---

Aladdin 阿拉丁
Snow White 白雪公主
personality 人物、名人

指引、传授

profile 格调

West End 西区

intimacy 亲密；密切

cater for 满足、接待

preserve 独享的活动

systematic 有系统的、有条不紊的
deferential 恭敬的
congregate 集合、聚集

as former colonies India, Australia, New Zealand and Barbados. The most popular overseas holiday destinations for Britons in 2009 and the numbers going to them were: Spain (10.7 million), France (8.9 million) and the US (2.7 million).

The summer is pop and rock festival season in Britain, and they have become a feature of youth culture. Glastonbury is the largest greenfield music festival in the world, and is famous not only for hosting the latest acts but also for putting on comedy, dance and theatre shows. In 2007 nearly 180,000 people attended, and there were over 700 acts on 80 stages. Additionally, art festivals take place annually in most large cities, and some smaller places even have their own opera festival.

Furthermore, British leisure time is also spent on visitation of such public institutions as museums and art galleries. In the past, such visits were mostly made by people of high culture society. Now, they have become places of **obligatory pilgrimage** for school children who in the course of their subsequent lives may never return.

New Patterns in Leisure

There is now a noticeable preference by young people for **inanimate** over animate source of entertainment. This is evident not just in the decline of such live arts as theatre or home pastimes like card playing or in the preference of nightclubs. **Technophiliac** "Generation X" often prefers things to people: cash machines to bank cashiers; computers to socializing; **cyber cafes** to coffee houses; virtual reality to reality. Nor do people just prefer TV and cinema to live entertainment. Within electronic media they prefer cartoons to "real" representations of people. Technology has proved that it can deliver "the real world", and yet people want less "real" images than are contained in traditional representation. For instance, they prefer their TV **adverts** to contain animated characters rather than real ones.

---

obligatory 义务的

pilgrimage 拜谒、人生的一段经历

inanimate 无生命的、无生气的

technophiliac 技术狂

cyber cafe 网吧

advert (英口) 广告

Another notable change in the pattern of Britons' leisure is a move away from socializing at home to frequenting public places of entertainment: "fun pubs", and **multiplex**es. There are regional variations, but generally the fact that British socializing took place in the pub or club made it difficult for new people to **integrate into** British society. Asians in particular preferred to socialize at home, and this **exacerbate**d cultural differences and separated people. In time, however, as in so many other aspects of cultural life referred to elsewhere, while young mainstream people adopted immigrants' practices, young people from minority backgrounds joined the move to socialize outside the home. So young people of all ethnic origins now tend to mix in places of public entertainment, while the older generation continues to opt for home entertainment, watching TV, DVD or surfing on the Internet.

Most recently, the National Lottery has become an important social and cultural phenomenon though Britain was the last country in Europe to introduce it (1994). Betting on the sport of the rich like horse racing has always been practiced by the working rather than the middle class. Many people, once a year, will place a bet on the Grand National or the Derby, but with the Lottery, everyone has a bet week by week. Online betting has become a major industry, with nine out of ten adults claiming to buy tickets on occasions. A lot of the criticism of the Lottery has been made, mostly based on the fear that one class will be **subsidiz**ing another's pleasures. What **irk**s many people is that winning the Lottery goes against their idea of "**natural justice**", as defined by middle classes, in terms of the work ethic. After all, to middle classes, there should be a clear distinction between "earned" and "unearned" money, but so far their complaints seem to **have fallen on deaf ears**.

multiplex（拥有6个或6个以上银幕的）多功能放映厅影院

integrate into 融入

exacerbate 使恶化、使加重

subsidiz 资助、补助

irk 使烦恼、激怒

natural justice 天然公平原则

fall on deaf ears 未被理睬

Unit Fifteen Leisure Life in Britain

Notes

Netball—In Britain and some other countries, netball is a game played by two teams of seven players, usually women. Each team tries to score goals by throwing a ball through a net on the top of a pole at each end of the court.

Nelson Mandela(1918—2013)— was a South African politician and activist. On April 27, 1994, he was made the first President of South Africa elected in a fully represented democratic election, as well as the first black President of his country.

Geoffrey Chaucer(1343—1400)—Known as the Father of English literature, Chaucer is widely considered the greatest English poet of the Middle Ages. Among his many works, which include *The Book of the Duchess*, The *House of Fame*, *The Legend of Good Women and Troilus and Criseyde*, he is best known today for *The Canterbury Tales*.

Ye Olde Cheshire Cheese—It is one of a number of pubs in London to have been rebuilt shortly after the Great Fire of 1666. There has been a pub at this location since 1538. This pub continues to attract interest due to the curious lack of natural lighting inside which generates its own gloomy charm.

Samuel Johnson (1709—1784)—Often referred to as Dr Johnson, Johnson was an English writer who made lasting contributions to English literature as a poet, essayist, moralist, literary critic, biographer, editor and lexicographer.

Oliver Goldsmith (1728—1774)—was an Anglo-Irish novelist, playwright and poet, who is best known for his novel *The Vicar Wakefield* (1766), his pastoral poem *The Deserted Village* (1770), and his plays *The Good-Natur'd Man* (1768) and *She Stoops to Conquer* (1771, first performed in 1773). He is thought to have written the classic children's tale *The History of Little Goody Two-Shoes*, the source of the phrase "goody two-shoes.

Charles John Huffam Dickens (1812—1870)—was an English writer and social critic. He created some of the world's best-known fictional characters and is regarded as the greatest novelist of the Victorian era. His works enjoyed unprecedented popularity during his lifetime, and by the twentieth century critics and scholars had recognized him as a literary genius. His novels and short stories enjoy lasting popularity. His masterpieces include: *A Christmas Carol*, *Oliver Twist*, *Great Expectations* and *A Tale of Two Cities*.

West End theatre—This is a common term for mainstream professional theatre staged in the large theatres of "Theatreland" in and near the West End of London. Along with New York's Broadway theatre, West End theatre is usually considered to represent the highest level of commercial theatre in the English-speaking world.

The Royal National Theatre(generally known as the National Theatre)—is one of the United Kingdom's three most prominent publicly funded performing arts venues in London, alongside the Royal Shakespeare Company and the Royal Opera House.

The Grand National—It is a National Hunt horse race held annually at Aintree Racecourse in Liverpool, England. It is the most valuable jump race in Europe, with a prize fund of £1 million in 2014.

Exercises

Ⅰ. Multiple Choices

The following are questions or incomplete sentences. Below each sentence or question four possible answers marked A, B, C and D are provided. Choose the ONE that best completes the sentence or answers the question.

1. _____ is the most important cultural exchange medium in Britain.
   A. television   B. radio   C. computer   D. cell-phone
2. Which of the following is NOT a popular sport in Britain?
   A. basketball   B. rugby   C. football   D. cricket
3. The minimum age for entering a public bar for consuming alcoholic drinks is _____.
   A. 14   B. 16   C. 17   D. 18
4. In Britain, rugby is the great sport of the British _____, while football is for the British _____.
   A. working-class/middle class   B. middle class/working class
   C. middle class/upper class   D. upper class/working class
5. Ye Olde Cheshire Cheese is a pub frequented in the past by some England's literary giants except _____.
   A. Geoffrey Chaucer   B. Samuel Johnson
   C. Oliver Goldsmith   D. Charles Dickens
6. Pantomimes constitute an important aspect of British cultural experience especially during Christmas for children.
   A. Thanksgiving Day   B. New Year's Day

C. Easter Day   D. Christmas

7. With the increasing openness and democratization in British society, many sports were transformed from being upper-class to something available to the majority of the population, including _____.

A. women and black sportspeople

B. black and disabled sportspeople

C. Asian and disabled sportspeople

D. Both A and C

8. According to a study published by the Office for National Statistics, the most popular sports among the four-fifths of British men are in the order of _____.

A. walking, snooker, cycling and swimming

B. walking, cycling, swimming and snooker

C. cycling, snooker, walking and swimming

D. swimming, walking, snooker and cycling

9. "Generation X" often prefers _____.

A. bank cashiers to cash machines

B. socializing to computers

C. coffee houses to cyber cafes

D. virtual reality to reality

10. Which of the following statements is NOT true about National Lottery?

A. Britain was the last country in Europe to introduce National Lottery.

B. Everyone has a bet every week.

C. National Lottery is an important social and cultural phenomenon in Britain.

D. The introduction of National Lottery is welcomed and praised by people from all walks of life in Britain.

Ⅱ. True and False

Read the following statements carefully and then decide whether they are true or false. Put a "T" if you think the statement is true and an "F" if it is not.

1. When pubs introduced large-screen TVs for specific sports events, it was a huge hit and attracted numerous customers.

2. Any hobby pursued by a Briton, no matter how minor it is, is accompanied by magazines.

3. Book buying in Britain is stimulated by television.

4. Much time previously devoted to reading is now spent, particularly by the young, on television.

5. Through supporting a team, a spectator can express his personal and group identity.

6. Traditionally, soccer players were of higher-social-status, while rugby players were looked down upon.

7. Cricket is largely a gentlemen's game.

8. The degree of health consciousness, fitness and dietary awareness is as high among the British young as among the Americans.

9. People patronized the snug because they preferred not to be seen in the public bar.

10. Visitation of museums and art galleries also consumes much of British leisure time, especially for school children.

Ⅲ. General Questions

1. Where are pantomimes staged?

2. What kind of stories are most pantomimes about? Name just a few.

3. What are the two major organized/spectator sports today in Britain?

4. Why aren't most British people fond of some American sports?

5. Why are there so many sports spectators in the UK?

6. According to the passage, how did British and Asian socialization differ from each?

7. Why is the number of pubs in Britain declining? Name one of the reasons.

8. Which sport do both Eton and Harrow field more? Rugby or soccer?

9. What kind of new role are some British pubs trying to play?

10. Where are Britons more likely to spend their two-week annual holiday abroad?

Ⅳ. Essay Questions

1. Television is the dominant medium for cultural exchange in Britain. Why?

2. Variations occur in the terminology used to describe people watching leisure entertainments. Those who watch soccer, rugby, cinema, TV, theatre or opera are known respectively as "crowds", "spectators", "audiences", "viewers" and "theatre-goers". Try to explain the implied cultural meanings of these terminologies.

Unit Fifteen Leisure Life in Britain

Reference Answers

Ⅰ. Multiple Choices

1. A   2. A   3. D   4. B   5. A   6. D   7. D   8. A   9. D   10. D

Ⅱ. True and False

1. F   2. F   3. T   4. F   5. T   6. F   7. F   8. F   9. T   10. T

Ⅲ. General Questions

1. Pantomimes are usually put on in theatres, village halls and community centers of all sorts.

2. Fairy stories and Oriental tales are among the most common, and traditional titles include *Aladdin*, *Cinderella* and *Snow White*.

3. The two major spectator sports in today's Britain are rugby and football (soccer).

4. To most British people, some of American sports are just not masculine enough. For example, baseball looks like grown men playing a variant of the children's game rounders, while basketball seems to be similar to the schoolgirls' game netball.

5. For many spectators sport is not just leisure—it is a way of expressing personal and group identity.

6. British socializing took place in the pub or club, but Asians tended to socialize at home.

7. The reason for the decline of pubs in number is manifold, one of which is the growing percentage of men and women who never drink alcohol at 15 and 20 respectively.

8. They field more soccer than rugby teams.

9. Some British pubs are finding a new role to play, for instance, performing the function of community meeting place.

10. Whenever possible, Britons are more likely to spend their two-week annual holiday in places they used to own, such as former colonies India, Australia, New Zealand and Barbados.

Ⅳ. Essay Questions

1. TV is a powerful social adhesive in Britain. Following stories on TV provides people with topics of conversation, allows them to get to know one another's tastes and

preferences, and enables them to explore the current social and cultural preoccupations that TV directs them towards. Workmates and friends are bonded together by their responses to the news, sitcoms, dramas or soaps that they have seen on TV.

2. These terms form part of a spectrum of cultural snobbery. Soccer fans are traditionally working class and are called "crowds", suggesting they are amorphous. Middle-class people who watch rugby are "spectators", because they are dispassionate onlookers. "Audiences" are more sophisticated, because they just listen. "Viewers" is a euphemism which suggest the passivity of the TV "couch potato". "Theatre-goer" implies some form of dynamism.

Unit Sixteen   Social Services

Focal Points

welfare state
maternity benefit
personal social service

social security
child benefit
social work

national health service
Beveridge Report
social care

Discussion Questions

What is the significance of welfare state in a capitalist country like Great Britain?

Text

The British social services system primarily comprises the National Health Service, the personal social services, and social security. Before World War II, state-funded services in Britain were either slow or **erratic**. Not until the Labor Party won victory in the general election of 1945, were a series of legislative and policy reforms made in the UK, establishing an effective and comprehensive social services network nationwide. Since then, the people of the United Kingdom have been taken care of by the welfare state **"from the cradle to the grave"**.

The Welfare State: An Overview

"Welfare" means "health, comfort and freedom from want". By "welfare state", it means that the state attempts to give all of this to every member of the community, paying the

---

erratic. 不规则、游移的

from the cradle to the grave 从生到死、一生

cost out of taxes of various kinds. It is like an **immense** insurance company with which every single citizen is **compulsorily** insured. In Britain, the welfare state comprises expenditures by the government of the United Kingdom intended to improve health, employment, living conditions and social security.

Historically speaking, the United Kingdom has a long history of welfare, notably including the English Poor laws which date back to 1536. Before the Industrial Revolution, welfare was the responsibility of local communities or religious organizations. Besides, charitable and voluntary organizations also played a major role in helping the poor, sick and disabled: this fine tradition continues even till today. It was not until 1601 that the first comprehensive legislation—The Poor Relief Act 1601 for relief of the poor was enacted by the Parliament of England, which marked the beginning of the state's direct involvement in social welfare and created a national poor law system for England and Wales.

The modern British welfare state, as we know it now, was **anticipated** by the Poor Law 1832, which was found to be subject to widespread abuse and promoted **squalor**, idleness and criminality in its recipients, compared with those who received private charity. Accordingly, the **qualifications** for receiving aid were tightened up, forcing many **recipients** to either turn to private **charity** or accept employment. The New Poor Law, passed in 1834, for example, significantly modified the existing system of poor relief. Prior to 1834, the system's administrative unit was the individual **parish**, which provided relief for orphans and the poor who were sick or aged and was paid for by **levying** local **rates** on rate payers. It also provided aid for those "deserving poor" who were able to work but became victims of economic circumstances beyond their control. The new **statute** altered the Poor Law system from one which was administered **haphazardly** at a local parish level to a highly centralized system which encouraged the large-scale development of workhouses, where

---

immense 巨大的
compulsorily 强制地

anticipate 先于…前行动
squalor 肮脏

qualification 资格、先决条件
recipient 接受者
charity 慈善

parish(主教管区下有自己教堂和牧师的)教区
levy 征收(税)
rates 不动产税、地方税
statute 法令、法规
haphazardly 随意地、无计划地

Unit Sixteen　Social Services

people did very unpleasant jobs in return for food and shelter. Most were employed on tasks such as breaking stones, crushing bones to produce **fertilizer**, or picking **oakum** using a large metal nail known as a **spike**. Conditions in workhouses were made harsh to discourage people from **claiming**. Later in the 19th century, conditions in the workhouses improved, due to the growth of humanitarian concern. The Poor Law system remained in operation until the emergence of the modern welfare state.

To a great extent, the British modern welfare state began to **take shape** after the general election of 1906, when the Labor Party became more influential and powerful. Additionally, other forces also contributed to the formation of the modern welfare state. For one thing, governments which had seen the wave of Communism were keen to ensure that deeper reforms reduced the risk of mass social unrest. For another, the phenomenon of industrial unemployment in the 20th century showed that poverty was more a structural economic problem than the fault of those unemployed. For still another, both government and industrial leaders were made to realize that modern complex industry had more need for a healthy and educated workforce than older industries had; hence, the need for "welfare". Finally, the experience of almost total state control during the Second World War had **inured** the population to the idea that the state might be able to solve problems in wide areas of national life. It seems that the government's role in mass evacuation of children, as well as the services it provided for the armed forces, had increased support for welfare among the middle classes of the country.

Subsequently, social welfare services and social security schemes were established, which not only replaced workhouses altogether in the first half of the 20th century, but also covered retirement and medical costs for a large portion of the population. All this was made possible by a government report published in 1942, entitled Social Insurance and Allied Services. Written by Sir William Beveridge, a highly regarded economist and expert on unemployment problems, the Beveridge Report **identified** five "Giant Evils" in society: squalor, ignorance, want, idleness and disease, aimed to provide a comprehensive system of social insurance "from the cradle to the grave".

  Specifically speaking, it recommended a national, compulsory, **flat rate** insurance scheme which would combine health care, unemployment and retirement benefits. Additionally, it also proposed that all working people should pay a weekly contribution to the state. In return, benefits would be paid to the unemployed, the sick, the retired and the widowed. Beveridge wanted to ensure that there was an acceptable **minimum** standard of living in Britain below which nobody fell. However, Beveridge was also careful to emphasize that unemployment benefits should be held to a **subsistence** level, and after six months would be conditional on work or training, so as not to encourage abuse of the system.

  In many ways, the Beveridge Report was the result of long-term changes in the attitudes of politicians and the British public toward social welfare. As was mentioned previously, at earlier times in Britain it had been common to lay the blame for poverty and unemployment on the individuals. Besides, since a variety of **charitable** organizations existed, it was not felt that the state needed to provide a comprehensive system of welfare support. However, beginning in the early years of the 20th century, the British government, in response to growing public demands, started to take a more positive position on social welfare issues, culminating eventually in the Beveridge Report. On the basis of this report, Britain has thereby established its modern welfare state, the fundamental principle of which is the provision of assistance against economic insecurity through government programs. Ever since then, the British government has been held responsible to provide health, employment and social security

---

identify 识别、确定

flat rate 统一价格、统一收费率

minimum 最低的

subsistence 维持生计

charitable 慈善的

for the people of the United Kingdom.

The Welfare System

The British welfare system covers a wide range of areas, including, among other things, social security, maternity and child benefits, and health care.

Social Security

Social security is used largely to refer to social insurance, but more generally it is a term used for personal financial assistance, in whatever form it may take. Generally speaking, social security may refer to: 1) social insurance, which provides people with benefits or services after they have paid contributions to an insurance scheme. These benefits typically include provisions for retirement pensions, disability insurance, survivor benefits and unemployment insurance; 2) income maintenance, which mainly refers to distribution of cash when employment is interrupted, including retirement, disability and unemployment.

Maternity Benefits

There are different benefits for families to help with the extra costs of children. These include benefits for women who are pregnant or who have just had their baby, benefits for the partners of women who have given birth, benefits for people who adopt, and benefits, tax credits and other help for people who have responsibility for a child or young person. Given the limited space here, only two types of benefits will be discussed.

When a woman is having a baby, she may be able to get **Statutory Maternity** Pay or Maternity **Allowance**. This will depend on whether one is employed or not, and how long she has been working. Most pregnant working women can receive their Statutory Maternity Pay directly from their employer, which can be paid for up to 39 weeks. For women who are **ineligible** for Statutory Maternity Pay, say if they are self-employed, have changed jobs or are unemployed, may qualify for Maternity

Allowance, which, depending on each individual's case, varies from one person to another. One may either get 90 percent of her average weekly earnings or £139.58 a week for 14 weeks, effective 6 April, 2015.

Child Benefits

The main benefits for children are Child Benefit and Child **Tax Credit**. Most people living in the UK can claim Child Benefit for their children. If a child's parents cannot look after a child, the person who does care for the child may be able to claim **Guardian**'s Allowance as well. Many parents can also claim Child Tax Credit for their children. They may get this whether or not they are working, depending on their income and how many children they have. If they have a child who is disabled, they may be able to get extra money included in their benefits, and they may be able to claim Disability Living Allowance **in respect of** their child.

As a rule, Child Benefit is a tax-free benefit paid to most people with children. Parents do not need to have paid any national insurance contributions to get Child Benefit, and indeed get it regardless of their income. However, if parents are getting Child Benefit and have income above a certain level, they may have to pay extra tax because of it. At any rate, parents can claim Child Benefit as long as they are responsible for a child aged under 16, or a young person aged under 20 if they are still in full-time education up to A level or equivalent, or on certain approved training courses.

NHS

Overseas visitors in Britain are often surprised to find that when they have an accident in the UK or they need to visit the hospital in an emergency, they do not need to pay for their treatment. This is made possible by the National Health Service, a publicly-funded healthcare system in the UK that provides free healthcare to all residents. It started operating in 1948 as a result of the reforms initiated by the Beveridge Report

---

tax credit 课税扣除

guardian 监护人

in respect of 关于、至于、就…而言

mentioned above. It was introduced by the Labor government in the mid-1940s, promising Britons a **"peace dividend"** which would include "cradle to grave" welfare services. Before then, health care had been private or charitable and almost impossible for ordinary people to afford. People demanded it because they wanted a complete change from the unequal and unfair society which had existed before the war.

Ever since the establishment of the NHS, certain sections of British society, notably the Establishment, represented by right-wing newspapers, have persistently attacked it. They criticize it for being bureaucratic, wasteful, inefficient and expensive. They say that it is **prey** to **spongers** and **malingerers** and "welfare tourists" from other countries, arguing that a privatized healthcare system would be more efficient and provide better service. In response to such criticisms, both Labor and Conservative governments have **tinkered with** the original idea behind it, and **charges** have been introduced for things like **prescriptions**, glasses and dental care, and at every election the different parties **vie with** each other to see who can be toughest on NHS spending while still promising that "the NHS is safe in our hands". What is clear from the public opinion is that any attempt to privatize UK healthcare system would be deeply unpopular with most British people.

The NHS is divided throughout the UK into regional primary healthcare trusts, and employs millions of people. According to the rule, each British resident is registered with a **GP** (general practitioner), or local family practitioner, who is the **first port of call** when the case is not an emergency. The idea of the family doctor has always been strong and remains so. When a person needs medical attention, the family doctor gives him/her treatment or prescribes medicine first. If the matter is serious and cannot wait, people should go directly to the **A&E** (Accident and Emergency) department and get treatment there. One **recurring** complaint is that there are great variations in the standard of care and cleanliness of hospitals, and that there is a **post-code lottery**, which means that in some areas patients get access to certain treatments that patients in other areas do not. Some people also claim that the NHS is under extreme pressure because of increased immigration. The fact is, though, that many of the doctors, nurses and **ancillary** staff in the NHS are from Commonwealth or other countries, and that the NHS would **grind to a halt** without them.

post-code lottery "邮政编码大乐透",即各地区医疗条件和治疗水平相差较大,病人是否获得高质量医疗完全像买彩票一样凭运气

ancillary 从属的、辅助的

grind to a halt 完全停止、慢慢地停止

Due to enormous expenditures on social security, the social security system has become the biggest item on the budget of the national government. Between 1995 and 2001, for example, almost one third of annual government spending was devoted to social security programs. In 2011-12, the UK government spent £166.98 billion, of which £159 billion was spent on benefits—an increase of 1.1% on the previous year. That is 23% of all public spending.

Housing and Personal Social Services

In general, housing in Britain **falls into** public and private sectors, with the majority of domestic **dwellings** belonging to the private sector. Specifically speaking, however, housing can be divided into private, council properties, and property **let** by "social" landlords or **housing associations**. In the private sector, the individual pays the market rate to rent or buy a property. As for **council properties**, they may be free or a low rent may be payable depending on the tenants' means. Waiting lists for council properties tend to be very long and, although the local authority has a duty to house people who would otherwise be homeless, this could mean providing a single room. Usually, priority will always be given to families and those with special needs. Regarding property let by "social" landlords or housing associations, the rent for such properties is likely to be considerably lower than the market rate but potential tenants may have to satisfy certain criteria. Apart from being on a suffi-

fall into 分为、归入

dwelling 住宅、寓所

let 出租

housing association 住房协会

council property 市政会所属公房

ciently low income, there could be other requirements such as suffering from a particular type of disability. On the whole, the vast majority of the British people live in houses or **bungalows** and the remainder in flats and **maisonettes**. Houses have been traditionally divided into **detached**, **semi-detached** and **terraced**, with the more expensive and prestigious ones in the detached category.

The idea that owning one's own home is the right thing to do is so deeply **ingrained** in British culture that it goes without question. Indeed, compared with many other Europeans, the British seem to have an **obsession** with property ownership. Relative to other European countries, Britain has incredibly cheap mortgages, and **on top of** that, both the Conservative and Labor governments tend to give help-to-buy **inducements**. Consequently, Britain has a pretty high home ownership rate. In 2005, its home ownership, for example stood at 70 percent. However, in the wake of the 2008 financial crisis, UK home ownership began to fall, undoing much of the work by Margaret Thatcher toward her dream of a property-owning democracy. According to the EU's official statistics bureau Eurostat, home ownership in Britain was 64.6 percent in 2013, compared to 70 per cent of the EU average home ownership of the same year. Apparently, with house prices rising faster than earnings, and with the average age of first-time homebuyers increasing, housing in the UK is likely to be more difficult for a significant portion of the population to afford, pushing more and more Britons into the rental sector, such as afore-mentioned council properties and property let by "social" landlords or housing associations.

While housing service in Britain shows little sign of improvement, personal social services in recent years have experienced similar problems as a result of shortage of funding. In Britain, "personal social services" refer to provision of practical help and support for elderly people, disabled people, people with learning disabilities or mental illness, families facing special problems and **offenders of justice**. These statutory services are provided by local social services authorities.

Strictly speaking, there is no clear or **coherent category** of "personal social services", which in reality covers both social work and "social care" services to people who fall outside the **remit** of health services. By "social work", it is to some extent defined by the activities of the personal social services and the client groups they deal with. Those who provide such services are called social workers, whose services include, but not limited to, problem solving (as advisor, broker or **advocate**), psycho-social **therapy**, changing behaviour, crisis intervention, and meeting the functional tasks of the agency. By "social care", it is largely defined as the provision of personal care, protection or social support services to children or adults in need or at risk, or adults with needs arising from illness, disability, old age or poverty. Mostly, if not all, social care is provided by the community; hence, the concept of "Care in the Community", first introduced by the Conservative and later expanded by the Labor governments. Care in the community includes care that is not in an institution, care in ordinary housing, and independence, all provided through social networks, community services and informal carers.

In recent decades, with the growing elderly population, the rising flow of immigrants, and the swelling ranks of the disadvantaged, personal social services in Britain have been under enormous public pressure. Since the 1990s, numerous attempts have been made in Britain to establish a framework for the funding and provision of personal social services. The Royal Commission on Long Term Care 1999; the Wanless Review in 2002; and Shaping the Future of Care Together (2009) all recommended reforms for personal social services. Most recently, on 11 July 2012, the Cameron Coalition Government published its long awaited White Paper and Draft Social Care Bill, aimed to initiate major

offender of justice 犯法者

coherent 一致的、协调的
category 种类、类别

remit 职权范围

advocate 拥护者、提倡者
therapy 治疗、疗法

reform of the social care system in England and Wales. Apparently, personal social services in Britain, like other social welfare programs, need to strike a good balance between growing public demand on the one hand and shrinking public funding on the other. Otherwise, neither of them can sustain itself for long.

Notes

William Beveridge (1879—1963)—was a British economist, noted progressive and social reformer. He is best known for his 1942 report *Social Insurance and Allied Services* (known as the *Beveridge Report*) which served as the basis for the post-World War II welfare state put in place by the Labor government elected in 1945.

Margaret Thatcher (1925—2013)—was the Prime Minister of the United Kingdom from 1979 to 1990 and the Leader of the Conservative Party from 1975 to 1990. She was the longest-serving British Prime Minister of the 20th century and is the only woman to have held the office. A Soviet journalist called her the "Iron Lady", a nickname that became associated with her uncompromising politics and leadership style. As Prime Minister, she implemented policies that have come to be known as Thatcherism.

Exercises

I. Multiple Choices

The following are questions or incomplete sentences. Below each sentence or question four possible answers marked A, B, C and D are provided. Choose the ONE that best completes the sentence or answer s the question.

1. The British social services system primarily consists of _____.
   A. the National Health Service   B. the personal social services
   C. social security   D. all the above

2. It was _____ that introduced a series of legislative and policy reforms in post-WWII Britain, leading to the establishment of an effective and comprehensive social services network nationwide.
   A. the Liberal Party   B. the Conservative Party
   C. the Labor Party   D. the Liberal Democrats

3. What does "welfare state" mean?

A. It means that the state provides "health, comfort and freedom from want" to a vast majority of the community, paying the cost out of taxes of various kinds.

B. It means the state provides "health, comfort and freedom from want" to every member of the community, paying the cost out of taxes of various kinds.

C. It means that the state provides "health, comfort and freedom from want" to a small majority of the community, paying the cost out of taxes of various kinds.

D. It means that the state provides "health, comfort and freedom from want" to a big majority of the community, paying the cost out of taxes of various kinds.

4. Before the Industrial Revolution, welfare was the responsibility of _____ or _____.

A. local communities/local governments

B. local governments/local religious organizations

C. local communities/local religious organizations

D. local governments/local political organizations

5. The Poor Relief Act 1601 for relief of the poor was enacted by _____.

A. the Parliament of England

B. the Parliament of Scotland

C. the Parliament of Wales

D. the Parliament of Northern Ireland

6. What does the "deserving poor" refer to?

A. It refers to those were so poor that they deserved relief aid from the state.

B. It refers to those who were willing to work hard but unable to get a job.

C. It refers to those who were able to work but became victims of economic circumstances beyond their control.

D. It refers to those who had worked hard before but then lost all their money.

7. Prior to the passage of the New Poor Law of 1834, conditions in workhouses were made harsh to _____.

A. punish the poor people working there

B. help the poor people learn to learn how to endure hardships

C. discourage the poor people from claiming

D. prepare the poor people to compete for tough jobs in the job market

8. To a great extent, the British modern welfare state began to _____ after the general election of 1906, when the Labor Party became more influential and powerful.

A. take off   B. take a great leap forward

C. take on   D. take shape

9. The five "Giant Evils" identified by the Beveridge Report in British society were: _____.

A. filth, squalor, ignorance, want and idleness

B. disorder, ignorance, want, idleness and disease

C. squalor, ignorance, want, idleness and disease

D. pollution, squalor, ignorance, want and idleness

10. It is on the basis of _____ that Britain has established its modern welfare state.

A. the Poor Relief Act of 1601   B. the Poor Law of 1832

C. the New Poor Law of 1834   D. the Beveridge Report

Ⅱ. True and False

Read the following statements carefully and then decide whether they are true or false. Put a "T" if you think the statement is true and an "F" if it is not.

1. The Beveridge Report was the result of quick ad immediate changes in the attitudes of politicians and the British public toward social welfare.

2. In Great Britain, social security mainly refers to social insurance and income maintenance.

3. Maternity Benefits include only Statutory Maternity Pay or Maternity Allowance.

4. Pregnant women or women who have given baby get Statutory Maternity Pay from the local government.

5. Most people living in the UK can claim Child Benefit for their children.

6. Under no circumstance can British parents claim Child Benefit once their child reaches the age of 19.

7. Foreign visitors in Britain have to pay twice as much as Britons do when visit the hospital for medical treatment in the event of an accident or an emergence.

8. Since the establishment of the NHS, it has received unanimous approval and support from all Britons across the country.

9. When Britons need medical attention, they usually go and see their practitioner, or local family practitioner first when the case is not an emergency.

10. Britons are quite satisfied with the medical treatment they receive in hospitals everywhere throughout the UK, because there is little variation in the standard of care and cleanliness of hospitals.

Ⅲ. General Questions

1. What does "post-code lottery" mean in the text?

2. Where do many of the doctors, nurses and ancillary staff in the NHS come from?

3. How many categories can housing in Britain be divided into?

4. Are council properties free of charge?

5. Of the three kinds of houses in Britain, detached, semi-detached, and terraced, which is properly the most expensive one?

6. How do Britons view home ownership?

7. What can we infer from the passage about Margaret Thatcher's view on housing?

8. Was British home ownership rate higher than that of the EU average home ownership in 2013, according to Eurosat?

9. Who are responsible for the provision of "personal social services"?

10. What kind of services do social workers in Britain provide?

Ⅳ. Essay Questions

1. What were the main factors that contributed to the formation of the modern welfare system in Britain?

2. How is the NHS administrated?

Reference Answers

Ⅰ. Multiple Choices

1. D 2. C 3. B 4. C 5. A 6. C 7. C 8. D 9. C 10. D

Ⅱ. True and False

1. F 2. T 3. F 4. F 5. T 6. F 7. F 8. T 9. T 10. F

Ⅲ. General Questions

1. It means what kind of medical treatment a patient in Britain receives is largely a matter of luck, because in some areas patients have access to certain treatments that patients in other areas do not have.

2. Many of the doctors, nurses and ancillary staff in the NHS are from Commonwealth or other countries.

3. Housing in Britain can be divided into three categories, namely private, council properties, and property let by "social" landlords or housing associations.

Unit Sixteen Social Services

4. It depends. They may be free or a low rent may be payable depending on the tenants' means.

5. The detached house is the most expensive one.

6. The British seem to have an obsession with property ownership, convinced that owning one's own home is the right thing to do.

7. We can infer from the passage that Margaret Thatcher worked hard to help Britons own their own houses, viewing it as an expression of democracy.

8. According to the EU's official statistics bureau Eurostat, home ownership in Britain was lower than that of the EU average home ownership in 2013.

9. Local personal social services authorities are in charge of "personal social services".

10. They provide such services as problem solving (as advisor, broker or advocate), psycho-social therapy, changing behaviour, crisis intervention, and meeting the functional tasks of the agency.

IV. Essay Questions

1. There were several factors that worked together to help the modern welfare state to take shape in mid 20th-century Britain. First, governments which had seen the wave of Communism were keen to ensure that deeper reforms reduced the risk of mass social unrest. Secondly, the phenomenon of industrial unemployment in the 20th century showed that poverty was more a structural economic problem than the fault of those unemployed. Thirdly, both government and industrial leaders were made to realize that modern complex industry had more need for a healthy and educated workforce than older industries had. Fourthly, the experience of almost total state control during the Second World War had inured the population to the idea that the state might be able to solve problems in wide areas of national life, winning both confidence and support for welfare among the middle classes of the country. Finally, the Labor Party had been a strong advocate of national welfare system since the beginning of the 20th century.

2. The NHS is divided up throughout the UK into regional primary healthcare trusts, and employs millions of people. According to the rule, each British resident is registered with a GP (general practitioner), or local family practitioner, who is the first port of call when the case is not an emergency. When a person needs medical attention, the family doctor gives him/her treatment or prescribes medicine first. If the matter is serious and cannot wait, people should go directly to the A&E (Accident and Emergency) department and get treatment there.

Bibliography

Reference Books on the United States:

Aguirre, Adalberto, Jr. and Turner, Jonathan H., *American Ethnicity: The Dynamics and Consequences of Discrimination*, New York: McGraw-Hill, third edition, 2001.

Althen, Gary, *American Way*, Maine: Intercultural Press, 3rd edition, 2011.

Baran, Stanley, *Introduction to Mass Communication: Media Literacy and Culture*, New York: McGraw Hill, 3rd edition, 2003.

Barnes, Gregory A., *The American University*, Philadelphia: ISI Press, 1984.

Bellab, Robert N., et al., *Habits of the Heart: Individualism and Commitment in American Life*, New York: Harper & Row, 1985.

Bromhead, Peter, *Life In Modern America*, New York: Longman Publishing, third edition, 1998.

Campbell, Neil and Kean, Alasdair, *American Cultural Studies: An introduction to American Culture*, London: Routledge, 1997.

Corbert, Julia Mitchell, *Religion in America*, New Jersey: Prentice-Hall Inc., fourth edition, 2000.

Day, Phyllis J., *A New History of Social Welfare*, second edition, 1989.

Eck, Diana L., *A New Religious America: How a "Christian Country" Has Now Become the World's Most Religiously Diverse Nation*, San Francisco: HarperCollins Publishers, 2001.

Mauk, David and Oakland, John, *American Civilization: An Introduction*, London: Routledge, second edition, 1997.

Moore, John A. Jr. and Roberts, Myron, *The Pursuit of Happiness*, New York: Macmillan Publishing Company, 1985.

Mitchell, Jeremy and Maidment, Richard, ed., *Culture: The United States in the Twentieth Century*, London: Hodder & Stoughton, 1995.

Olson, David H., DeFrain, John, *Marriage and Families*, Boston: McGraw-Hill Higher Education, fourth edition, 2003.

Skolnick, Arlene, *Embattled Paradise: The American Family in an Age of Uncertainty*, New York: Harper-Collins Publishers, 1991.

Stevenson, D. K., *American Life and Institutions*, Washington D. C.: United States Information Agency, 1989.

Stewart, Edward C. and Bennett, Milton J., *American Cultural Patterns*, Maine: Intercultural Press, Inc., revised edition, 1991.

Woloch, Nancy, *Women and the American Experience*, New York: McGraw-Hill, 2000.

Zelinsky, Wilbur, *The Cultural Geography of the United States*, New Jersey: Prentice-Hall Inc., 1973.

Reference books on Great Britain

Anderson, Janice, and Edmund Swinglehurst: *Britain: Yesterday & Today*. London: Carlton. 2003.

Banker, Leslie, and William Mullins: *Britannia in Brief: the Scoop on All Things British*. New York: Ballantine Books, 2009.

Biressi, Anita, and Heather Nunn, *Class and Contemporary British Culture*, 2013.

Bryson, Bill, *Notes from a Small Island*, London: Black Swan, 2012.

Champion, A. G., and Alan R. Townsend, *Contemporary Britain: a Geographical Perspective*. London: Edward Arnold, 1st edition, 1991.

Childs, Peter, and Mike Storry, *Encyclopedia of Contemporary British Culture*, 2014.

Fox, Kate, *Watching the English: The Hidden Rules of English Behavior*. Boston: Nicholas Brealey Publisher, 2008.

Higgins, Michael, Clarissa Smith, and John Storey, *The Cambridge Companion*, Hampshire: Palgrave Macmillan. 2010.

Morley, David, and Kevin Robins, *British Cultural Studies: Geography, Nationality, and Identity*. Oxford: The Oxford University Press. 2001.

Norbury, Paul, *Culture Smart! Britain*. London: Kuperard, 2007.

Scotney, John, *Scotland*. London: Kuperard, 2010.

Storry, Mike, and Peter Childs,. *British Cultural Identities*, London: Routledge, 2013.

Turner, Graeme.. *British Cultural Studies: An Introduction*. London: Routledge, 1996.

Websites

Websites on the United States

http://www.kidport.com/RefLib/UsaGeography/UsaGeography.htm
http://www.let.rug.nl/~usa/GEO/index.htm
http://www.cdc.noaa.gov/USclimate/states.fast.html
http://www.villagemagazine.ie/article.asp?sid=1&sud=38&aid=3169
http://en.wikipedia.org/wiki/New_England
http://www.answers.com/topic/the-south
http://historyplace.com/unitedstates/revolution/rev-early.htm
http://historyplace.com/civilwar/index.html
http://www.ecb.org/tracks/mod9.htm
http://www.bergen.org/AAST/Projects/depression/
http://en.wikipedia.org/wiki/Cold_War
http://www.answers.com/topic/progressive-era
http://www.bergen.org/AAST/projects/Immigration/
http://www.trinity.wa.edu.au/plduffyrc/subjects/re/bible/discrim.htm
http://www.unu.edu/unupress/unupbooks/uu12ee/uu12ee0o.htm
http://en.wikipedia.org/wiki/WASP
http://www.ahsd25.k12.il.us/Curriculum%20Info/NativeAmericans/index.html
http://www.marcusschenkenberg.info/translationtext07.html
http://www.usconstitution.net/const.html
http://usinfo.state.gov/products/pubs/outusgov/
http://www.historylearningsite.co.uk/america_and_elections.htm
http://www.historylearningsite.co.uk/supreme_court.htm
http://en.wikipedia.org/wiki/Separation_of_powers
http://lexrex.com/enlightened/AmericanIdeal/yardstick/pr6.html
http://crf-usa.org/bria/bria14_3.html#swedish
http://www.answers.com/topic/centres-for-medicare-and-medicaid-services
http://www.answers.com/topic/social-security

http://www.huduser.org/publications/pubasst/transform.html
http://www.aflcio.org/issues/healthcare/whatswrong/
http://www.associatedcontent.com/article/1608/healthcare_in_america_medicaid_and.html
http://en.wikipedia.org/wiki/Education_in_the_United_States
http://plato.stanford.edu/entries/affirmative-action/
http://www.commondreams.org/views02/0710-02.htm
http://usinfo.state.gov/journals/itsv/1105/ijse/costs.htm
http://usinfo.state.gov/journals/itsv/1105/ijse/ekman.htm
http://www.servintfree.net/~aidmn-ejournal/publications/2001-11/PublicEducationInTheUnitedStates.html
http://www.loc.gov/exhibits/religion/
http://www.theocracywatch.org/separation_church_state2.htm
http://www.newreformation.org/relfree.htm
http://www.wfu.edu/~matthetl/perspectives/three.html
http://www.wfu.edu/~matthetl/perspectives/seventeen.html
http://www.religion-online.org/showbook.asp?title=1663
http://www.digitalhistory.uh.edu/historyonline/plife_overview.cfm

Websites on the United Kingdom
http://www.en.wikipedia.org/wiki/United_Kingdom
http://www.uk.cn/bj/index.asp?lang=e
http://www.cia.gov/cia//publications/factbook/geos/uk.html
http://www.statistics.gov.uk
http://www.scotland.gov.uk
http://www.nio.gov.uk
http://www.wales.gov.uk
http://www.thecommonwealth.org
http://www.europa.eu.int
http://www.britishcouncil.org/studies.english
http://ethnos.co.uk/what_is_britishness_CRE.pdf
http://ethnos.co.uk/decline_of_britishness.pdf
http://www.ukstudentlife.com/Britain.htm - 11k
http://www.britannia.com/history/

http://www.great-britain.co.uk/history/history.htm
http://www.spartacus.schoolnet.co.uk/Britain.html
http://www.british-history.ac.uk/
http://british-history-101.blogspot.com/
http://www.dca.gov.uk
http://www.royal.gov.uk
http://www.privy-council.org.uk
http://www.parliament.uk
http://www.ukonline.gov.uk
http://www.number-10.gov.uk; www.pmo.gov.uk
http://www.cabinetoffice.gov.uk
http://www.northernireland.gov.uk; www.nio.gov.uk
http://www.ni-assembly.gov.uk
http://www.electoralcommission.org.uk
http://www.direct.gov.uk
http://www.dwp.gov.uk
http://www.doh.gov.uk
http://www.homeoffice.gov.uk
http://charity-commission.gov.uk
http://www.womenandequalityunit.gov.uk
http://www.vexen.co.uk/religion/uk.html
http://www.church-of-england.org
http://www.cofs.org.uk/3colos.htm
http://www.tasc.ac.uk/cc; www.catholic.org.uk
http://www.brijinel.org.uk
http://www.jewish.co.uk
http://www.muslimdirectory.co.uk
http://www.direct.gov.uk
http://www.dfes.gov.uk
http://www.educationuk.org
http://www.isis.org.uk
http://www.open.ac.uk
http://www.ost.gov.uk
http://www.rcuk.ac.uk

Websites

http://www.cst.gov.uk

http://www.culture.gov.uk

http://www.britishcouncil.org

http://www.uksport.gov.uk

http://www.mediauk.com

http://www.bbc.co.uk

http://www.itc.org.uk

http://www.pad.press.net

http://www.the-times.co.uk

http://ww.guardian.co.uk

http://www.telegraph.co.uk

http://www.statistics.gov.uk/socialtrends